THE PRAGMATIC TURN IN PHILOSOPHY

THE PRAGMATIC TURN IN PHILOSOPHY

Contemporary Engagements between Analytic and Continental Thought

Edited by

William Egginton and Mike Sandbothe

STATE UNIVERSITY OF NEW YORK PRESS

Published by
State University of New York Press, Albany

For information, address State University of New York Press,
90 State Street, Suite 700, Albany, NY 12207

Production by Diane Ganeles
Marketing by Michael Campochiaro

Library of Congress Cataloging-in-Publication Data

The pragmatic turn in philosophy : contemporary engagements between analytic and
    Continental thought / edited by William Egginton and Mike Sandbothe.
        p. cm.
    Includes bibliographical references (p.) and index.
    ISBN 0-7914-6069-X (alk. paper) ISBN 0-7914-6070-3 (pbk.: alk. paper)
        1. Pragmatism—History—21st century. 2. Pragmatism—History. 3.
    Philosophy—History—21st century. I. Egginton, William, 1969– II. Sandbothe, Mike,
    1961–

B832.P7525 2004
144'.3—dc22   2003059026

10 9 8 7 6 5 4 3 2 1

Contents

Introduction

In recent years the classical authors of Anglo-Saxon pragmatism have gar-nered a renewed importance in international philosophical circles. In the aftermath of the linguistic turn, philosophers such as Charles S. Peirce, William James, George H. Mead, Ferdinand C. S. Schiller, and John Dewey are being reread alongside, for example, recent postmodern and deconstructivist thought as alternatives to a traditional orientation toward the concerns of a represen-tationalist epistemology. In the context of contemporary continental thought, the work of Jacques Derrida, Jean-Francois Lyotard, and Gilles Deleuze comprises just a few examples of a culturewide assault on a metaphysical worldview premised on what Michel Foucault called the empirico-transcendental doublet, and presents a wealth of potential exchange with the pragmatist critique of representationalism. In both cases, aspects of pragmatist thought are being used to add flexibility to the conceptual tools of modern philoso-phy, in order to promote a style of philosophizing more apt to dealing with the problems of everyday life. The hope for a pragmatic "renewing of phi-losophy" (Putnam) evidenced in these trends has led to an analytic reexami-nation of some of the fundamental positions in modern continental thought as well, and to a recognition of previously unacknowledged or underappreciated pragmatic elements in thinkers like Kant, Hegel, Nietzsche, Heidegger, and Wittgenstein.

Within the current analytic discussions, a wide spectrum of differing and at times completely heterogeneous forms of *neo*pragmatism can be distinguished, which for heuristic purposes can be grouped into two general categories according to the type of discursive strategy employed. The first of these consists in a conscious *inflation* of the concept of pragmatism in order to establish it as widely as possible within the disciplinary discourse of philosophy. The second consists in a *deflationary* application of the concept, in order to distinguish it from the professional self-image of academic philosophy in a marked and even provocative way. What each variant has in common is its tendency to criticize as "representationalist" the debate between realism and antirealism.

At the center of this debate, which has left its imprint on twentieth-century thought, lies the problem of whether our mental representations should be understood realistically, as pictures of some externally existing reality, or antirealistically, as constructions of that realm. For the deflationists, this debate is seen as a case of fruitless bickering around the quasi-religious question of a sublime, metaphysical reality that—whether from the outside or from the inside—is believed to determine the contours of our speech and thought. Instead of searching ever further for this ultimate authority or foundation, the deflationists recommend that we view our knowledge as a collection of tools for the democratically-oriented transformation of reality, for which we alone are responsible (Rorty). In contrast to this political and humanistic critique, the inflationists formulate their critique of the debate between finding and making from a logical and analytic perspective. Their response to representationalism is an antirepresentationalist epistemology whose foundations are developed in such frameworks as normative pragmatics (Brandom), undogmatic empiricism (McDowell), or interpretational theories of truth (Davidson).

The contributions to *The Pragmatic Turn in Philosophy* explore how these various discursive strategies are related and what their pertinence is to the relationship between pragmatism and philosophy as a whole. Perhaps the primary importance of this collection, however, lies in its demonstration that, in light of the current reinvestment in pragmatic thinking, the fabled divisions between analytic and continental thought are being rapidly replaced by a transcontinental desire to work on common problems in a common idiom. Of course, much of the work of deconstructing the continental/analytic divide remains to be undertaken, and imposing obstacles remain. Idiom and style, to mention two, would seem to transcend categorization as merely external or secondary differences. Analytic philosophers tend to dismiss continental philosophers as being too literary, tend to fault their lack of rigor, of clarity, of precision. Continental thinkers, in turn, often ridicule analytic philosophy for its pretensions to scientificity and spurn it as positivistic, dry, irrelevant. Richard Rorty once characterized, in his inimitable way, the difference between continental and analytic philosophy as being little more than the difference between those philosophers who thought what was important was to read the history of philosophy and those who thought what was important was to read the last ten years of journal articles; and, indeed, in American departments of philosophy those who pay attention to thinkers of the continental tradition are referred to more often than not as historians.

What this volume puts forth is a potential ground for a meeting between these idioms, a common ground of concern and place for interaction. It is our conviction that the century from which we have emerged has born witness to a sea change in philosophy, irrespective of on which side of the divide one stands. Recognized as such or not, a pragmatic philosophy has gained ascendancy over the traditional concerns of a representationalist epistemology that has determined much of the intellectual and cultural life of modernity; we believe that the philosophy of the next century will emerge from this recognition, and that the practice of this emergence is well underway. Moreover, in the age of globalization, an ecumenical philosophy represents an important contribution to the task of bringing together the autonomous disciplines into a transdisciplinary network of knowledge practices; perhaps a reenergized pragmatism will provide the philosophical support for this project.

In the first piece in this volume, "The Insistence on Futurity: Pragmatism's Temporal Structure," Ludwig Nagl focuses on the question of time and temporality that figures so centrally in the thought of William James. He begins by arguing that the pragmatist test of whether a theoretical question makes any practical difference does not primarily serve to abolish the big metaphysical questions, but rather serves to distinguish the concerns of a real and living humanity from the intellectualistic pseudoproblems of professional philosophy. James's pragmatic reflections on temporality should be thought of in this way: as breaking through the appearances of speculative reason in order to create a space for "the Will to Believe." Beyond physicalist ontologies and aprioristic intellectualizing, James stood for a temporalization of time whose realization would entail the opening up of a multiplicity of time-horizons. This becomes the basis for James to throw a pragmatically-selective light on old metaphysical controversies, such as those between materialism and spiritualism, or between free will and determinism. Nagl concludes by bringing James's pragmatic logic of hope to bear on current discussions in the philosophy of religion, specifically in the work of the French political historian Marcel Gauchet. For Gauchet, we are living in a postreligious age in which hope for the future has become a meaningless openness to whatever comes, totally lacking the stabilizing force of a utopian ideal. Nagl counters this notion with James's "insistence on futurity," which in no way leads to the leveling out of the ever-receding other of the future, but rather makes visible the borders of the kind of humanistic "inner transcendence" so important to the thought of writers like Habermas, Rorty, and Gauchet himself.

The pertinence of James to contemporary moral concerns continues to be at stake in Hilary Putnam's contribution, "Philosophy as a Reconstructive Activity: William James on Moral Philosophy." Putnam seeks to locate in the work of William James the basis for a pragmatic theory of morals that would try neither to assume a transcendental authoritative status nor to dissolve ethical questions into an empirical cultural anthropology. In an early essay, "The Moral Philosopher and the Moral Life," James ties such metaphysical questions as the nature of "obligation," of "good," and of "ill" in a relativistic fashion back to the existence of sentient beings, while at the same time making clear that the truth of moral judgements presupposes a standard external to the subject. This standard, however, is by no means transcendent, because it is based on an intergenerational consensus and on an evolutionary reconciliation of ideals. The "metaphysics of morals" to be found in James's work, therefore, is itself built on the grounds of a consensus-based "metaphysics of truth." Putnam underscores, however, that James's moral philosophy has much to offer even if we do not share the theory of truth that implicitly supports it, and he proceeds to highlight those aspects of James's moral theory that are not dependent on the consensus theory of truth or that in fact contradict it, especially his emphasis on the standpoint of the agent. This last point leads Putnam back to the thesis, formulated by Albrecht Wellmer in the eighties, that an emphasis on the standpoint of the agent is incompatible with the idea (which he associates with both Habermas and James) that the last consensus is a necessary and adequate determination of truth. For Wellmer, whereas truth is entirely public, intersubjective consensus presupposes each particular subject's individual recognition of truth. As a possible objection to Wellmer, Putnam reconstructs James's argument that the recourse to the individual subject of action is only a condition for consensus insofar as I myself must be involved in the inquiry, in order to be able to judge whether it was correctly carried out. The last criterion of truth, then, remains a public inquiry carried out under ideal research conditions and guided by the most recent consensus. Putnam presents this Jamesian riposte to Wellmer with the cautionary note that the utopian idea of the last consensus is just as untenable as the theory of correspondence so rightly criticized by James, though this should not lead us to trivialize the philosophical thematic of truth, but rather to endeavor, with Frege and the late Wittgenstein, to achieve a philosophical clarification of *what we do* when we make mathematical, ethical, and other claims.

In her contribution, Antje Gimmler looks for a progenitor of pragmatism a century before James and on the other side of the Atlantic. She begins her examination of the "Pragmatic Aspects of Hegel's Thought" by clarifying some of the differences between classical pragmatism and neopragmatism, and by noting the centrality of antirepresentationalism to both, which she in turn relates to the priority of praxis over theory. Following the work of Robert Brandom, she distinguishes between a normative and an instrumental pragmatism, but stresses that a neopragmatism worthy of its name would have to grant both orientations equal weight. Against this background, Gimmler argues that it was Hegel who set out the tasks for a pragmatic philosophy, which have to date only been partly undertaken by neopragmatism. While Brandom has made explicit Hegel's theory of intersubjective recognition as a basis for a use-theory of meaning—according to which the constitution and application of concepts interweave with one another in the space of a normative practice of experience—his blind spot consists in the fact that he defines experience solely as the practice of recognition and not of appropriation. For Gimmler it is precisely the relationship between recognition and appropriation that forms the center point of Hegel's pragmatism, and in her concluding section she demonstrates the importance for Hegel's theory of self-consciousness of the instrumental-creative dimension of subjectivity produced by the transformative relation to things. In his critique of Kant, Hegel carries out a turn toward anti-representationalism, on the basis of which he develops a nonreductive notion of knowledge as tool, which he embeds in an interactive notion of experience exemplified in the relation between the master and the slave. Whereas the master has a contemplative and representational relationship to things, the slave carries out the movement of reconstructing the world of objects, and in this way may be taken as the paradigm for how, in Hegel's thought, self-consciousness is rooted in universality and transsubjectivity, not only through relations of recognition, but also and just as importantly through the practical interrelations of poiesis.

According to the authors of the next four contributions' anti-representationalism, the roots of which Gimmler identifies in Hegel's critique of Kant, provides the theoretical keystone of neopragmatism. In "The Pragmatic Twist of the Linguistic Turn," Mike Sandbothe identifies another—pragmatic—turn toward antirepresentationalism in the twentieth century's "linguistic turn." This pragmatic turn is revealed in three ambivalences related to that turn: the first having to do with the status of the linguistic method; the second with the determination of its goals; and the third—and in Sandbothe's view preeminent—with the metaphilosophical presuppositions informing the desire for an autonomous philosophical method. This latter ambivalence provides the stage for a confrontation between a transformative pragmatism in Rorty's sense and the language-analysis projects of formal or normative pragmatics. If one takes this fundamental distinction to heart, authors like Quine, Sellars, and the (early and in some ways also the late) Wittgenstein appear as thinkers who contributed to the pragmatic turn without overcoming the dualistic signature of professional philosophy and the methodological understanding of the discipline that it supports. Donald Davidson, on the other hand, presents the possibility of another sort of philosophical activity, one no longer oriented toward the traditional, epistemological views of the discipline, but rather endeavoring to determine anew the task of philosophical thought in conjunction with the sciences. Nevertheless, according to Sandbothe, Davidson's program remains primarily one of describing the specific truth theories of different natural languages, whereas Rorty's thought is focused on the possibilities of provoking a sociopolitically effective change in common sense.

In "The Debate about Truth: Pragmatism without Regulative Ideas," Albrecht Wellmer argues that the fundamental error of correspondence theories of truth consists of the attempt to think the idea of correspondence as independent of our justification practices. Instead, he argues, we should try to develop a theory of truth that starts out from the notion of an internal relationship between truth and justification, without thereby reducing truth to justification. Wellmer's contribution to the debate about truth consists of demonstrating how the internal relation of truth and justification must be thought together with the ineradicable grammatical difference between "true" and "justified." To this end Wellmer considers suggestions offered by Putnam, Habermas, and Apel. Against Apel's idea of an ideal communication-community's final consensus, Wellmer notes Derrida's objection that communication refers in a regulative way back to a metaphysical ideal that puts into question the material, finite, and temporal conditions of the possibility of communication itself. Wellmer does not want to draw from this the conclusion that truth ought to be understood in a disquotation-theoretical sense as a semantic concept rather than in a justification-theoretical sense as an epistemic concept, but rather argues in the paper's concluding section for the possibility of grounding a normative concept of truth without recourse to regulative ideas. He begins spelling out such a concept by arguing that a language-pragmatic version of Tarski's "convention T" presupposes taking into account "the difference between the perspective a first person (a speaker) has of him or herself and the first person's perspective on *another* speaker." Whereas I do not necessarily recognize as true the reasons that I attribute to the other's justification of his or her convictions, I will always recognize the reasons underlying my own justifications as true. This is so, according to Wellmer, precisely because I cannot imagine myself as myself outside my own convictions, reasons, and evidences. Consensus cannot therefore be the criterion for identifying reasons as good, because consensus for its part rests on the normative recognition of those reasons in discussion as good or true reasons only as recognized by the individual interlocutors. This makes clear that there is no need for the regulative idea of consensus as a standard for adequately describing our distinction between "true" and "justified."

From the notion of truth we move to that of objectivity, the central theme of Arthur Fine's "The Viewpoint of No-One in Particular." Fine's paper focuses on pragmatic aspects of the modern philosophy of science and represents a critical confrontation with the realist positions of Thomas Nagel and Bernard Williams. This realist position grants the natural sciences a special distinction in the pursuit of human knowledge, a privilege based on the ostensible methodological neutrality and impartiality of their "view from nowhere." On the basis of the democratic conception of the natural sciences developed by Paul Feyerabend in connection with the ideas of John Stuart Mill, Fine argues for a pragmatic testing of those conceptions coming out of concrete research that are held to be scientifically objective, a testing that leads him to distinguish between "objectivity as product" and "objectivity as process." Whereas realists like Nagel and Williams tend to confound the difference between the process and the product, Fine argues that procedural objectivity is not a characteristic of the product, but of our attitude toward the product. Objectivity, in this view, turns out to lack the importance it has traditionally been granted in distinguishing the realm of the natural sciences, being neither reserved for them nor excluded as soon as we have to do with human or spiritual matters.

At the outset of his article "A Pragmatist View of Contemporary Analytic Philosophy," Richard Rorty identifies a fundamental resonance between the arguments of Arthur Fine, whom he calls his favorite philosopher of science, and those of his "favorite philosophers of language," Robert Brandom and Donald Davidson, a resonance he sees as "marking a breakthrough into a new philosophical world." The agreement among these thinkers involves the obsolescence of the realism/antirealism debate and the conviction that we should no longer be thinking of how language or indeed how science works as having anything to do with the process of representing reality. In the second part of his essay, Rorty remarks on some of the metaphilosophical consequences he sees resulting from the pragmatic approach to science and language adopted by the above-mentioned thinkers. These consequences include, on the one hand, a tendency to stop thinking of reality as containing an essence that it is incumbent upon humans to grasp and to stop believing that the hard, natural sciences have an advantage over the soft, human sciences in this regard. On the other hand, such a pragmatic approach leads philosophers to stop thinking in terms of "recurrent philosophical problems"—a symptom of what Rorty considers the over-professionalization of philosophy—and to speak rather of "imaginative suggestions for redescription of the human situation." Nevertheless, for Rorty, one's choice of representationalism or antirepresentationalism remains based on "reasons of the heart," for neither one provides a philosophical ground on which to disprove the arguments of the other.

Rorty's position on several key topics of neopragmatism form the background for the last four pieces of the volume. Barry Allen's contribution, "What Knowledge? What Hope? What New Pragmatism?", takes the form of a polemic response to Rorty's book *Philosophy and Social Hope*. To begin with, Allen argues that Rorty uses the term "philosophy" in a variety of ways that need to be distinguished. "Philosophy" stands for: first, meta-physics—the tradition of abstract absolutes inherited from Plato; second,

epistemology—philosophy as a theory of representation; third, therapy—
deflating the notion that there is such a thing as a "philosophical problem";
and finally, poetry—philosophy as a process of imaginative redescription
aimed at self-creation rather than self-knowledge. Clearly, when Rorty uses
philosophy in the former two senses he means it disparagingly, whereas the
latter two are terms of praise. In light of this classification, Allen challenges
what he sees to be the principle argument of *Philosophy and Social Hope:*
namely, that hope is more important, and more relevant, for a philosophy of
the fourth—positive—kind, than is knowledge. For Allen, Rorty's mistake
lies in his tendency to *replace* the question of knowledge entirely with that
of hope. For if "hope replaces knowledge, failure loses its disconfirming
power." This abandonment of the question of knowledge leads Rorty to a
politics that shies away from a "revaluation of tenacious presumptions," such
that, in the end, "Rorty forgets about imagination, diminishes the power of
redescription, and dismisses the work of those who try to make serious alternatives
seem urgent if not always hopeful."

Wolfgang Welsch's basic thesis in "Richard Rorty: Philosophy beyond
Argument and Truth?" is that Rorty, in particular in *Contingency, Irony, and
Solidarity,* transgresses his own restrictive thesis concerning the limits of
philosophy, according to which typologically distinct conceptions of
philosophy have nothing to say about each other's truth claims. According to Welsch, Rorty demonstrates—through argumentation—that the
representational model of knowledge rests on certain conceptual errors.
The fundamental thesis of representationalism, whether it serves as the
foundation for a realist or antirealist theory of knowledge, is that reality be
thought of as something prior to, external to, and independent of our
efforts to relate to it. The presupposition of such an "alpha-reality" is,
however, contradictory, because it is itself a specific construal of reality, and
therefore already interprets reality in a determined and hardly self-evident
way—namely, as interpretation-independent—thereby bringing about a
determination on the performative level that was negated at the level of
content. Nevertheless, although Rorty is correct in maintaining that
incommensurable foundational arguments are useless for the refutation of
other foundational arguments, according to Welsch this does not mean
that particular aspects or details of a conception of philosophy that share
a certain transversal commonality with another, typologically distinct,
conception may not be brought into conversation with them. It is precisely
the challenge for a philosophical thought oriented toward problems of
reason and truth to explore such transversal possibilities of communication.

In "Keeping Pragmatism Pure: Rorty with Lacan," William Egginton
argues that Rorty's philosophy has succumbed to a temptation he has often
warned others against, namely, the temptation of purity. According to
Egginton, Rorty's attraction to nominalism, and in particular to the conviction

that "nothing is better than a something about which nothing can be said," has led him to dogmatically reject the meaningfulness of any notion of experience as distinct from language. Egginton argues that Rorty's "pure" nominalism is a case of "using Occam's razor to cut your own wrists," for not only is the denial of lived, or first-person, experience absurd in its own right, it ultimately cripples pragmatism's *raison d'être*, its focus on usefulness, because it deprives pragmatism of a conceptual tool needed to confront one of the most prevalent and relevant experiences of human beings: desire. Nothing is better than a something about which nothing can be said, unless, of course, there is something to be said about that "something about which nothing can be said." As it turns out, the experience of not being able to say anything about something, ineffability, is not at all uncommon to human experience and is a central aspect of more than a few alternative conceptions of philosophy. Egginton then turns to ineffability's place in French psychoanalyst Jacques Lacan's theory of desire as offering a useful corrective to a pragmatism purified of the ineffable.

In the volume's closing piece, "Cartesian Realism and the Revival of Pragmatism," Joseph Margolis argues that, under the cover of a pragmatist vocabulary, neopragmatists like Rorty, Putnam, and Davidson are in fact reproducing old Cartesian problems at the same time as they continuously checkmate each other over the issue of truth. Margolis criticizes Rorty's ostensible dismissal of epistemological truth problems for overlooking the fact that a theory of truth can have value as an explanatory tool in discussions about knowledge. For Putnam, on the other hand, Rorty's dismissal of truth slides into relativism, because Rorty throws out the consensus-based theories of truth developed by Peirce, James, and Dewey along with traditional theories. Putnam's earlier adherence to such theories is in turn criticized by Rorty and Davidson for falling back into a Cartesian scientism. Putnam points out, furthermore, that neither Davidson's causal nor Rorty's sociological naturalism entails a philosophical foundation for the development of a normative and meaningful notion of truth, which is nevertheless needed in order to avoid a naturalistic reproduction of Cartesian problems. As an alternative to these options, Margolis suggests a third way, consisting of a return to a constructive realism. The foundations for this are to be found for the most part in the thought of "the original pragmatists," which Margolis locates in the anti-Cartesian insights of continental European post-Kantians. His program of constructive realism consists in a revival of Hegel's critique of Kant in the context of current philosophical discourse. From this revival the insight emerges, that the critique of representationalism à la Rorty and Davidson depends on a notion of *tertia*, or mediating terms between subjects and objects, as a kind of internal representations or "epistemic intermediaries." Against this dismissal of all *tertia*, Margolis advances a notion of interpretive intermediaries "as historicized, variable, artifactual, and open to the puzzle of reconciling realism and, say, relativism or incommensurabilism." Such an understanding of *tertia*, Margolis concludes, saves a realism that is, not objectivist but constructivist through and through.

Putting together a volume such as this one is nothing short of a group effort. The editors would like to express their gratitude to all of those who contributed in any way to making this possible. To begin with, some of the essays included here first appeared in German, in *Die Renaissance des Pragmatismus* (ed. Mike Sandbothe, Weilerswist: Velbrück Wissenschaft, 2001); we would like to thank those authors for allowing their work to be translated or, in some cases, for allowing us to publish the original versions. Thanks as well to those who wrote completely new essays for this volume. We are also grateful to those who translated or assisted in the translation of these pieces: Andrew Inkpin, Eric Little, Lowell Vizenor, and Bernadette Wegenstein; to the Julian Parks Fund of the University at Buffalo, for a grant supporting the translations; to Kevin Heller, for his proof-reading prowess; to Miguel Fernández Garrido, who spent a summer looking up quotations in their original languages; to Ana María Olagaray for creating the index; and finally to Henry Sussman, who directed us to SUNY Press, and to our editors Jane Bunker and Diane Ganeles, whose patience and care made this all possible. While credit is to be fully shared with them for anything edifying that may emerge from these pages, they cannot shield us from the inevitable opprobrium inspired by errors of fact, judgment, organization, or taste, all of which, lamentably, are our own.

Mike Sandbothe, William Egginton

1

༄

Ludwig Nagl

The Insistence on Futurity: Pragmatism's Temporal Structure

In his lectures of 1906, *Pragmatism, A New Name for Some Old Ways of Thinking*, William James announced that Pragmatism, "from looking backwards upon principles [. . .] shifts the emphasis and looks forward [. . .] The really vital question for us all is, What is this world going to be?"[1] This shift in perspective is the topic of this essay, in which I will investigate James's insistence on futurity, his emphasis on action and on its horizon: hope, and his accompanying strategy of de-dramatizing "intellectualistic" questions of metaphysical origin.

My essay has three parts: After briefly assessing the influence of James's "paradigm change" on neopragmatic discourse (part 1), I will deal, in the main part of my essay (part 2), with selected aspects of James's emphasis on futurity. In section 2.1, James's overall project—his "pragmatism"—will be described, somewhat riskily, as a "de-transcendentalized" version of Kantianism. Within this frame of reference I will then analyze, in section 2.2, James's failed attempts to conceptualize time-experience psychologically and will try to connect, en passant, James's pragmatic resituation of temporality within the European debate around (what was recently called) the "temporalizability" of time. After this, two of James's "pragmatic considerations" that hinge on temporal arguments will be examined: in section 2.3 I will deal with his attempt to relocate the quarrel between materialists

11

and theists within a logic of hope, and in section 2.4 I will look at his effort
to undermine the aporetical dispute between the advocates of determinism
and the defenders of free-will by reflecting upon the future-relatedness of
our pragmatic *Lebenswelt*. In the concluding section of the essay (part 3), I
will compare James's pragmatic strategy (that paves the way for our "right to
believe") with a new French contribution to notions of the "future" and
religion: Marcel Gauchet's thesis—presented in his book *The Disenchantment
of the World. A Political History of Religion*[2]—that "after the end of ideology"
we have entered "the phase of 'pure future,'" where society starts to structurally
"absorb its other"—an "other" that was conceived, in premodern times, as
"transcendent." This structural change, Gauchet argues, induces "a postreligious" era in which—masking the imminent "end of religion"—a
"widespread adherence to privately practiced beliefs, including syncretic
reconstructions" characterize the age of "man after religious man."[3] How
does James fit into this picture? Is Gauchet's thesis corroborated by James's
pluralistic "logic of hope"? Or can we trace elements in James's pragmatic
exploration of time that contradict Gauchet's ambivalent theory of "religion's
aftereffects"? I will finally conclude with a critical assessment of the Gauchet-
James link, based—in part—on arguments from the Canadian philosopher
Charles Taylor.

1. "FUTURE" AS A TOPOS OF
CONTEMPORARY NEOPRAGMATIC DISCOURSE

James's theme resounds through neopragmatic philosophies. For instance,
both Richard Rorty and Hilary Putnam find James' insistence on futurity
inspiring. Let us begin with a brief look at Rorty.

1.1

In his 1993 Viennese Lectures, *Hoffnung statt Erkenntnis. Eine Einführung
in die pragmatische Philosophie,* Rorty's *leitmotif* is "anticipation": "If there is
anything distinctive about pragmatism, it is that it substitutes the notion of
a better human future for the notions of 'reality', 'reason', and 'nature.'"[4]
Rorty returns to this theme in his 1997 essay "Religious faith, responsibility,
and romance"[5] (where he characterizes pragmatism, with James, as "a kind
of religious faith [. . .] in the future possibilities of mortal humans"), as well
as in his 1998 book *Achieving our Country. Leftist Thought in Twentieth-
Century America,*[6] where he sides with Walt Whitman and Dewey—who
(poetically and philosophically) explore mankind's "future"—and contrasts
their outlook to the perspective of people who take "refuge in self-protective
knowingness about the present."

1.2

Rorty is not the only neopragmatist who is impressed by James's move; Hilary Putnam finds it congenial, too. Although he is very critical of Rorty's—rhetorically exaggerated—claim to replace "reason" and "reality" by "hope," Putnam—like Rorty—focuses on those temporal shifts that form the core of pragmatic reflection. In his 1995 book *Pragmatism: An Open Question*, Putnam argues that the central emphasis of pragmatism is the "emphasis on the primacy of practice."[7] This sea-change unsettles all reified concepts of time, and (re-)enables questions concerning the complex—future-bound, and past-related—interplay of any individual's "becoming who she or he already is."[8] Putnam reinstates, postanalytically, a set of questions that reformulate, in late analytic discourse, Kant's "What should I do" and "What can I hope for." Such questions, according to Putnam, are located on the margin of our standard concepts of objectivity and intersubjective "assertibility." In *Pragmatism. An Open Question* he writes: "James and Wittgenstein would have asked us to remember that what is publicly verified (or even what is intersubjectively 'warrantedly assertible') is not all of what any human being or any culture can live by: James in *The Varieties of Religious Experience* and Wittgenstein in *Lectures and Conversations on Aesthetics, Psychoanalysis, and Religious Belief* and *On Certainty* explore the problems posed by what may be called the limits of intersubjectivity [. . .] There is plenty for philosophy to do in exploring those needs."[9] Putnam takes interest in those "horizons of anticipation" that structure our individual actions. In this, his interest is different from Rorty's: while for Rorty pragmatism is "kind of an atheist's religion," Putnam's "logic of anticipation" comes closer to James' own position, which does not rule out the "overbelief" in a "transcendent other."[10]

2. JAMES'S REDEPLOYMENT OF "A GENUINE METAPHYSICAL DEBATE" WITHIN THE "HORIZON OF ANTICIPATION"

Pragmatism is primarily esteemed, by its positivist heirs, as a critical method of testing theories in view of their results: only "differences which make a difference" survive the pragmatic test. This is, most certainly, the first effect of Peirce's and James's "pragmatic turn": the interest in "fruits and results" renders obsolete all "dead" metaphysical "opposition vocabularies" that have no conceivable influence upon our actions. But pragmatism is not to be reduced to this first, negative business. James as well as Peirce claim that there is a "genuine metaphysical debate" that survives the (negative) "pragmatic test." (In Peirce, systematic attempts to investigate questions of this sort are found in his "semiotics," as well as in his "phaneroscopic" doctrine of the categories, and in his cosmology). James, in his lectures on *Pragmatism*, expounds the second, positive side of pragmatic reflection in considerations dealing with the temporal horizon of our actions. Any universalization of a causalistic *ratio*, according to James, reduces what will come to the mere continuation of what was (and is). In Lecture VII of *Pragmatism* he explicitly opposes his "humanism" to theories that underrate "that the world stands really malleable, waiting to receive its final touches at our hands."[11] For the pragmatist, reality is not—as for the determinist—"ready made and complete from all eternity," but is rather "still in the making, and awaits part of its complexion from the future."[12]

2.1 James's pragmatism: a de-transcendentalized Kantianism?

This emphasis on the agent (and on her or his "temporal horizon") has a familiar ring. Some historians of philosophy, most notably Murray Murphey, claimed early on that the Cambridge pragmatists—Peirce and James, in particular—were influenced by Kant to such an extent that they could rightly be called "Kant's children." This assertion, although exaggerated, points to some similarities between Kant's *Critiques* and core arguments of pragmatists and neopragmatists alike. James himself would certainly have disliked Murphey's assessment, because he once wrote: "As Schiller, Dewey and I mean pragmatism, it is *toto coelo* opposed to either the original or revived Kantianism [. . .] It is irreconcilable with anything in Kant—only the most superficial resemblance obtaining."[13] If one scrutinizes James's writings closely, however, this self-assessment becomes dubious. As recent studies have shown,[14] arguments from all three of Kant's *Critiques* did influence James—albeit in a "de-transcendentalized" form and restructured by ideas that he imported from Darwin's theory of evolution. As Robert Brandom pointed out in his "Pragmatics and Pragmatism,"[15] it is more promising, in any case, to reread pragmatism in the light of Kant (and "the early Heidegger, the late Wittgenstein and such figures as Quine, Sellars, Davidson, and Rorty") than to restrict its reception to the internal history of "Peirce, James and Dewey" and the narrow framework of an "instrumentalism," analytically read. James's first move, his attack on the dead-end "intellectualism" of metaphysics, has a distinctly Kantian ring. Kant calls conceptual "differences which make no difference" *bloße Gedankendinge*: phantoms, i.e., produced by the self-destructive "dialectics" of "pure" reason! But also James's second, positive move—his attempt to reopen, *modo pragmatico*, a "genuine metaphysical debate"[16]—actualizes, in a post-Kantian form, Kant's transition (in his ethics and philosophy of religion) from "theoretical" arguments to arguments situated within the realm of "practical reason." (The "unmistakably Kantian sound" of James's moves was noted recently by Hilary Putnam.[17]) James's pragmatics of "hope"—like Kant's second *Critique*—hinges on "postulates." (The postulates of "God" and "free-will," in James's reading, will be presented in parts 2.3 and 2.4 of this essay). In spite of this indebtedness to Kant, however,

James's pragmatism is innovative, because he explicitly rejects Kant's "transcendental" method; as a "fallibilist," James is a determined critic of all a prioris. In his pragmatic redeployment of Kantian motifs, he avoids, at all times, claims of the kind Kant raises in his transcendental deduction. This double-bind—to stick, on the one hand, to Kant's "architectonic," and to methodically subvert Kant's "rigid" project on the other—leads to interesting new arguments even in James's psychology of time, as we will now see.

2.2 Conceptualizing time-perception:
"intellectualistic" aporiae and a pragmatist's way out

As a thinker influenced by Kant, James is fascinated by temporality; as a pragmatist, however, he avoids any of the (Newtonian and metaphysical) implications of Kants "transcendental aesthetics": Kant's theory of "intuition," for James, suggests a time "monism" of untenable rigidity.

James explores time perception—on a theoretical level—in his *Principles of Psychology*,[18] focusing there on what he calls "the specious present": Time is "specious" in the sense "that it is not strictly present but is rather a constant slipping into the past and yielding to the future."[19] "Duration," in contrast, is defined as a block within which time-as-succession becomes perceivable. But this metaphor turns out to be treacherous, too. "When the specious present is conceived as an unchanging block of time analyzable into 'fine grained subdivisions', the resulting picture is a time line choked with minute successions but having no flow." James tries to defuse this problem in the following way: "If each subdivision is 'a felt time', then each overlaps or compenetrates with the next, generating a flow that is more than mere succession." Any such reading of temporality is threatened again with falling prey to its spatial implications. As James's critics were quick to point, to conceptualize time as a sequence of subdivisions, i.e., of parts on a time line, "plainly confuses the relations of succession and compenetration. If felt moment M occurs before felt moment N, and we are aware that N succeeds M, we register the succession of two distinct moments which [since they remain next to each other] cannot be identified as melting, overlapping, or compenetrating."[20]

On the cognitive level of time psychology, James thus gets stuck in mentalistic versions of those aporiae which—since St. Augustine's *Confessions*—keep resurfacing whenever the temporal *ekstases* of past, present, and future are "objectivized." Most of these aporiae result from our deep urge to "spatialize" temporality: if we yield to it, we are held captive by the "false picture" of time as a flowing movement of (extended) "now"-points on a time line. The bewildering consequences of this "objectivistic" *Holzweg* are instructive, however: by spatializing time we create a set of (secondary, neometaphysical) puzzles that turn out to be as unenlightening as they are irresolvable. James the pragmatist—at least in his best moments—tries to escape from this (theory-induced) prison. Like Wittgenstein—in his remark on St. Augustine in *Philosophical Investigations*, and in the lengthy passage on temporality in the *Blue Book*—James resituates, in his *Pragmatism* lectures, temporal experience within our everyday action horizon and language use. Without "ontologizing" time through a physicalistic notion of "Temporality" with a capital T—Ilia Prigogine's project, today—and without postulating a hermeneutico-"transcendental" framework of time that is incompatible with and presupposed by any concept of time in physics—Paul Ricoeur's phenomenological Kantianism—James, where he is at his best, interprets time—in equidistance from transcendental philosophy and physicalism—as a plurality of times. Myers accurately recapitulates what James's extensive psychological inquiries into time resulted in on the cognitive, theoretical level: "The only time we know, the overlapping times of immediate experience, resist any attempt at adequate formulation."[22]

James the pragmatist, however, when facing this aporetic result of "intellectualistic" concepts of time, does not withdraw from analyses of temporality. Instead, he learns to live with "times"—and, for that matter, with the open plurality of time vocabularies that cannot be reduced to one consistent theory of time. In his pragmatic reflections on "our" temporal horizon, James thus comes pretty close to the most advanced, third position in recent temporal discourse: to the idea, i.e., that a sufficiently sophisticated concept of temporality must "temporalize time" itself.[23] This "temporalization"/"pragmatization" implies, first, the de-ontologizing and, second, the de-transcendentalizing of temporal experiences: it thus resituates all time discourses within the open plurality— and historical malleability—of our time vocabularies. Such a move frees us, according to its proponents, from the age-old fantasies surrounding the metaphysical problem of time. What James suggests in his third *Pragmatism* lecture—that we reconsider "older metaphysical problems" in the light of our practices and their temporal horizon—prefigures, in interesting ways, this current mode of anti-"foundationalism." In the following, I will analyse two of James's "considerations" in *Pragmatism, Lecture Three*. Both of them, while reflecting on our temporality (and, especially, on its horizon of futurity), avoid every "intellectualistic" notion of time, whether a physicalistically redimensioned spatial concept or—equally aporetical—the offspring of a "transcendental aesthetics." First let us examine how James rereads, in this spirit of antifoundationalism, the old problem of matter and mind in his *Pragmatism* lectures.

2.3 Materialism versus Spiritualism: a stagnant discourse pragmatically resituated within the temporal horizon of hope

According to James, pragmatism is able to first, destroy and second, relocate the old, and insistently recurring, antagonism between matter and mind.

How can pragmatism achieve this double result: the destruction of false (theoretical) opposition-vocabularies on the one hand and the rescue of their "genuine" content on the other?

2.3.1 Exposition of the problem

James reads "materialism" as the project to explain "higher phenomena by lower ones" and thus to leave "the destinies of the world at the mercy of its blinder parts and forces."[24] Within the old paradigm of speculative metaphysics, "materialism" is opposed to "spiritualism" (or "theism"), which claims "that mind not only witnesses and records things, but also runs and operates them: the world being thus guided, not by its lower, but by its higher element."[25] There is no way to decide—resorting to either speculation or empirical "theory" alone—which of these two positions is true. If the "theist" rejects materialist reduction as mere oversimplification, he underrates, according to James, its capacity to explore the "infinitely and incredibly refined" structure of matter. Materialism, on the other hand, generates more problems than it solves, since it subverts—due to its causalistic premises— our basic self-understanding as agents: a self-understanding that is deeply embedded in our everyday world-orientation, as well as in the project of science itself, insofar we understand it as a form of enlightenment and liberation.

2.3.2 Pragmatic method and the dimension of time

The controversy between materialism and theism terminates, in its meta-physical form, in a cluster of "dead oppositions." "Instead of resting in principles after the stagnant intellectualist fashion," therefore, James, asks: "What practical difference can it make now that the world should be run by matter or by spirit?"[26] To answer this question, he introduces a thought experiment that alters the temporal dimension of our experience: if we were creatures who were able to register the past (up to the present) only, it would not make "a single jot of difference [. . .] whether we deem [the world] to have been the work of matter or whether we think a divine spirit was its author."[27] Had the universe come to an end now, both hypotheses (materialism and theism)—as justifying the given facts by different stories—explain nothing but the *status quo*: Quarrels between two rival theories that account for the same present equally well are "idle and insignificant" quarrels, unable to pass the "pragmatic test": they rest on differences which make no difference.[28]

James's thought experiment demonstrates *ex negativo*, i.e., by making apparent the deficiency of its construction principle, that "our world," *in concreto*, has an altogether different time structure: We are not objects, placed within a "linear," monodirectional temporal scheme, where the present is

chained to the past: our world is not a world of facts that are "given," but
a world "that has a future that is yet uncompleted whilst we speak."[29] "In this
unfinished world," according to James, the old metaphysical quarrel reappears
in transformed mode: once we recognize the abstractness of our thought
experiment and recomplete our temporal framework, "the alternative of
'materialism' vs. 'theism'" proves to be "intensely practical."

In refocusing upon "our" temporal horizon in its fullness—on its action-
relatedness, i.e., and on its three "ekstases"—James opts for a nonreductive
concept of the universe. No "false picture" will do: neither in metaphysics
nor in science can we "protocol" the world "objectively," or "as if complete"—
any such "God's Eye View" (as Hilary Putnam says) is out of reach. All our
theories contain temporal markers: they are (limited and falsifiable) attempts
to prepare—by anticipations, intentions, and prediction—for a future that
we shape, although we are only imperfectly able to foretell and to "make" it.
Theories are thus, constitutionally, embedded in (finite) practices. Viewed
from this perspective, the old distinction between "materialism" and
"spiritualism" regains significance. The "theist" and the "materialist" "horizons
of anticipation" are not at all equivalent hypotheses with respect to "our"
future. On the contrary. According to James, any materialist reading of "what
is to come" drastically limits the range of our hope, since it rules out for
futurity anything not already contained in materialism's formative principle:
contingency. In a contingent world "the laws of redistribution of matter and
motion" [. . .] "are fatally certain to undo their work again, and to redissolve
everything that they have once evolved . . . [in the long run thus] matter will
know itself no longer."[30] All our moral striving is built on quicksand. The
ultimate perspective of materialist reduction—which we should not mix up
with the short-term optimism of the operational logic of "forecasting"—is
("as at present understood") "utter final wreck and tragedy."[31] Materialism is
not "too gross," as its opponents, the "intellectualistic" spiritualists say: the
operational gains made possible by the prognostic potential of modern science
are convincing. What turns materialism, "pragmatically conceived," into a
problem is that any univerzalisation and ontologization of its reductive
methodology subverts, in a thorough way, our self-understanding as agents
who shape a (socioculturally mediated) life-world. The everyday world of
actions and plans, of communications and institutions, is neither "founded"
in—or, for that matter, perfectly explicable by—"scientistic" or metaphysical
theoria. Theory is always embedded, and thus has a secondary, derivative
status only. World-orientation cannot be reduced to cognition: "description,"
on every level, is embedded in webs of practices, of anticipations, and of
hopes—and is thus (always already) ethically charged. James, in a
(post)Kantian, pragmatic manner, makes room for "practical reason": he
reinterprets materialist reduction as an abstract, and fallible, scheme which,
in spite of its functional value, is devoid of "ontological" dignity.

But he goes even further: compared with the bleak horizon of "materialist reduction"—where "meaning" ends where it started: in "contingency," and "materialism's sun sets in a sea of disappointment"[32]—"spiritualistic faith" (once it gets de-ontologized) can make a real difference, because it strengthens our efforts to act in such a way that a better world can be the result. Even if the notion of God—James is at this point rather close to standard "positivist" thought—may be inferior in clearness "to those mathematical notions so current in mechanical philosophy," it has "this practical superiority over them, that it guarantees an ideal order that shall be permanently preserved. A world with a God in it to say the last word, may indeed burn or freeze . . . [but] where He is, tragedy is only provisional and partial, and shipwreck and dissolution not the absolutely final thing."[33]

These considerations are hope-functional only: they deal exclusively with rival "grand theories" of the world in view of their motivational force. James defends the "realm of ends" (as Kant would say) against the threat of sheer "contingency." Neither for him nor for Kant is "God" a concept that can be theoretically secured: its validity can neither be "deduced" from metaphysical "essences"—e.g., from the concept of "substance"—nor can it be "induced"—or, for that matter, "eliminated"—by scientific arguments. Kant's criticism of theology in *Critique of Pure Reason* has shattered such "intellectualistic" options once and for all. This is a well-established result for James. "The bare fact," as he writes in *The Varieties of Religious Experience*, "that all idealists since Kant have felt entitled either to scout or to neglect [the proofs for the existence of God] shows that they are not solid enough to serve as religion's all-sufficient foundation."[34] The structure (and force) of the religious language game can be fairly evaluated *modo pragmatico* only: "Here then, in these different emotional and practical appeals, in these adjustments of our concrete attitudes of hope and expectation and in all the delicate consequences which their differences entail, lie the real meanings of materialism and spiritualism—not in hairsplitting abstractions about matter's inner essence, or about the metaphysical attributes of God."[35] Pragmatism is, therefore, not just meaning-critical "positivism." The rejection of "dead" opposition vocabularies—of concepts, i.e., that entail no possible consequences—is accompanied by a second pragmatic reflection of an affirmative nature, which unfolds and explores, within a logic of hope, those questions that resist debunking and insistently recur. Such questions, according to James—as opposed to Rorty[36]—cannot, however, be answered only in a privatistic manner—i.e., without any connection to (public) argument. James tries to show this in his much misunderstood essay "The Will to Believe," where he defends "our right to adopt a believing attitude in religious matters." The exercise of this "right," according to James, implies an act of choice: to decide in favor of a "living option"—which is "living" because it is embedded in a sufficiently plausible context of interpretation. This choice is justified only where decidability on "intellectual grounds" alone has come to an end. (Such a choice thus presupposes intellectual discourse on various levels and does not at all discredit *theoria* in an "anti-intellectualistic" move.) It takes place under the "unavoidable" (or "forced") condition of uncertainty—because theoretical reason alone cannot decide which option to choose—and it concerns a "momentous," i.e. nontrivial, option.[37] When Rorty suggests, in his reading of James's essay[38] that we should strictly separate "private" (hope-related) and "public" (assertibility-related) language games, he overlooks—as far as I can see—that postulates always already imply interpretations and arguments. James, unlike Rorty, is aware that any rigid—and one might say: schizophrenic—separation of "private" and "public" realms is unworkable when he writes in his third *Pragmatism* lecture: "[. . .] truths clash and try to 'down' each other. The truth of 'God' has to run the gauntlet of all our other truths. It is on trial by them and they are on trial by it. Our final opinion about God can be settled only after all the truths have straightened themselves out together. Let us hope that they shall find a *modus vivendi*."[39]

This Jamesian project—that our beliefs ought to become compatible with the other validity claims that we raise as citizens of an enlightened world—runs counter not only to Rorty's (privatized) notion of hope, but also to Habermas's understanding of religion—as raising claims that are "holistic and universal," but not "true" in any philosophically relevant sense.[40] For James, pragmatism makes room for our multiple "logics of hope." His strategy of reintroducing, in a positive-pragmatic manner, questions concerning our horizon of action may, however, seem a sheer anachronism. Is it not commonly agreed, in our enlightened age, that we are better off neglecting those "perennial" riddles that will not be solved in a forseeable time? James, like Kant, avoids this avoidance strategy. For James, any question that is "genuine" survives the negative pragmatic test by recurring insistently; problems that have this stature need our special attention: "The absolute things, the last things, the overlapping things, are the truly philosophic concerns: all superior minds feel seriously about them, and the mind with the shortest views is simply the mind of the more shallow man."[41] It doesn't seem promising, therefore, to displace these questions—"positivistically" (as the Vienna Circle did) or "post-philosophically" (as neopragmatic Rortians do)—and to reallocate them in the realm of "private" emotions and aestheticised games. To focus on futurity also implies, for James, to think philosophically about "ultimate things."

2.4 "Free-will" and futurity

Temporal reflection is prominent in another of James's attempts to "pragmatically reconsider an old metaphysical problem": in his analysis, i.e., of the opposition between determinism and free-will. James starts, as he does most of the time, with a de-transcendentalized Kantian exposé. He argues that the problem of free will, inner-theoretically considered, proves to be irresolvable. "The real ground for supposing free-will is pragmatic [. . .]."[42] Before we start analyzing this claim, a quick excursion into James's biography is needed. As a young man, trained in the natural sciences, James read the world as an unbroken chain of causal connections. In 1869 he wrote to a friend: "I am swamped in an empirical philosophy. I feel that we are nature through and through, that we are wholly conditioned, that not a wiggle of our will happens save as the result of physical law; and yet, not withstanding, we are *en rapport* with reason. How to conceive it? Who knows?"[43] James was deeply affected by this problem and suffered from depressive moods. He managed to overcome his crisis while studying the works of Charles Renouvier. An entry in James's diary of April 30, 1870, documents this: "I think that yesterday was a crisis in my life. I finished the first part of Renouvier's 2nd Essay, and saw no reason why his definition of free will—the sustaining of a thought because I choose to when I have other thoughts—need be the definition of an illusion. At any rate I will assume for the present—until next year—that it is no illusion. My first act of free will shall be to believe in free will."[44] James justifies this decision later in his correspondence with Renouvier—in quite Kantian terms—as the result not of intellectualistic deductions but of a *Postulat*: "I believe more and more that free will, if accepted at all, must be accepted as a postulate in justification of our moral judgment that certain things already done might have been better done. This implies that something different was possible in their place [. . .] So, for entirely practical reasons, I hold that we are justified in believing that both falsehood and evil to some degree need not have been."[45]

This complex argumentative move forms the background of James's defense of free-will in his third *Pragmatism* lecture, where he expresses his critique of determinism in explicitly temporal terms: "Free-will pragmatically means novelties in the world, the right to expect that in its deepest elements as well as in its surface phenomena, the future may not identically repeat and imitate the past."[46] Any abstract "necessitarianism" (this was already Peirce's conviction) subverts the option-space that makes possible pragmatic procedures. In focusing upon "fruits" and "results," the pragmatic method rests on anticipation (and thus always already presupposes free-will): if we were unable to think up new experiments, the core question of pragmatism, "Which option will bear fruits?" (or "better" fruits, for that matter), could never be asked.

"Intellectualistically" conceived, the opposition between determinism and free-will proves to be irresolvable. The claim that we can choose has to be defended on a different plane. Even if we are unable to provide conclusive theoretical proof for or against it, we can perfectly reasonably defend freedom as the precondition of any "melioristic" anticipation. The belief in free-will is pragmatically embedded in a doctrine that "holds up improvement as at least possible, whereas determinism assures us that our whole notion of possibility is born of human ignorance, and that necessity and impossibility between them rule the destinies of the world." "Free-will," for James, is structurally anchored in "a general cosmological theory of promise."[47]

Postulates, like free-will, however, are powerful ideas only if they are not "posited" in an abstract way (e.g., as mere consolation or as the result—for James's critics—of a "will to deceive"). Their motivational force depends upon contextual integration; they are able to "bear fruits" only if they are embedded in a "language game" that interprets—within a narrative that can count as a "living option"—situations of significance that are theoretically irresolvable. Nevertheless, even postulates that are "acceptable" by these standards only have a limited validity. They are, for James as for Kant, valid only in regard to our horizon of action. "Other than this practical significance, the words God, free-will [. . .] etc., have none. Yet dark though they be in themselves, or intellectualistically taken, when we bear them into life's thicket with us the darkness there grows light about us."[48]

James, like Kant, tries to "make room for faith." No gesture of quasi-deduction, and no pretense of certainty, urges his readers to follow him into this room. James's analysis of "hope" is embedded in the liberal structure of an enlightened constitutional culture. Rorty articulates this democratic basis of James's defense of belief as follows: "We latest heirs of time are lucky enough to have considerable discretion about which options will be live for us and which not."[49] Pragmatism, for James, "has no obstructive dogmas, no rigid canons of what shall count as proof [. . .] She will entertain any hypothesis, she will consider any evidence. It follows that in the religious field she is at a great advantage both over positivistic empiricism, with its anti-theological bias, and over religious rationalism with its exclusive interest in the remote, the noble, the simple, and the abstract in way of concepts."[50]

James defends, as a "right," the full articulation of hope through a pluralistic spectrum of "expectations and promises": At any present our articulations of hope are incomplete; and they cannot be restricted to religious images in the narrow sense. Hope, for instance, also contains what Rorty calls "romance": "a kind of atheist's religion" that explores, via literature, "the future possibilities of mortal humans." As Rorty says, "Romance, this fuzzy overlap of faith, hope and love [. . .] may crystalize around a labour union as easily as around a congregation, around a novel as easily as around a sacrament, around a God as easily as around a child."[51] In the closing part of this essay I will return briefly to this claim.

3. James after Gauchet: The "insistence on futurity" in the light of "pure future," or, religion after the "end of religion"?

James's attempts to pragmatically resituate our "genuine metaphysical problems" within a logic of hope can be related to, and questioned by, another—and, it may seem, more radical—concept of futurity. Marcel Gauchet, the French philosopher and political historian of religion, puts forward in his book *The Disenchantment of the World* the assertion that after an "age of ideology," where future had a direction that we believed to know and control,[52] we now have entered the phase of "pure future": i.e., a future "whose content is completely undetermined."

This is the time, for Gauchet, when we begin to enter a "postreligious age." In his reading Christianity is, generally speaking, "the religion which brings about the exit from religion," because it introduces—after "emptying the cosmos and confining the holy to God alone"—into modern secular society "a form of life in which the key temporal dimension is the future seen as something that we must shape."[53] This radical insistence on futurity, which privileges innovation and becoming and invalidates origin and past, dramatically alters the cultural coordinates of humanity. Charles Taylor, in his introduction to the English translation of Gauchet's book, characterizes futurity on its way to "pure future" as follows: "We are indeed at the antipodes of the original religious society, which was riveted to the past. And yet the very nature of this controlling activity renders this future less and less definitively conveivable."[54]

In many respects the temporal axes of James's "pragmatic turn" seem to fit hand in glove into Gauchet's framework. This casts an interesting light on James's "logic of hope." Societies that structure themselves on the principle of "pure future" do not only invalidate older concepts of religion (while congenially tolerating them); "pure future" also has a destabilizing effect on those ideological "substitute faiths" that attempted—"in an intermediary moment where the new had to follow a familiar process and compromised with the old"[55]—"to assure [themselves] of the future, to clearly chart [their] direction, and to subordinate [their] production to works of a fully conscious will."[56] This disappearance of traditional religions as well as of ideologies has for Gauchet, however, a paradoxical nature, because religion does not vanish altogether but rather survives in the postreligious age. Taylor summarizes Gauchet's analysis as follows: "The old Feuerbachian (and Marxist) idea that humans return out of their religious and material alienations into a full possession of themselves [. . .] is condemned by Gauchet as illusion." Even if society—in the age of an "open future"—starts to exclusively act upon itself, "our self-understanding and sense of agency still relate us to something 'other', to something we do not understand and cannot transparently control."[57] In the "post-religious world"—i.e., in the Western world of "ex-Christendom" (and of postideology in the ex-socialist states)—all the difficult questions about who we are and what is the meaning of things—questions preempted by traditional religions and political utopias—are still around: "Le réligieux après la réligion" is structurally dependent upon the promises, as well as the insecurities, of an "open future" not stabilized by utopian concepts of control. When traditional religious cultures and classical ideologies wane, "each individual is faced with these difficult questions. This makes for a great unease [. . .] People will search everywhere, quarrying, among other places, the religious ideas of the past." James, it seems, is an important philosophical voice in this situation, because his highly individualized and pluralistic "logic of hope" corresponds to, and philosophically reaffirms, "le réligieux après la réligion." Gauchet's analysis forbids, however, any one-dimensional reading of this situation and confronts us with the question whether religion—in the friendly climate of advanced liberalism where it superficially thrives—has started, de facto, to come to an end: i.e., a quiet end, at the very moment where spiritual searches seem to regain strength, sympathetically supported by attentive politico-constitutional discourses and by postmodern reflections that dissolve the older, all-out criticism of religion. Does the neopragmatic restructuring of temporal horizons—which formerly, in metaphysics, were tied to "principles and origins"—within a "temporalized" (and fallible) concept of time (see 2.2) *nolens volens* undermine, on a depth-structural level, those religious energies that pragmatists like James and Putnam seek to strengthen? Or can these energies—in the age of "pure future"—be redeployed without significant loss as an—ethically charged—"transcendence from within," and thus fuel our advanced "project of modernity," as Jürgen Habermas asserts?[58] Those who do not trust the "elegance" of this solution will object that any transformation of the Habermasian type—a transformation that Rorty advocates, too, when rendering sacrament and poetry exchangeable—is simply a category mistake resulting from an inability to draw appropriate conclusions from the massive implosion of "substitute faiths" in our postideological age.

But how close are Gauchet's and James's concepts of hope, anyway? James, it seems, is more complex, because he leaves important questions undecided that Gauchet claims to have answered, although he didn't even ask them. James's "emphasis on futurity" is nowhere tied to an exaggerated idea of society's self-reflective—and "other"-absorbing—capacity. James isn't convinced that the "humanistic" internalization of "the other"—even if it has a postideological stature—will work. Religion, in James—when he is at his best—is a sensorium that registers the bounds of modernity's "transcendence from within." James's analysis of the "pragmatic environment" of hope runs deeper than Gauchet's culturalistic—and "constructivist"—story of the rise and imminent fall of religion. He nowhere pretends that hope is simply the outgrowth of mankind's illusion-producing capacity. Unlike Gauchet, he leaves the question open as to how to understand the "existence" claim at the bottom of all religious hope: for James, all religions "unequivocally testify" that "we can experience union with something larger than ourselves."[59] This depth-structure of hope—that its promise is seen *not* as our construct *only*, but as something situated on (and transgressing) the limits of our capabilities to bring about effects—is nowhere "unmasked" in James, as it is in Marx or Freud's criticisms of "mankind's religious illusions." Gauchet's theory is more advanced, however, than Marx's "projection" theorem, because it takes into account the fact that—once the aporiae of modernity's "ideological" projects have become obvious, and we become convinced that there is no way to clearly chart the direction of the future "and to subordinate its production to works of a fully conscious will"[60]—we still face future's "otherness." For Gauchet, however, this "other" of an "open future"—which is insistently redeployed—has to be constantly (re)"absorbed" into society itself. He expresses this (radicalized) "humanistic" reading of hope—which is not dissimilar to Habermas's and Rorty's humanism—as follows: Even if it became obvious—after the demise of ideology—"that men are not gods,"[61] i.e., that "men will not necessarily always know what they are doing [. . .], they cannot fail to recognize that they themselves have brought about whatever comes to pass. At the center of the structuring relation between the actual visible and the invisible future, lies the practical certainty that the causes of social progress are to be found within society itself distributed among its components."[62]

James, certainly, would be in sympathy with those aspects of Gauchet's "humanism" that affirm democracy and "meliorism"; but it is also clear that he would not be willing to subscribe to Gauchet's theorem of a self-referential—and (exclusively) self-empowering—society. His logic of hope centers around a different image of "the other": an image that avoids the idea of the other's "absorbability"—the claim, i.e, "that the causes of social progress are to be found exclusively within society itself." In his last *Pragmatism* lecture James introduces, instead, his well-known and charming metaphor of the finiteness of our nature: "I firmly disbelieve, myself . . . that our human experience is the highest form of experience extant in the universe. I believe rather that we stand in much the same relation to the whole of the universe as our canine and feline pets do to the whole of human life. They inhabit our drawing-rooms and libraries. They take part in scenes of whose significance they have no inkling. They are mere tangents to curves of history the beginnings and ends and forms of which pass wholly beyond their ken. So we are tangents to the wider life of things."[63]

Is this a "Swedenborgian" image only: an image which—although it has poetic qualities—is, soberly judged, as indefensible as it is regressive? Or does James's analogy contain a critical potential that can help us become aware of the closure induced by any theory that overrates society's capacity to absorb "the other": an "other" which is "its"—society's—other always only in part?

NOTES

1. *Pragmatism* (Cambridge, Mass.: Harvard UP, 1975), 62.

2. Marcel Gauchet, *The Disenchantment of the World. A Political History of Religion* (Princeton: Princeton University Press, 1997).

3. Ibid., 300.

4. Richard Rorty, *Hoffnung statt Erkenntnis. Eine Einführung in die pragmatische Philosophie* (Vienna: Passagen Verlag, 1994), 16.

5. Richard Rorty, "Religious faith, responsibility, and romance," *The Cambridge Companion to William James*, ed. Ruth Anna Putnam (Cambridge: Cambridge University Press, 1997), 84–102.

6. Richard Rorty, *Achieving Our Country. Leftist Thought in Twentieth-Century America* (Cambridge, Massachusetts, and London, England: Harvard University Press, 1998).

7. Hilary Putnam, *Pragmatism. An Open Question* (Oxford, UK, and Cambridge, Mass.: Blackwell, 1995), 52.

8. Hilary Putnam, *Renewing Philosophy* (Cambridge, Mass., and London, England: Harvard University Press, 1992), 191.

9. Putnam, *Pragmatism*, 75.

10. James, *The Varieties of Religious Experience* (Cambridge, Mass.: Harvard University Press, 1985), 515.

11. James, *Pragmatism*, 123.

12. Ibid.

13. See Ralph Barton Perry, *The Thought and Character of William James*, 2 volumes (Boston: Little, Brown, and Company, 1935); and Thomas Carlson, "James and the Kantian Tradition," *The Cambridge Companion to William James*, ed. Ruth Anna Putnam (Cambridge: Cambridge University Press 1997), 363–383.

14. Ibid.

15. Robert Brandom, "Pragmatik und Pragmatismus," in *Die Renaissance des Pragmatismus*, ed. Mike Sandbothe (Weilerwist: Velbrück Verlag, 2000).

16. James, *Pragmatism*, 52.

17. Hilary Putnam (with Ruth Anna Putnam), "William James's Ideas," *Realism with a Human Face*, ed. James Conant (Cambridge, Mass., and London, England: Harvard University Press, 1990), 217–231; 227, 218ff.

18. James, *Principles of Psychology* (Cambridge, Mass.: Harvard University Press, 1981).

19. Gerald E. Myers, *William James. His Life and Thought* (New Haven, Conn., and London: Yale University Press, 1986), 144.

20. Ibid., 152 ff.

21. *Philosophical Investigations*, trans. G. E. M. Anscombe (New York: MacMillan, 1968), sec. 89; *The Blue and Brown Books* (New York: Harper and Row, 1965), 26 ff.

22. Myers, 159.

23. By pointing out three basic tendencies in contemporary philosophies of time (Prigogine, Ricoeur, and Heidegger/Rorty) I follow Mike Sandbothe's *The Temporalization of Time. Basic Tendencies in Modern Debate on Time in Philosophy and Sciences* (Lanham, Md., and New York: Rowman & Littlefield, 2002).

24. James, *Pragmatism*, 49.

25. Ibid.

26. Ibid., 50.

27. Ibid.

28. This argument is quite convincing, although James, later on, raises an objection against its general validity: a "soulless body" (or "automatic sweetheart"), he says (probably with Offenbach's marionette "Olympia" in mind), can never be a "full equivalent" for a "spiritually animated maiden." *Pragmatism*, 296, footnote 2. Even in a world that is restricted to the time dimensions of past and present, we look for "sympathy and recognition" where we love, and this renders impossible the exchangeability of a materialist and spiritualist "reading" of the beloved person: would we believe that our love is just a machine, then this would alter our attitude toward her.

29. Ibid., 52.

30. Ibid., 54.

31. Ibid.

32. Ibid., 56.

33. Ibid., 55.

34. *Varieties*, 437.

35. *Pragmatism*, 55.

36. Cf. Richard Rorty, "Religious faith, responsibility, and romance," *The Cambridge Companion to William James*, ed. Ruth Anna Putnam (Cambridge: Cambridge University Press 1997), 84–102; 91.

37. Hilary Putnam defends James's argument in *Renewing Philosophy*: Although the "Will to Believe" has "received a great deal of hostile criticism, I believe that its logic is, in fact, precise and impeccable." *Renewing*, 191 ff.

38. Rorty, "Religious Faith."

39. *Pragmatism*, 56.

40. Well-informed critics of Habermas, like Maeve Cooke, object at this point that Habermas' theory—in opposition to James's, we may add—suffers from a "reduction of the notion of 'experience' to empirical experience based on observation or controlled scientific experiments." A less reductionist framework, according to Cooke, "would allow religious experience as well as ethical and aesthetical experience to count as evidence when participants in discourses argue on disputed matters of validity." Maeve Cook, "Inspiration or Illusion? The Place of Religion in a Critical Theory of Society" (unpublished paper, 1999), 25.

41. *Pragmatism*, 56.

42. Ibid., 60.

43. *The Letters of William James*, 2 vols. Edited by Henry James. (Boston: Atlantic Monthly Press, 1920), vol. I, 152 ff.

44. *Letters*, 147 ff.

45. Perry, I, 682 ff; Carlson, 372–378.

46. *Pragmatism*, 60.

47. Ibid., 61.

48. Ibid.

49. Rorty, "Religious," 99.

50. *Pragmatism*, 44.

51. "Religious," 96.

52. Gauchet, 178 ff.

53. Charles Taylor, "Foreword" to Marcel Gauchet, *The Disenchantment of the World*, ix–xv; xiii.

54. Ibid.

55. Gauchet, 178.

56. Ibid., 179.

57. Taylor, xiii.

58. Jürgen Habermas, "Transzendenz von innen, Transzendenz ins Diesseits," *Texte und Kontexte* (Frankfurt: Suhrkamp, 1991), 127–156; 127.

59. *Varieties*, 525.

60. Gauchet, 179.

61. Ibid., 199.

62. Ibid., 191.

63. *Pragmatism*, 134 ff.

2

~

HILARY PUTNAM

Philosophy as a Reconstructive Activity: William James on Moral Philosophy[1]

In his "Introduction: Reconstruction as Seen Twenty-Five Years Later" to the second edition of *Reconstruction in Philosophy*,[2] John Dewey wrote,

> Today Reconstruction *of* Philosophy is a more suitable title than Reconstruction *in* Philosophy. For the intervening events have sharply defined, have brought to a head, the basic postulate of the text: namely that the distinctive office, problems and subject matter of philosophy grow out of the stresses and strains in the community life in which a given form of philosophy arises, and that, accordingly, its specific problems vary with the changes in human life that are always going on and that at times constitute a crisis and a turning point in human history.[3]

Both Dewey and his philosophical ally William James shared the conception of philosophy as a reconstructive activity, an activity that aims at making a difference to the way we understand and the way we live our scientific, aesthetic, educational, religious, and political lives, one comprehensive and durable enough to deserve the name of a "reconstruction." But by the time Dewey wrote the words I have just quoted, philosophy was going in a very different direction or set of directions, which is why Dewey writes that we need "reconstruction *of* philosophy" and not just reconstruction *in* philosophy.

31

And he goes on to lament that contemporary philosophy—in the 1940s, when those words were penned—is "concerned for the improvement of techniques" and with "erudite scholarship about the past that throws no light on the issues now troubling mankind" at the expense of "substantial content," and in a way that involves "a withdrawal from the present scene."[4]

Today, however, a half century after Dewey's "Reconstruction as Seen Twenty-Five Years Later" was written, the willingness to consider that the pragmatist tradition may say something worth listening to seems to be on the rise (although, unfortunately, not always for the best of reasons).[5] In the present essay, I shall explore the way in which such a conception of philosophy informs the thinking of one great pragmatist. My pragmatist of choice today, however, will be not John Dewey but the ally I mentioned, William James, whose reconstructive conception of philosophy is still less often noted than is Dewey's.

Before I turn to James, let me say one further word. I am troubled by the way in which contemporary moral philosophy still seems to have what one might call a "Queen of the Sciences" conception of philosophy ("sciences" in the sense of "knowledges" or "Wissenschaften," that is, not natural sciences). When I read today's distinguished moral philosophers, the conception of the subject I often encounter is that the moral philosopher will provide a set of principles—to be sure, very general and abstract ones—which *hoi polloi* are then to apply. In a recent and brilliant study, Michelle Moody-Adams—who acknowledges Dewey as a predecessor—has criticized both this conception and the various recent attacks on the very idea of moral theory:

> An effective challenge to . . . skepticism about the relevance of moral theory to moral life must begin by relinquishing the vain insistence on the authoritative status of philosophical moral inquiry—along with the implausible notion that moral philosophy produces moral expertise. There is a middle way between the skeptical anti-theorist view on which moral philosophy should be *replaced* by some other discipline—such as cultural anthropology, or experimental psychology, or literature, or some combination thereof—and the unsupportable view that moral philosophy is the final court of appeal on questions of moral justification. That middle way involves thinking of moral philosophy as a valuable and distinctive participant in the ongoing process of moral inquiry.[6]

As we shall see, what bothers Moody-Adams today also bothered William James, and her idea that moral philosophy can be a "valuable and distinctive participant" without claiming "authoritative status" is one that James anticipated. But my aim is not simply to celebrate James today (for some of his metaphysical assumptions were certainly problematic), but to see what were the insights and what were the problems in the ways in which a great, if still neglected, philosopher thought about the problem of "reconstruction in philosophy." For the most part, my discussion will be based on the essay in which James discusses the status of moral philosophy at greatest length, and in which he connects that status explicitly with his own pragmatist theory of truth—"The Moral Philosopher and the Moral Life"[7]—and I shall read that essay in the light of my own exegetical work on James's theory of truth, as revealed in the whole course of his writing.[8]

1. THE "CASUISTIC QUESTION"

James distinguishes three questions within the general field of moral philosophy, which he calls respectively the psychological question, the metaphysical question, and the casuistic question.[9] By "the casuistic question" James has in mind the task of working out a specific moral code. As we shall see, he regards the task as a paradoxical one—and especially so for the philosopher!

James begins by making the important point that the philosopher already has a moral ideal of his own simply by virtue of being a philosopher, namely the moral ideal of a *system*. (It is not often remarked that the desire for a moral system is itself a moral ideal, is it?) Next, James tells us that we stand ourselves at present in the place of that philosopher, the philosopher who has the ideal of a comprehensive system of ethics, a system of ethical truths that we can discover if we take pains. But, he goes on, "We must not fail to realize all the features that the situation comports. In the first place we will not be skeptics. We [hold to it] that there is a truth to be ascertained." And he continues: "But in the second place we have just gained the insight that that truth cannot be a self-proclaiming set of laws, or an abstract 'moral reason', but can only exist in act or in the shape of an opinion held by some thinker really to be found. There is, however, no visible thinker invested with authority."[10]

This is what makes the problem of moral philosophy, or, more specifically, "the casuistic question," paradoxical in James's view: on the one hand, we are to seek what moral philosophers have always sought, a system of moral truths, but we must do so without relying on the faith that there is an abstract moral reason or a self-proclaiming set of moral laws. "Shall we then simply proclaim our own ideals as the law-giving ones?" James asks. "No! For if we are true philosophers, we must throw our own spontaneous ideals, even the dearest, impartially in with that total mass of ideals which are fairly to be judged."[11]

That is, the task assigned to moral philosophers is to seek not an Archimedean point, but a point of some impartiality. They must begin by looking at all the ideals that human beings have, or at least at all the ideals that men and women of good will have. We are to throw all our ideals, even the dearest, impartially in with the total mass of ideals and then try to judge them impartially.

> But how then can we as philosophers ever find a test? How avoid complete moral skepticism on the one hand, and on the other escape bringing a wayward personal standard of our own along with us, on which we simply pin our faith? The dilemma is a hard one, nor does it grow a bit more easy as we revolve it in our minds. The entire undertaking of the philosopher obliges him to seek an impartial test. That test, however, must be incarnated in the demands of some actually existent person. And how can he pick out the person, save by an act in which his own sympathies and predilections are implied?[12]

That was James's problem, and it is our problem today: to find a route to objective ethical truths not in a Platonic realm of independently existing values, nor yet in a faculty of pure practical reason, as in Kant, but starting with the demands of actually existing persons—and to do this without simply pinning our faith on "a wayward personal standard of our own."

2. THE "METAPHYSICAL QUESTION"

Now let us turn to what James calls "the metaphysical question." James somewhat misleadingly—that is, misleadingly for us today—describes this as the question of what we mean by the words "obligation," "good," and "ill." Speaking of this as the question of what we "mean" suggests conceptual analysis; and that is not really what James means. What James means is rather an inquiry into the nature of obligation, good, ill, and so on—a metaphysical inquiry (which is very often what analytic philosophers also mean, even when they claim to be only "analyzing concepts").

First of all, James argues that there cannot be any good or bad in a universe without sentient life. Perhaps only G. E. Moore at his dottiest would have disagreed with this. "The moment one sentient being, however, is made a part of the universe, there's a chance for goods and evils really to exist."[13]

However, James does not say merely, as would most philosophers, that there would be no goods and evils in a world without sentient beings; he maintains the metaphysical premise that obligations—all obligations, including epistemic ones—and all standards, including epistemic ones, can only arise from the demands of sentient beings. When something is "required of us," it *is* literally required—"demanded" is James's word for this—by some sentient being or other, and it is, so to speak, the will of the other that we experience as a demand upon us, and nothing more than this.

James makes a remarkable metaphysical move: "The moment one sentient being, however, is made a part of the universe there is a chance for goods and evils really to exist. Moral relations now have their *status* in that being's consciousness. So far as he feels anything to be good, he makes it good."[14]

If we stopped there, this would fit all the subjectivist and relativist readings of James. If we ignored the context, we might really read this as meaning, "if it satisfies him, it is good." In a sense James says that—but he inflects it in a very unexpected way. "It *is* good, for him; and being good for him is absolutely good. For he is the sole creator of values in that universe. And outside of his opinion, things have no moral character at all."[15]

Again, if we stopped there, we would have as relativist or subjectivist a doctrine as one can find. But now listen: "In such a universe as that, it would of course be absurd to raise the question of whether the solitary thinker's judgments of good and ill are true or not. Truth supposes a standard outside of the thinker to which he must conform. But here the thinker is a sort of divinity subject to no higher judge. Let us call the supposed universe which he inhabits a moral solitude."[16]

This one sentence—"Truth supposes a standard outside of the thinker to which he must conform"—constitutes a one-line statement of what has often been taken to be "Wittgenstein's private language argument." I have argued elsewhere[17] that Wittgenstein did *not* in fact have a "community standards" view of truth; but James *did*, provided you are willing to count as the community the whole of the human race up to what James calls "the last man." More precisely, what James had was an "ultimate consensus" view of truth; while James's philosophy has many facets, one important facet is his insistence, early and late,[18] that truth requires what he calls "ultimate consensus," that what is true is what becomes "coercive" over opinion in the long run, what becomes "the whole drift of thought."[19] But in the passage I just quoted, James is adding an important qualification: meaningful consensus requires something more than convergence in the opinions of one person (or, as we immediately see, even in the independently arrived at opinions of persons who do not communicate). Meaningful consensus presupposes *community*.

James makes this point explicitly by imagining a world in which there are two sentient beings who are indifferent to one another. Of such a world he says,

Not only is there no single point of view within it from which
the values of things can be unequivocally judged, there is not
even the demand for such a point of view, since the two thinkers
are supposed to be indifferent to each other's thoughts and acts.
Multiply the thinkers into a pluralism, and we find real for us in
the ethical sphere something like that world which the antique
skeptics conceived of, in which individual minds are the measures
of all things, and in which no one objective truth, but only a
multitude of subjective opinions can be found. But this is a kind
of world with which the philosopher, so long as he holds to the
hope of a philosophy, will not put up. [I don't know of any place
where James more clearly rejects Rortyian relativism.] Among
the various ideals represented there must be, he thinks, some
which have the more truth or authority, and to these the others
ought to yield so that system and subordination may reign.[20]

At this point, James begins to develop his own moral views. I don't
want to go into the details of those views. What I want to point out is the
important statement that truth presupposes a standard external to the
thinker—a standard however, that is not transcendental. James is quite explicit
on that. In the same essay, he writes that even if there is a God, "still the
theoretic question would remain, What is the ground of the obligation even
here?"[21] (Shades of Kant!) And that ground must be a real claim, one which
is felt as real. "The only force that appeals to us, which either a living God
or an abstract ideal order can wield, is found in the everlasting ruby vaults
of our own human hearts as they happen to beat responsively or not
responsively to the claim. So far as they do feel it, when made by a living
consciousness it is life answering to life."[22] What we want is an ethical
standard external to the subjective opinions of any one thinker, but not
external to all thinkers or all life.

Needless to say, the two metaphysical assumptions I have isolated are
deeply problematic ones. The idea that obligation can be *reduced* to demand
is not one that is likely to find adherents today—apart from the Utilitarians,
who are, of course, still with us. James's way of attempting the reduction
turns on the attractive idea that the problem in ethics is ultimately the
reconciliation of ideals.[23] To the further question of what makes a reconciliation
objectively right, James's answer would be: just what makes the outcome of
any inquiry right, that the particular reconciliation, or the particular outcome,
becomes the "ultimate consensus." This answer, however, presupposes that
truth *can* be identified with ultimate consensus, and that view also has few
adherents. (I myself have criticized it more than once,[24] and I shall criticize
it again later in this paper.) James's metaphysics of morals stands or falls
(unfortunately) with his metaphysics of truth.

Why then should we who do *not* think that truth can be defined as "ultimate consensus" be interested in James's moral philosophy? For at least two reasons: first, even if truth is not the same thing as what the human community will converge to in the long run, nevertheless James was right to see a connection between the existence of community and the possibility of distinguishing between subjectivity and objectivity. The connection is not as simple as James's metaphysical account would have it, but, in fact, it is only through the experiences we have of winning others over through argument, of being won over ourselves, of searching for consensus between individuals with different temperaments, different funded knowledges, and different ideologies, that we come to have and to appreciate such notions as *good reason*. Perhaps the existence of community is not a "logical" prerequisite for the existence of objective justification, but it is an existential and phenomenological prerequisite for the existence of the only forms of objective justification we know. And, second, because James is right to remind us that if objective resolutions to controversial questions require ongoing "experiments"[25] and a continual attempt to arrive at consensus, then there is something deeply wrong with the idea of "an ethical philosophy dogmatically made up in advance." I now turn to this second aspect of James's thought.

3. Truth about Middle-Sized Dry Goods versus Truth in Ethics

We are in the position that all of us claim general validity for our moral views, or whatever views, while at the same time we don't all agree. Let me qualify that. On some things we do agree. In fact, though epistemologists may disagree on what the standards are for saying that there are enough chairs for us all to sit on, we don't really disagree about that very often. We may disagree about what Roderick Chisholm wrote in a philosophy paper, or what Quine writes in a philosophy paper, but these disagreements *literally play no role in our lives*. Nobody checks whether Memorial Hall still exists *one bit differently* because of all the thousands of pages that have been written using that sort of example. Nobody checks whether there is a book on this table *one bit differently* in spite of all the thousands and thousands of pages, the thousands and thousands of *books*, that have been written on how we know there is a book on the table. To be sure, a philosopher might say "It is not clear what is meant by pragmatist talk, James's talk or Quine's talk, of the best trade-off between predictive power, preserving founded beliefs, and elegance, even in the case of 'There's a book on the table'"; but the fact is that we are in agreement concerning the standards for that, at least when direct perceptual verification is concerned. In the law court, when it is a question of indirect verification, we may disagree. But ultimately the truth in such a case is determined by the possibility of direct verification, as James says. And on direct verification we are in agreement—in agreement as shown by our lives, not by our philosophical words.

As James tells us in the opening paragraphs of this essay,[26] however, there are certain kinds of matters, especially moral and political matters, that are so problematic that we not only often disagree, but even if we were to come to agreement, we might not be sure whether the agreement would last or was a temporary phase in the evolution of society. We cannot really be sure in these sorts of cases, James says, "until the last man has had his experience and said his say," which is to say we will never be sure in the case of these matters beyond all possibility of changing our minds.

James, to be sure, recognizes that "abstract rules can indeed help" in such moral and political matters,[27] but he also cautions that "the ethical philosopher must wait on facts," and furthermore, that

> he only knows if he makes a bad mistake, the cries of the wounded will soon inform him of the fact. In all this the philosopher is just like the rest of us non-philosophers, so far as we are just and sympathetic instinctively, and so far as we are open to the voice of complaint. His function is in fact indistinguishable from that of the best kind of statesman at the present day. His books on ethics, therefore, so far as they truly touch the moral life, must more and more ally themselves with a literature which is confessedly tentative and suggestive rather than dogmatic—I mean with novels and dramas of the deeper sort, with sermons, with books on statecraft and philanthropy and social and economical reform. Treated in this way ethical treatises may be voluminous and luminous as well; but they can never be *final*, except in their abstractest and vaguest features, and they must more and more abandon old-fashioned, clearcut, and would-be 'scientific' form.[28]

I see James, in this passage, as revoking—rather than simply contradicting—his earlier statement that "if we are true philosophers, we must throw our own spontaneous ideals, even the dearest, impartially in with that total mass of ideals which are fairly to be judged." The writing in "The Moral Philosopher and the Moral Life" is, as James' writing always is, highly "literary." James takes us along with him on a mental journey, a musing, in the course of which a number of twists and turns take place. At the end of the journey, we have to see that James is telling us that the moral philosopher with which he started, the moral philosopher who has no ideal of her own except the ideal of a "system" will come up empty-handed—or come up with nothing but "the abstractest and vaguest features" of morality. The price of ethical treatises that really *treat* the moral life is the willingness to take a stand that does not pretend to the total impartiality that led to the seeming paradox that moral philosophy is required to produce a whole moral world practically *ex nihilo*. In this James is being true to his perpetual insistence on the agent point of view as the only one ultimately available to us, as well as to his pragmatic insistence that the standards by which inquiry is conducted themselves emerge from the give and take, the conflict of ideals and points of view, and cannot be laid down beforehand.

4. SOME PROBLEMS WITH A NORMATIVE CONSENSUS THEORY OF TRUTH

Let us now consider some criticisms that might be made of consensus views of either truth or rationality. The consensus that Peirce and James had in mind and that today's consensus theorists also have in mind was an unforced consensus, a consensus reached after experimentation and discussion. One might ask, "Well, why should we identify truth with the outcome of open and free discussion? Why not identify it with the will of the strongest? If somebody has the power to impose his view forever, if some super-Hitler can impose his view forever, that would show the super-Hitler is the strongest. Why shouldn't we say truth is just the will of the stronger?" This is the question raised by Thrasymachus in Plato's *Republic*.

One answer would be that a "truth" that is accepted only out of fear of the tyrant is the "truth" of a moral solitude. "Truth supposes a standard outside the thinker to which he must conform," and the tyrant acknowledges no such standard. Just as in the universe with only a single thinker, "it would of course be absurd" to raise the question of whether the tyrant's judgments of good and ill are true or not, unless it be from the point of view of the tyrant's subjects (assuming *they* form a community, and are not held together only by a common fear of the tyrant). You cannot have a community, James thinks, if you are deaf to "the cries of the wounded." In addition, both Peirce[29] and James argue that any attempt to impose answers to our questions—no matter of what sort—by sheer authority—including the authority of allegedly a priori truths—will fail in the long run.

What Peirce argued,[30] and what James is building on in Peirce's thought, is the claim that we won't, in fact, arrive at beliefs that can withstand criticism, that can withstand refutation, if we "block the paths of inquiry." As a matter of human experience, the "Method of Authority" and the "Method of What Is Agreeable to Reason" have met failure. They haven't led to consensus. They have led to disagreements and to much less pragmatic success than we've had in the three hundred years since Bacon.[31] The pragmatist line is to argue that, even if the notions James employs in *Pragmatism*[32] of true ideas "carry[ing] us prosperously from any one part of our experience to any other part, linking things satisfactorily, working securely . . ." are vague, they are not empty: we know from experience that we don't do as well when we block the paths of inquiry. The pragmatist refusal to tell us once and for all exactly how to conduct scientific inquiry or exactly how to conduct moral inquiry is not accidental; it is intrinsic to the view that standards of inquiry should be expected to change in the course of inquiry itself.

5. IS JAMES'S INSISTENCE ON THE AGENT POINT OF VIEW COMPATIBLE WITH HIS CONSENSUS THEORY OF TRUTH?

Sometimes philosophers who are a little surprised that I "work on" James have asked me what I have *learned* from James. Of course, I feel that my debts to James are too long to list in a paragraph. But when I am asked the question, I think more or less immediately of two things: first, the idea that we must not be afraid of offering our own philosophic picture, even though we know that our picture is fallible (and based on "our own ideals") and that it always needs to be discussed with and by others, seems to me much needed at a time when the image of philosophy as a sort of final authority still dominates so much moral philosophy. It is this aspect of James that I have been stressing in this essay. And second—but not in importance—I have been impressed and strongly influenced by the stress in James on the agent point of view.[33]

That stress is complementary to the insights I've been talking about, the Peircean insights in James. James always has a "we" in mind, his theory of truth is a theory of truth for "us"; various forms of the first-person plural pronoun occur again and again in James. But in James, the emphasis on the "we" is always balanced by an emphasis on the "I." James simultaneously connects truth with the ideal of rational consensus and insists on our right, indeed our responsibility, to *take a stand*, an individual stand. Not surprisingly, that too is justified by a *pragmatic* argument. We will not do as well as we could do in morality unless we are willing to take a stand *in advance* of the evidence, to commit ourselves to ideas that *we cannot yet* intersubjectively validate.[34]

Of course, James is not the first or the last philosopher to have such an idea. Some years ago I discovered a very interesting paper in which Albrecht Wellmer argues that the emphasis on the agent point of view is actually *incompatible* with the Habermasian (and Jamesian) idea of ultimate consensus as a *necessary and sufficient condition* for truth.[35]

In this paper, Wellmer begins by discussing the notion of rationality, then criticizes Richard Rorty's sharp distinction between "rational argument," operating within a system, and irrational or arational "invention." The point I just referred to occurs when Wellmer discusses rational consensus as a criterion of truth.[36] He writes,

> What I've said comes close to some of the considerations which Habermas has put forward in support of a consensus theory of truth. Truth, according to this theory, is the content of a rational consensus; and a consensus can be called 'rational' if it has been achieved under conditions of an ideal speech situation. As I have already indicated above, however, I do not believe that a consensus theory of truth and the peculiar account of discursive rationality which goes with it can be justified. Truth, as I've argued elsewhere,[37] cannot be defined in terms of a rational consensus, even if truth in *some* sense implies the possibility of a rational consensus. For to put it in a nutshell: although truth is public, the *recognition* of truth is always *my* recognition: i.e. *each of us* must be convinced by arguments if a consensus is to be called rational. But then the consensus cannot be what convinces us of the validity of a truth claim.

Certainly, we can't decide if something is true by asking what other people think—by taking votes, taking a poll, and counting the votes. Thus, Wellmer asserts, "Although truth is public, it is not decided on publicly: I *myself* have to decide in each single case whether I ought to take an argument seriously or not, whether an objection is serious or irrelevant, or whether a truth claim has been justified. In short: it is always 'I myself' who has to evaluate what the others say—their truth claims, arguments and objections; and as far as these evaluations are fallible, they cannot become infallible by becoming collective."[38]

In one sense, of course, this last remark is too strong (especially the "in each single case"). In practice, once I have decided that certain people are rational, I *do* accept their consensus for truth on many matters—on what I read in an atlas, on what my doctor tells me, on most scientific matters, etc. But if I myself am one of the sources of the relevant information, one of the people whose task it is to inquire into the matter, then Wellmer is right.

Wellmer is saying that if one is inquiring into whether something is true, e.g., whether there is life in another galaxy, one cannot conduct the inquiry by looking to see *if other people are converging on the view that there is life in the other galaxy*; one has to look at the other galaxy, at the astronomical, biological, etc. evidence, and make up one's *own* mind. At first blush the argument may seem unfair; after all, Habermas, just as much as Peirce and James, thinks of truth as what we converge on *if we use the right method* (the scientific method in the ordinary "narrow" sense of "scientific method," in the case of the question "Is there life in the other galaxy?"), not as what we converge on if we use the Method of What Is Agreeable to Reason, for example. But Wellmer's point is deeper than it looks. For, even if we all use the scientific method, still, as scientists, we do not decide if there is life in the other galaxy by *seeing if other scientists are converging on the view that there is*; even in an ideally-scientific community—especially in an ideally-scientific community—each scientist has to make up his or her own mind. But if "It is true that there is life in the other galaxy" *means* that other people, using the right method, will converge on the view that there is, then it would be perfectly appropriate to look at other people to determine the truth of the sentence.

But is this argument effective against James? Although, in *The Meaning of Truth*, absolute truth is characterized by James as membership in an "ideal set" of "formulations" on which there will be *"ultimate consensus"*[39]—a very Peircean formulation—James never claims that "ultimate consensus" is what "true" *means*. Metaphysics, in James's view, consists of hypotheses; metaphysical truths are not analytic. On the other hand, even if we take truth to be only contingently identical with "ultimate consensus, provided inquiry is conducted in the right way," it may seem that the problem Wellmer raises does not wholly go away. For if I ever come to believe, to accept, this "theory of truth," why should I *then* not determine if there is life in the other galaxy *by investigating the conclusions the others are coming to*, rather than by investigating that galaxy? But this is a question to which James has an answer.

The answer is that *whether an inquiry is conducted in the right way*— which, for James, means with attention to concrete fact, and particularly when the inquiry is a moral one, with attention to "the cries of the wounded," fallibilistically, etc.—is itself a question that cannot be answered from a nonengaged point of view. "I myself" have to say whether the inquiry is properly conducted or not, and I cannot do this without participating in the inquiry myself. (This would also be Habermas's answer to Wellmer.[40])

While this *may* meet Wellmer's objection, there remain serious objections to the theory that being true is the same thing as being part of the "ultimate consensus," not the least being the possibility that there will *be* no ultimate consensus, not even on the question whether there ever was a conference on "Philosophy, Education and Culture" in Edinburgh. (And Peirce's counterfactual version of the ultimate consensus theory is even more problematic.)

We should not, then, accept the Peirce-James view—that truth is to be identified with the tremendously Utopian idea of "the ultimate consensus"— of the theory to be reached (and to become coercive) at the end of indefinitely continued investigation. Nevertheless, a great deal that James wants to deny *should* be denied. James is right to tell us that we do not have to think of truth as presupposing a single—and therefore mysterious—"relation of agreement with reality"—*one and the same relation in all cases*—or as presupposing some mysterious Absolute—an infinite mind able to overcome the limitations of all limited and finite points of view (as in Absolute Idealism)—or some other piece of transcendental machinery *beneath* our practice of making and criticizing truth claims that makes that practice possible. Insofar as a general account of truth is possible at all, it seems to me that it was given by Frege: to call any content (any Fregean "thought") true is to make the very same claim that one makes by asserting that content. (But substitute "sentence" for "content" (*Gedanke*) in that formula, as today's "disquotationalists" do, and one loses the entire point Frege was trying to make!) Frege's point was not that "true" is just a word that we attach to marks and noises[41] that we assert, but that what connects descriptive judgments to the world is the *content* of those judgments; a descriptive judgment is intrinsically about some part or aspect of the world—that's what makes it the judgment it is. To think of a judgment as a mere *representation* that has to be put into "correspondence" with the world is a disastrous error. But Frege's point also applies to judgments that are not descriptions—to mathematical judgments, normative judgements, etc., to give an account of "truth in mathematics," or "truth in ethics," etc., what is required is to give an account of the content of mathematical, ethical, etc. judgments; or, as Wittgenstein would have put it—eliminating any lingering metaphysical moments in Frege's thought—of what we *do* when we make mathematical, ethical, etc. claims—but without succumbing to the temptation to think that an account of "what we do" must be a *reductive* account.[42]

In short, we must not think that rejecting metaphysical accounts of truth is the same as rejecting the notion of truth (or treating it as a mere "adjective of commendation"). On the contrary, giving up the idea that there must be a single metaphysical account that (simultaneously) accounts for the use of "true" in ethics as well as in particle physics, in connection with the tables and chairs as well as in connection with works of art, in religion as well as in cooking, can and should free us to see that we need no better ground for treating moral assertions as capable of truth and falsity than the fact that we can and do rationally discuss them, that we can and do treat them as capable of warranted assertability and warranted deniability. But to unpack that remark I would have to turn to the writing of yet another pragmatist—John Dewey.[43]

1. As so often in the past, once again I owe a debt of gratitude to Ruth Anna Putnam for her criticism of an earlier draft and for her valuable suggestions.

2. Dewey, *Reconstruction in Philosophy* (New York: Henry Holt and Co., first edition 1920, enlarged edition 1948).

3. Ibid., v–vi.

4. All quotes in this paragraph are from ibid., vi–vii.

5. E.g., Rorty has tried hard to connect pragmatism with the rejection of the notion of objective truth, as well as the rejection of any notions of justification that is not purely "sociological," while Richard Posner and Stanley Fish use "pragmatism" as a label for a form of utilitarianism and for unapologetic opportunism, respectively.

6. Michelle Moody-Adams, *Fieldwork in Familiar Places: Morality, Culture and Philosophy* (Cambridge, Mass.: Harvard University Press, 1997), 176. See epilogue as well.

7. "The Moral Philosopher and the Moral Life," in *The Works of William James; The Will to Believe and Other Essays*, Frederick H. Burkhardt and Fredson Bowers eds. (Cambridge, Mass.: Harvard University Press, 1979). All quotations are from this edition. The opening sentence of the essay (141)—"The main purpose of this paper is to show that there is no such thing possible as an ethical philosophy dogmatically made up in advance. We all help to determine the content of ethical philosophy so far as we contribute to the race's moral life"—is the very point that Michelle Moody-Adams makes in the passage I quoted.

8. Cf. my "James' Theory of Truth," in Ruth Anna Putnam ed., *The Cambridge Companion to William James* (Cambridge: Cambridge University Press, 1997).

9. "Moral," 142.

10. Ibid., 151.

11. Ibid.

12. Ibid., 151–152.

13. Ibid., 145.

14. Ibid., 145–146.

15. Ibid., 146.

16. Ibid.

17. "On Wittgenstein's Philosophy of Mathematics," *The Aristotelian Society*, Supplementary Volume LXX (1996): 243–264.

18. See "James' Theory of Truth" for the evidence for this claim.

19. See "James' Theory."

20.   "Moral," 146–147.

21.   Ibid., 148.

22.   Ibid., 149.

23.   This idea is developed in section III of "The Moral Philosopher and the Moral Life."

24.   See "Pragmatism," *Proceedings of the Aristotelian Society*, xcv, part 3 (1995): 291–397; also my "James' Theory of Truth."

25.   "Moral," 156–157.

26.   The first paragraph of "The Moral Philosopher and the Moral Life" runs as follows: "The main purpose of this essay is to show that there is no such thing possible as an ethical philosophy dogmatically made up in advance. We all help to determine the content of moral philosophy so far as we contribute to the race's moral life. In other words, there can be no final truth in ethics any more than in physics, until the last man has had his experience and said his say. In the one case as in the other, however, the hypotheses we now make while waiting, and the acts to which they prompt us, are among the indispensable conditions which determine what that 'say' shall be" (141).

27.   Ibid., 158.

28.   Ibid., 158–159.

29.   That there is a strong Peircean strain in James's views on truth is argued in "James' Theory of Truth."

30.   In "How to Make Our Ideas Clear" and "The Fixation of Belief," reprinted in Charles Hartshorne and Paul Weiss eds., *The Collected Papers of Charles Sanders Peirce*, vol. 5 (Cambridge, Mass.: Harvard University Press, 1965).

31.   Although Peirce also argues that the "Method of Tenacity"—which is common to both the appeal to Authority and the appeal to what is Agreeable to Reason—makes "true" little more than an emotive word for beliefs one likes, and this could, perhaps, be regarded as a "conceptual" argument.

32.   *The Works of William James; Pragmatism*, Frederick H. Burkhardt and Fredson Bowers eds. (Cambridge, Mass.: Harvard University Press, 1975), 34.

33.   See, in particular, the closing pages of my *The Many Faces of Realism* (LaSalle, Ill.: Open Court, 1987).

34.   "The Will to Believe" and "The Sentiment of Rationality," in *The Works of William James; The Will to Believe and Other Essays.*

35.   Albrecht Wellmer, "Intersubjectivity and Reason," in L. Herzburg and J. Pietanen, eds., *Perspectives on Human Conduct* (Leiden/New York: E. J. Brill, 1988), 128–163.

36.   Ibid., 157.

37.   Wellmer is probably referring to his *Ethik und Dialog* (Frankfurt: Suhrkamp Verlag, 1986), 69–102.

38.   "Intersubjectivity and Reason," 157–8.

39.   *The Works of William James: The Meaning of Truth*, Frederick H. Burkhardt and Fredson Bowers eds. (Cambridge, Mass.: Harvard University Press, 1975), 143–4.

40.   See, for example, Habermas's *Theory of Communicative Action* (Boston: Beacon Press, 1984) 1: 113 ff. Habermas is discussing the stance that an ideal social scientist must take, but, in his view, this is just the stance that anyone interesting in understanding for its own sake must take.

41.   "Marks and noises" is Rorty's expression for our assertions, but all "disquotationalists" from Ayer and Carnap on have supposed that "true" is a predicate of such syntactic objects. Tarski's view, to which they often appeal, is more nuanced: on the one hand, he agrees with them in viewing sentences as syntactic objects, characterizable apart from their meaning—which is a mistake—on the other hand, he presupposes that the terms in our sentences have what he calls "concrete meanings," and he does not attempt to reduce our grasp of these meanings to the mastery of assertability conditions, as today's disquotationalists all do. For a detailed discussion of the difference between Frege's view and the disquotationalist views with which it is so often confused, see my "*The Dewey Lectures 1994*: Sense, Nonsense and the Senses; An Inquiry into the Powers of the Human Mind," *The Journal of Philosophy* XCI, no. 2 (Sept. 1994): lecture III.

42.   I discuss the error in reductionist readings of Wittgenstein in my *Pragmatism* (Oxford: Blackwell, 1995), as well as in the paper cited in the previous note.

43.   In these closing sentences I have borrowed from the close of my "Are Moral and Legal Values Made or Discovered," *Legal Theory* 1, no. 1 (March 1995): 19.

3

ANTJE GIMMLER

Pragmatic Aspects of Hegel's Thought

Translated by Reinhild Steingrover–McRae

While the analytical philosophical tradition since the turn of the century has generally considered Hegel's thought to be meaningless and has only regarded selected aspects as interesting for larger connections, it appears that this situation is currently changing. An increase of recent publications that engage Hegel's philosophy in problem-oriented approaches can be noted.[1] Questions regarding future directions focus primarily on the relevance and the pioneering aspects of Hegel's legacy.[2] This currently noticeable Hegel renaissance in continental and Anglo-American Hegel research receives crucial impulses from a philosophical movement that gathers together under the title of neopragmatism such disparate thinkers as Nicolas Rescher, Richard Rorty, Hilary Putnam, Jürgen Habermas, Robert Brandom, and Donald Davidson. It furthermore counts Wittgenstein, Wilfrid Sellars, and Willard van Orman Quine among its members as well. The term "neopragmatism" refers to the contemporary, multifaceted philosophical movement that reconsiders and reutilizes basic themes and elements of classic American pragmatism in the context of the linguistic turn, i.e., in the service of an investigation of language and meaning as dependent on use and practice. It is especially this school of thought that assists Hegel research in defining new approaches and perspectives.

In order to explain Hegel's role in neopragmatism we can take as a first indication the reception of Hegel in classic pragmatism. Connections between Hegel's philosophy and the pragmatism of Charles S. Peirce and William James can be found; but a strong and positive reference to Hegel is most notable in the third party of the triad of classic American pragmatism, John Dewey. Dewey received his philosophical training under the Neo-Hegelian George Sylvester Morris and regarded himself in his early career as a Hegelian. This influence remains visible in his writings until the time of that classic text of pragmatism *The Quest for Certainty*, in which he describes his position as "a philosophy of experimental idealism."[3] But classic American pragmatism around the turn of the century has also constituted itself through the confrontation with Neo-Hegelian metaphysical conceptions, as represented, for example, by Josiah Royce or Francis H. Bradley. Thus the history of relations between Hegel, Neo-Hegelianism, and classic pragmatism can be characterized by both engagement and confrontation.

But more important than this multifaceted history of reception connecting Hegel, classic pragmatism, and neopragmatism—which in turn refers to classic pragmatism—is the actual relationship. Classic pragmatism—especially that of Dewey—already contains not only the explicitly Hegelian rejection of dualistic philosophy, but also an antirepresentationalism whose roots can be traced back to Hegel. This antirepresentationalism becomes central to neopragmatism. Various representatives of neopragmatism refer to Hegel because in Hegel's idealism the central themes of neopragmatism can already be identified as preconfigured, or at least can be traced to their origins: namely, the problematizing or rejection of a representational theory of epistemology and its related epistemological or ontological presuppositions. In this sense of a positive reference we may understand Sellar's much-quoted statement regarding Hegel: "that great foe of 'immediacy.'"[4] Such actual commonalties lead to a new consideration of Hegel's philosophy from a neopragmatic perspective: "Hegel himself was more of a pragmatist than is ordinarily granted."[5] But what is pragmatic about Hegel?[6] Is Hegel a genuinely pragmatic thinker?

A problematic aspect of a possible answer to this question is that no commonly shared, precise determination of what can be understood by "pragmatism" exists. For heuristic purposes I will first sketch out a typology of pragmatism in order to clarify the meaning of the terms "pragmatic" and "pragmatism" as they are used in current discussions. This typology should make it possible to specify the question of pragmatic aspects of Hegel's thought. Secondly, I will discuss two neopragmatic interpretations of Hegel. Thirdly, I will present elements of Hegel's pragmatic antirepresentationalism with reference to his critique of epistemology. The crucial point in this paper will be that the concept of experience, which was already central for classic pragmatism, should be revalidated. Hegel's concept of experience, a nonempiricist one,[7] has the potential to lead us out of neopragmatic restrictions because in its antirepresentational conception of experience it regards action in its linguistic as well as poietic expressions.

1. WHICH PRAGMATISM?

Various philosophical approaches have been gathered under the term "pragmatism." As early as 1908, Arthur Lovejoy critically differentiated thirteen types of pragmatism, and at least as many variations of neopragmatism can be identified today.[8] The lowest common denominator among these variants may be the general and unquestioned thesis that practice takes precedence over theory. This fundamental thesis is shared not only by classic American pragmatism as well as current neopragmatism, but also by hermeneutic or constructivist-culturalist schools of thoughts that work with basic pragmatic elements. The preference for practice over theory can be explained more precisely as a conviction that "knowing how" is preferable to "knowing that"—that practice maintains explicatory priority over theory. But opinions are divided as to how practice should be more precisely defined, what status theory should have, and how exactly the preference of practice over theory should be understood. In the following, therefore, I will proceed from a more general conception of pragmatism, encompassing neopragmatism and classic pragmatism, and will attempt to name the commonalties of the various directions. In doing so, I will initially grant little importance to the differences between classic pragmatism and contemporary neopragmatism.[9] For a more specific examination of the definition of the terms practice and theory in pragmatic philosophies, the differences between classic pragmatism (for which language was a topic but which had not yet encountered the linguistic turn) and neopragmatism, (which developed out of the linguistic turn and its postanalytic critical transformation), will become more important.

An initial clarification of how pragmatism will be defined in this paper can be gained by examining more closely the reversal of the traditional relationship of theory and practice. This reversal is accompanied in all pragmatic theories by a problematizing and rejection of a so-called representationalism. The devaluation of "knowing that," a type of knowledge claim traditionally at the center of philosophy, and the revaluation of the status of the practical "knowing how" is accompanied by a relinquishment of a privileged knowledge that enables and justifies the practice of all. One of the most fundamental characteristics of the various forms of pragmatic philosophy is, therefore, its antirepresentationalism.[10] Pragmatic criticism is first directed against a representationalism characteristic of the rationalist and empirical approaches of modern philosophy—that is to say against a preferably mental, epistemological representationalism. Secondly, it is directed against a representationalism that has been influential even for currents of modern language philosophy, which is marked not by an image theory but by Kantian-constructivism. Because Kant insisted on the idea that a world that is independent from consciousness needs to be paired up with a form of regulatory epistemology that guarantees certainty and objectivity, his theory is regarded by pragmatism as representationalist. Pragmatism and neo-pragmatism, moreover, criticize Descartes and Locke as well as Kant for their representationalist concept of "knowing that."

All forms of representationalism maintain that—as neopragmatists like Rorty and classic pragmatists such as Dewey emphasize repeatedly—the world, which is characterized by its independence from concepts, judgments, language, or spirit, is to be adequately imagined, represented, or structured by terms and judgments, signs, sentences, ideas, schemata, or concepts. This assumption leads to numerous problems, according to classic American pragmatism and neopragmatism, including further ontological obligations, e.g., toward directly or indirectly realistic or antirealistic assumptions about the material world; obligations concerning how to understand the nature of concepts, signs, ideas, or perceptions; as well as a correspondence theory of truth.

A further problem is the mentalistic vocabulary that is a necessary part of the representational concept, especially from Descartes to Hume. The world is divided here into objects and ideas of objects, into appearance and reality. It is the task of the "inner" world, the ideas and signs, to provide certainty for the statements about the "material" world. If representation through linguistic signs and ideas is to be successful, a further prerequisite for the verifying reference toward this inner representation is necessary. As opaque and mediated the access to the world appears on the one hand, so transparent should consciousness be for itself on the other. A privileged position for self-referentiality and transparent introspection is a necessary ingredient of representationalism. The other side of the coin of this "quest for certainty"[11] is skepticism. Epistemological skepticism becomes a permanent companion to an epistemology that struggles for certainty.[12] From the perspective of pragmatism, epistemological skepticism receives an intensification through the transcendental Kantian version of represen-tationalism—that is to say, through a strategy that, according to Kantian thought, proffers a certain knowledge against skepticism. The dual track of questioning that results from the Kantian approach—namely, regarding the transcendental vanishing point of the schematizing and formatting understanding on the one hand, and regarding the possibilities of getting beyond mere appearance (i.e., the limitations of the schematized) on the other—contains not just the danger of skepticism but also of relativism.

The pragmatic reaction to the—here only briefly sketched out—problem that is presented by representationalism is not an attempt to find a solution within the representational approach. Classic pragmatism and neopragmatism rather initiate a far-reaching and fundamental reorganization the result of which is that numerous problems of representational theories don't occur in the first place.[13] This reorganization pertains especially to the theoretical relationship of the subject of classic epistemology to the world, that is to say the preference of theory over practice. A theoreticist understanding of philosophy and a representationalist approach to cognition are mutually dependent. Cognition is for representationalism always contemplative, it is only concerned with the "knowing that." Dewey regards this claim for totality to which the theoretical and contemplative concept of cognition is bound as the "great intellectuallistic fallacy"[14] that philosophy has repeatedly made since the Greeks. Pragmatism changes the perspective entirely by refocusing attention on a practical-pragmatic relationship to the world. The "spectators' theory of knowledge,"[15] as Dewey has called it, is abandoned in favor of the engagement of the active subject with the world: "They are things *had*, before they are things cognized."[16] Dewey's classic pragmatism, according to its own definition, thus contains not an epistemology but a theory of experience and knowledge that encompasses cognition and action. Cognition and knowledge are not an end in themselves but part of a goal-directed action: experience is a slice of the practice of action. We are not uninvolved spectators but involved agents who shape the world experimentally through a process of experiences, and recognize it for this purpose. Experience means here the occurrence of cognitive-reflexive self-referentiality, which becomes possible through controlled, experimental action.

But how does pragmatism define practice and theory? A first differentiation in the concept of practice has to be made between a pragmatism that is oriented toward language practice and a pragmatism that thematizes the practice of language as well as of action. Language practice (e.g., Austin and Morris) partially considers the nonlinguistic practice of action, but does not regard it as a field for investigation itself and does not really consider it for the explanation of meaning. The second concept of practice, on the other hand, assumes that actions contribute in fundamental ways both in their linguistic and poietic form toward generating and determining the meaning of concepts as well as toward knowledge in general. For the second type, pragmatism with a comprehensive concept of practice, a further differentiation can be made that continues to define the understanding of practice for pragmatism. In the variant of classic pragmatism, especially Dewey, poietic and communicative action are understood as preceding and being foundational for theory. Questions regarding meaning appear here framed in an encompassing theory of knowledge. Even more important in relation to other variants of pragmatism is that practice is regarded as that for which theory is created in the first place. For this practice-supporting knowledge is interpreted in a strongly instrumentalized way according to the pattern of an ends-oriented mediating action. It is in this sense that Dewey's determination of language as the "tool of tools"[17] should be understood; the practice of this pragmatism is oriented towards making and producing.

In a second variant of this pragmatism's comprehensive concept of practice, the poietic or instrumental action is derived from the intersubjective linguistic practice of competent speakers, who execute the norms of utilizing and generating concepts. This is where I would situate the normative pragmatism of Robert Brandom and the theory of communicative action of Jürgen Habermas. Brandom himself has stressed this differentiation between a normative and an instrumental pragmatism.[18] Unlike Brandom, who regards the priority of the normative as fundamental, I will assume in the following that both directions, the normative and the instrumental, will have to be regarded as equally important.

What does the pragmatic understanding of theory look like? Here, too, we can differentiate between a pragmatic conception that gives theory the status of explaining the foundational structures or the functioning of practice, and one in which theory itself should be understood as instrumental and not as fundamental. The first type again gives theory a quasi-contemplative character, because it defines theory as the reconstruction of practice. I consider Brandom's approach typical of this. As the title of his book *Making it Explicit*[19] makes clear, what he wants to emphasize is what already occurs anyway: what he wants to reconstruct are the creativity and expressivity of reason and language. But the other variant of a strongly instrumentalized pragmatism demands a therapeutic and involved functioning of theory. In a thumbnail sketch of pragmatism, Dewey describes this as follows: "Pragmatism must take its own medicine. Cannot be a metaphysics in an old sense. Because, being itself a mode of knowledge, all its theories must be recognized to be only working hypotheses and experimental in quality. . . . Pragmatic value of free or pure theorizing. No progress possible without independent intellectual undertakings. Theory must, however, be a responsible division of labor and not usurp irresponsible sovereignty."[20] The instrumentalist understanding of theory includes the reflection of its own conditionality and function. In pragmatic philosophy according to Dewey, pure theorizing—the Platonic-Aristotelian "theoria"—is not completely abolished, but by being radically functionalized is made less powerful and deprived it of its foundational purpose.

From this briefly developed typology one problematic area in particular arises that needs to be addressed by the evolving pragmatic trend of thought. I will sketch out this question with regard to Hegel's position, and in a third part of this essay will then propose a conception of this pragmatism by means of an interpretation of Hegel's work. The differences between classic pragmatism and neopragmatism can be thematized in the relationship between action and language, action and knowledge. The latter relationship was at the center of classic pragmatism. Neopragmatism, which orients itself towards language philosophy, regards the practice of action—and with it technology, production, and the sociopolitical order—only implicitly in the framework of a theory of language.[21] Hegel, as well as classic pragmatism, always considered thinking and knowing as products of action and externalization and thus showed the possibility of an overlapping of concepts and poietic practice with what he called subjective, objective, and absolute spirit. Hegel establishes this relationship of knowledge and action in his *Phenomenology of Spirit* in the context of a theory of experience that is clearly antirepresentationalist in its critique of epistemology. Herein lies its proximity to the pragmatism of John Dewey, or rather it is here that Hegel's strongest influence on Dewey can be shown. Let us neglect for the moment the implications of the metaphysical concept of absolute spirit and its related theoretical claim. If we interpret Hegel's philosophy of spirit in a weaker sense, namely as the continuing reconstruction of our claims to truth and knowledge (that we have arrived at through intersubjectivity externalization, and practical action), then an extensive field of inquiry opens up for pragmatic philosophy.

2. RORTY OR BRANDOM—PRAGMATISM AS HISTORICISM OR IDEALISM?

Among the influential protagonists of neopragmatism who reconsider Hegel are Richard Rorty and Robert Brandom. Rorty regards Hegel's thought as a quarry from which to mine those elements that are relevant for his purpose while disregarding the remaining work. Brandom, on the other hand, proceeds from Hegel's own claims and attempts to apply these as a serious option in current debates. To put it succinctly: Rorty understands Hegel as the initiator of a far-reaching historicizing and contextualizing of reason, and in this he finds points of contact for neopragmatic approaches. Brandom, on the other hand, assumes that it is precisely Hegel's idealism that can be interpreted as the crucial pragmatic element.

Let us begin with Rorty's interpretation of Hegel as the initiator of a theory of the priority of the practical, which Rorty calls "pragmatic." He writes: "Once one starts to look for pragmatism in Hegel, one finds quite a bit to go on."[22] If one applies the strategy of de-absolutizing,[23] Hegel's pragmatism will emerge. As Rorty puts it, "Hegel himself, to be sure, had his Philosophical moments, but the temporalization of rationality which he suggested was the single most important step in arriving at the pragmatist's distrust of Philosophy."[24] The capitalized "Philosophy" refers to Hegel's idealism and his thinking of the absolute, the intention of which is to rethink the legacy of Greek philosophy under the terms of modern subject-philosophy. In order to solve this task, Hegel, according to Rorty, de-transcendentalizes the subject of cognition and contextualizes it in history and culture. Hegel, in other words, de-transcendentalizes reason by historicizing and con-textualizing it. For Rorty, this represents a first and important step toward a critique of the theory of absolute knowledge and its corresponding foundational philosophical efforts, which Hegel himself did not yet formulate.

This move introduces the consequences of a de-absolutized Hegel: the project of Hegel falls into two parts for Rorty, which cannot be consistently connected: on the one hand the claim to maintain the classic metaphysical ideal of a unitary and conclusive theory of reality; on the other the attempt to describe more adequately the contextuality, i.e., the relativity, of the foundational categories and modes of thinking through a theory of the sociocultural context of knowledge and its historical sequencing. Rorty regards Hegel's often quoted dictum from the *Philosophy of Law*—"So too is philosophy its time captured in thought"[25]—in precisely this contextual sense, but radicalizes this interpretation by maintaining, in *Contingency, Irony and Solidarity*, that Hegel has demonstrated that philosophical problems can only be meaningfully encountered by using a new vocabulary and by "changing the subject." Rorty thus regards Hegel as a Kuhnian revolutionary who has himself provided an example of revolutionary science in his *Phenomenology*, and arrives at an interpretation of the *Phenomenology* as a sequence of stories, told in contexts in which the subject reaches the self-understanding of its own conditions as being relative to the context. Hegel's *Phenomenology of Spirit* appears to Rorty, in short, as a brilliant piece of philosophical literature, as a collection of perspectives and worldviews whose sequence does not show an internal necessity. The historicizing and contextualizing of reason and the consistent radicalization of this movement, which is later executed by Kierkegaard, Nietzsche, and others, remain for Rorty, however, the only elements of Hegel's thought that can be connected to his variant of neopragmatism. The reasons for Rorty's rejection of further connections in Hegel lie, on the one hand, in the plausible repudiation of Hegel's insistence on the theory of absolute spirit (Rorty criticizes Hegel's sublation of the particularity of intersubjective community formation through the universality of absolute spirit as "talking about human communities as expressions of something greater than themselves"[26]). On the other hand, though, it is significant that it is precisely Rorty's critique of Dewey's concept of experience—which he judges to be an indecisive mix of idealism and empiricism and thus superfluous—that impedes a productive and affirmative perspective on the antirepresentationalist elements in Hegel's theory of knowledge. This is not the place to explain Rorty's reasons for his rejection of Dewey's concept of experience. But the interpretation of Hegel's concept of experience will show whether a pragmatic concept of experience will indeed return to us, as Rorty fears, all the representationalist problems of an epistemological "tertium" that mediates between us and the world.

Whereas Rorty arrives at a particularistic context by historicizing and relativizing Hegel's project and does not take it any further, Robert Brandom pursues an interpretation that tries to respect Hegel's basic intentions. For Rorty, our practices, culture, and language determine the limits of our knowledge and its claims. Brandom, meanwhile, begins his normative pragmatic approach with practice from the perspective of a participant. Rather than to demonstrate its particularity and relationality, his goal is to secure the objectivity of our claims for validity. The clarification of the validity of our practices leads Brandom to the "making explicit" of our language practices. Brandom has pursued this philosophical mega-project of a semantic-normative pragmatism, which attempts to integrate into itself the representationalist vocabulary with which we refer to something in the world, in his book *Making it Explicit*. For this work Hegel's role is that of the implicit provider of ideas; he is mentioned explicitly only in passing.

Brandom traces Hegel's contribution to his semantic-normative pragmatism more directly in his essay "Some Pragmatist Themes in Hegel's Idealism."[27] The basic thesis of semantic-normative pragmatism is "that the use of concepts determines their *content*, that is, that concepts can have no content, apart from that conferred on them by their use."[28] Brandom finds this use-theory of the meaning of concepts supported by what he identifies as Hegel's basic idealist thesis: "The structure and unity of the *concept* is the same as structure and unity of the *self*."[29] Brandom wants to show that semantic pragmatism is not only in agreement with the idealist thesis, but also that Hegel's basic thought can be conceptualized with recourse to a language-analytical vocabulary and its theoretical accomplishments.

Brandom assumes two further theorems that elaborate the above theses and situate them as markers of Hegel's specific idealist pragmatism. Firstly, it is the connection between the constitution and application of concepts in empirical judgments that describes the realm of practice. Concepts are determining and thus normative for Brandom, and he situates experience in this normative practice. Secondly, Brandom expands this realm of experience of the constitution and application of concepts by adding a theory of intersubjectivity and autonomy, i.e., a theory of the achievement of autonomy for the self on the basis of mutual recognition. This means that "the process of reciprocal specific recognition should be taken to provide the context within which concepts are both applied and their contents instituted and determined."[30] The determining, normative function of concepts is indivisibly connected with the social constitution of the self. "They *recognize* themselves as *mutually recognizing* one another,"[31] says Hegel in the master/slave chapter of the *Phenomenology of Spirit*, and with Brandom we could add: they recognize themselves as recognizing each other as users of concepts, which in turn determine the content of concepts through the recognition and negotiation of the connected commitments and entitlements. Brandom describes experience as "making an adjustment of one's conceptual commitments in the light of such a collision,"[32] a collision that occurs between users of concepts because of the latent agonistic structure of autonomy. Experience is thus a process that takes place among users of concepts for whom the relationship of the subject to the object is of minor importance.

Brandom identifies the pragmatic element particularly in Hegel's idealism. I would like to focus here only on one problematic decision in Brandom's theory, which concerns the concept of experience and is of importance for the understanding of pragmatism and the interpretation of Hegel as a pragmatic thinker. Brandom's conception of the self is supposed to refer to a linguistic practice that is constituted intersubjectively. But Hegel's concept of the subject and its related structure of subjectivity refer structurally to a wider concept of practice, which includes intersubjectivity and poietic action. Brandom's concept of practice is a practice of recognition, not appropriation—i.e., of externalization, objectivization, or transformation. But recognition *and* appropriation are the crucial structural characteristics of subjectivity and practice in Hegel. This is made clear by Hegel in the chapter on *master and slave*, where work, which means the externalization and objectivization in the other as thing, not just the other as person, enters the relationship of the recognizing subjects. As is well known, it is this that allows self-consciousness to experience the certainty of itself. Hegel's structure of subjectivity—which encompasses appropriation and recognition, the finding of oneself in the other as object and in the other as person—remains as underdeveloped in Brandom as does Hegel's concept of experience. Instead, it is the relationship between theory and normative language practice that constitutes the realm of experience for Brandom. There is no reflection of a practice that also includes a poietic activity. The exclusion of the instrumental-poietic dimension of the structure of subjectivity in favor of a normative practice of users and generators of concepts is notable. It should thus be asked whether a sophisticated pragmatic conception of experience should also take into consideration the externalization and objectivization of subjectivity in the world for the purposes of determining meaning—and that means, from a pragmatic point of view, for determining our knowledge and its claims for validity.

3. HEGEL'S PRAGMATIC CONCEPT OF EXPERIENCE

Already in the context of the twentieth century, Hegel appears as the philosopher of practice. In Marxist or neo-Marxist interpretations, often combined with existential-philosophical or existential-ontological approaches,[33] desire, recognition, and work become the markers of human self-becoming and historical practice. Hermeneutic philosophy (e.g., Hans-Georg Gadamer) also approaches Hegel from the perspective of practice. In this case however, the rejection of transcendental philosophy's foundational claims and intimations of an unconditioned status have priority, as does the primacy of human practice in the form of tradition.[34] These interpretations of Hegel's work may deliver several clues for our question, but they do not contain the genuinely pragmatic essence of a nonrepresentational concept of practice. Such an essence is contained in explicitly pragmatic approaches such as George Herbert Mead's theory of intersubjectivity, which constructively uses Hegel's theory of recognition as an element in its social philosophy. The same can be said for the pragmatic theories of truth of James and Dewey, for whom Hegel's conception of truth, described as "context-dependence of truth," is the key element, as Rolf-Peter Horstmann has pointed out.[35] Hegel's concept of work and action or his idea of tool and mediation, as he had developed it in the *Jenaer Systementwürfe*, offer further points of connection for the interpretation of Hegel as a pragmatic thinker.[36] I limit myself here to the metaphilosophical question concerning Hegel's antirepresentationalism and to the relationship of knowledge and action that results from his critique of epistemology.

Hegel's procedure in the introduction to the *Phenomenology of Spirit*, as well as elsewhere, is to connect critique with presentation. The critique is directed against the modern theory of epistemology and serves at the same time as a foil for presenting Hegel's own concept of experience. He takes Kant, as the protagonist of the theory of epistemology in its most advanced form, as his starting point. "It is a natural assumption that in philosophy, before we start to deal with its proper subject-matter, viz., the actual cognition of what truly is, one must first of all come to an understanding about cognition, which is regarded either as the instrument to get hold of the Absolute, or as the medium through which one discovers it."[37] The test of the faculty of cognition as a means or instrument to see the thing as it is in itself must fail according to Hegel, and he problematizes precisely this misuse of tools, in which he sees the specificity of Kant's epistemology: "what is really absurd is that we should make use of a means at all."[38]

But Hegel's treatment of the faculty of recognition as a tool or medium, i.e., as a medium or mediator between subject and object, is quite ambivalent. It is not a critique of the tool or the medium as such, as it might appear at first glance and as it is taken for granted by Hegel interpreters such as Heidegger.[39] The exclusively negative interpretation of Hegel's concept of the tool and the medium becomes implausible when one considers the meaning of the operating concept of "mediation," which has its roots, besides deriving from the middle term in the Aristotelian syllogism, in the concept of the tool in the *Jenaer Systementwürfe*. With his critique of the model of cognition as tool or medium, Hegel points to the representationalist preconditions that misunderstand the means as well as the relationship of subject and object.

Two preconditions that Hegel has critically uncovered are especially noteworthy. First, modern epistemology takes cognition as a tool intervening between "us" and the "object"; and here Hegel is referring again mainly to Kant. Cognition understood as an instrument in this way is something external to the relationship; it is as external to us and the object as the object is external to us in the representationalist model. This idea, according to Hegel, assumes "a difference between ourselves and this cognition,"[40] which in turn requires the mediation between cognition as an instrument and ourselves. The second precondition that Hegel points to in his critique of Kantian epistemology is connected to the mediation that must take place in this transcendental approach. The entire approach of this misunderstood instrumentalism depends on the possibility of examining the tool independently from its use. The transcendental approach to the forms of judgements that constitute knowledge in its self-definition can be clearly differentiated from empirical judgments in that the former depend on self-evidence. John Dewey, too, regarded this differentiation as one of the main difficulties of Kant's transcendental logic: "Kant never dreams, for a moment, of questioning the existence of a special faculty of thought with its own peculiar and fixed forms."[41] Only the creation of a separate transcendental realm of pure cognition enabled Kant to make objective statements about the characteristics of the tool, i.e., the faculty of cognition. But just as it is impossible to describe real tools such as saws or hammers in regard to their function without performing their function or knowing their function by former use, there can be no statement about the pure cognition of cognition. Hegel thus concludes that the entire description of cognition before cognition is fictive, maybe even self-deceptive, which makes clear why Hegel ironically compares the tendency of epistemology, which seeks to know something about knowing before it is known, with the wise plan "of Scholasticus to learn to swim before he ventured into the water."[42]

Hegel's own position—his depiction of experience that goes beyond this criticism and his nonreductionist concept of the tool—is already indicated here. Hegel's conclusion concerning the critique of epistemology consists in analyzing cognition in the introduction to the *Phenomenology* in such a way that cognition becomes a part of a comprehensive concept of experience. The process of cognition, its material and operative elements, cannot be deduced from the process; rather it *constitutes* cognition. Cognition thus becomes part of a process of experience in which object and concept represent the changing and externalized products of an interaction. William James and, after him, John Dewey have described this in strictly holistic terminology as the double-barreled structure of experience. Dewey writes: "It is double-barreled in that it recognizes in its primary integrity no division between act and material, subject and object, but contains them both in an unanalyzed totality."[43] Experience unites what is experienced and the experience of the experiencing as one. Experience's character of process, which Dewey describes in his pragmatic-experimental method,[44] appears in Hegel in a structurally similar form as the examination of consciousness. By applying the implications that he developed from the concept of knowledge, Hegel dissolves object and knowledge into one relation. For this Hegel uses terms such as being-in-itself, being-for-itself, being-for-another. Hegel writes: "Upon this distinction, which is present as a fact, the examination rests. If the examination shows that these two moments do not correspond to one another, it would seem that consciousness must alter its knowledge to make it conform to the object. But, in fact, in the alteration of the knowledge, the object itself alters for it too, for the knowledge that was present was essentially a knowledge of the object: as the knowledge changes, so too does the object, for it essentially belonged to this knowledge."[45] This structure of experience contains reflection on one's own action in a different way than Hegel finds it realized in traditional epistemology: the operation of cognition becomes integrated into the object; knowledge of an object is gained through a process; it is a knowledge that constantly corrects and expands itself. This transforms the static relationship of cognition into a dynamic one, which produces knowledge not only about an object but also about ourselves. This, taken together, constitutes "experience" for Hegel.

If thus far it is only the process-character of the structure of experience that has been described as a pragmatic aspect of Hegel's thought, I will now point to another pragmatic element in Hegel's concept of experience. The dynamic, process-character of experience is one side; the other side is that Hegel conceives of thinking as being active in this structure: i.e., it is strictly noncontemplative. Michael Theunissen has stressed this, although he draws different consequences from the analysis: "This congruence [of the object with its concept, A.G.] should be conceived as action, is as much active correspondence as the adaequatio, in which the intellectus attempts to adjust to the res; it is indeed a real event (Geschehen), not just a projection of the subjective activity onto the object."[46] Hegel repeatedly insisted that thinking changes reality in a very simple sense. "In this way, thinking asserted its validity in the actual world and exerted the most tremendous influence,"[47] he countered to those who conceived moral, ethical, and political reality as opposite to thought. But this point already makes clear an ambitious sense of this activity of thought. It was the epistemological presupposition of representationalism that reality should be understood as it is, should be merely depicted. But if thinking is conceptualized as interactive with its environment, if its concepts are only formed through this interaction, and if its activity effects appropriation and transformation, then its purpose is not contemplative but practical. Dewey has characterized that contemplative-theoretical relationship—which was prevalent with few exceptions in ancient as well as modern philosophy—as a so-to-speak aesthetic—i.e., one that is free of interest—consumption of objects in their finality.[48] According to the pragmatic view, we only gain knowledge about objects by inserting our theories or hypotheses about objects into the context of purposeful action and controlled manipulation. But this aimed intervention can fail. Hegel showed in his *Phenomenology of Spirit* that once the consequences of the claims of knowledge and truth in their respective contexts become clear, we see one aspect of our knowledge illuminated but we also become aware of its deficits. Hegel, in other words, made the cognitive processing of failure, disappointment, and doubt the principle of the process of education (Bildung) in the *Phenomenology of Spirit*.

Hegel demonstrates explicitly in the *Phenomenology of Spirit* that comprehending and justifying the utilized operative concepts can be achieved through applying and testing the validity of their truth claims. This is only introduced in its outline in the introduction to the *Phenomenology*, but is fully developed in the various chapters of that work. The relationship of self-consciousness, intersubjectivity and the active transformation of reality, i.e., work, is the topic of the chapter on *master and slave*.[49] Brandom has interpreted the theory of recognition and intersubjectivity that is to be situated in this section as the normative practice of the application of concepts, which is also a generating of concepts. But Brandom's interpretation misses one of Hegel's most antirepresentationalist points, namely, the understanding of epistemology as part of a comprehensive process of experience. Self-consciousness, according to the theory Hegel attempts to prove in his *master and slave* chapter, is first bound to a doubling of consciousness and secondly to externalization and objectivation.

Hegel demonstrates the dialectics of self-consciousness in two stages: the doubling of consciousness—consciousness for itself—leads each consciousness, inasmuch as it is a relation, to relate in the same way to the other consciousness. Hegel calls this relationship desire, its corresponding logical-operative term being negation. This desire has a twofold direction: at an object that itself is not desire and at an object that is itself desire. That desire, which completely takes in the other, i.e., negates the other completely, destroys itself in this process: "Each [consciousness] is indeed certain of its own self, but not of the other, and therefore its own self-certainty still has no truth."[50] The conclusion of the first round of argumentation is that each consciousness can only sustain itself as self-consciousness if the other consciousness has not been completely negated: "Each is for the other the middle term through which each mediates itself with itself and unites with itself; and each is for itself and for the other, an immediate being on its own account, which at the same time is such only through this mediation. They recognize themselves as mutually recognizing one another."[51] The unity of self-consciousness that refers to itself is only successful if the self-reference takes place through another self-consciousness performing the same self-reference. Hegel's goal, however, is not to outline a genetic theory of the constitution of self-consciousness, but instead to reconstruct the determinants of self-consciousness in order to reveal the structure of the "certainty-of-itself," which renders the much-discussed question of whether it is an internal doubling of self-consciousness or an external doubling, i.e., two empirical self-consciousnesses, rather secondary.[52]

In a second step Hegel demonstrates the dialectics of a self-sustaining relationship between the one who is recognized and the one who recognizes. In the introductory paragraph of the chapter, Hegel determined desire as directed not only to another subject but also to objects, which themselves are not subordinated to the structure of desire. This is where "the thing" enters into the nonreciprocal relationship of recognition. It is the object of desire for the master and the object of work for the slave. The slave was not able to maintain his independence in the struggle for recognition, which makes him dependent in relation to the master. The master, in turn, is dependent on the slave who works on the thing for the sheer pleasure of the master. The work on the thing produces complete self-referentiality, through which self-consciousness becomes the certainty of itself.

> Through work, however, the bondsman becomes conscious of what he truly is. [. . .] Work on the other hand, is desire held in check, fleetingness staved off; in other words, work forms and shapes the thing. The negative relation to the object becomes its form and something permanent, because it is precisely for the worker, that the object has independence. This negative middle term or the formative activity is at the same time the individuality or pure being-for-itself of consciousness, which now in the work outside of it, acquires an element of permanence. It is in this way, therefore, that consciousness, qua worker, comes to see in the independent being [of the object] its own independence.[53]

The constant struggle for recognition as the practice of intersubjectivity is thus complemented by a poietic practice. Only this allows subjectivity to attain certainty of itself, which Hegel suggests occurs in a concrete externalization and objectivation. Knowledge is sedimented in the tool, and only the tool enables the further reproduction and development of the process. If we understand master and slave as structural concepts, we can indeed interpret them as a metaphilosophical formulation of the alternative between representationalism and antirepresentationalism: it is to the master that Hegel grants a contemplative relationship to the thing. The master is—as Dewey has accused ancient philosophy—only focused on the consumption of objects in their finality. Not so the slave. He performs the movement of the transformation of the independent objectiveness and thus acquires a sedimentation of recognitions. Against the representationalist theories of self-consciousness of modern philosophy, and against his own idealist predecessors, Hegel's work contains the beginnings of a genuinely pragmatic theory of self-consciousness. Hegel makes pragmatic what is at the center of modern epistemology and the philosophy of consciousness—consciousness and the certainty of itself.

Epistemology and knowledge are thus placed in the context of a practice that is broadly defined. Hegel reconnects self-consciousness through poietic and linguistic, instrumental and normative contexts of practice to generality and transsubjectivity: "What still lies ahead for consciousness is the experience of what spirit is—this absolute substance which is the unity of the different independent, self-consciousnesses which, in their opposition, enjoy perfect freedom and independence: 'I' that is 'we' and 'we' that is 'I.'"[54] Hegel's theory of absolute spirit, however, in which the logical nature of reality has been conceptualized, assumes the finality of this process. All attempts to minimize this concept of spirit in its claim and thus to rescue Hegel's theory as a whole face this difficulty. While Hegel works in an antirepresentational manner in his critique of epistemology, he does not draw the same consequence for the understanding and the status of his own philosophy. If we adhere to Dewey's demand for self-application, we must conclude that Hegel hasn't taken his own medicine, and thus comprehended his philosophy only in very limited ways as the changeable instrument for the production of fulfilled lives in a reflected and directed human, social, scientific, and political practice. A pragmatic theory of experience, of the connection between knowledge and action, can build on the reconstruction—made possible by Hegel's antirepresentationalist turn—of our claims for knowledge in concrete contexts of human practice. Moreover, pragmatic philosophy claims not to remain in the seclusion of the Absolute but to generate orientation and knowledge for the controlled change of human practice—and this claim cannot be banned by Hegel's owl of Minerva.

Notes

1. Among the numerous publications I point only to: Pirmin Stekeler-Weithofer, *Hegels analytische Philosophie* (Paderborn: Ferdinand Schöningh Verlag 1992), as well as: Robert B. Pippin, *Idealism as Modernism: Hegelian Variations* (Cambridge: Cambridge University Press, 1997).

2. Cf. the special issue on *Hegel and His Legacy* of *The European Journal of Philosophy*, 7 (1999).

3. John Dewey, *Quest for Certainty*, in *Later Works*, ed. Jo Ann Boydston (Carbondale: Southern Illinois University Press, 1988), 1:134.

4. Wilfrid Sellars, *Empiricism and the Philosophy of Mind* (Cambridge, Mass.: Harvard University Press, 1997), 14.

5. Allen Hance, "Pragmatism as Naturalized Hegelianism: Overcoming the Transcendental Philosophy?" in ed. Herman J. Saatkamp Jr., *Rorty & Pragmatism, The Philosopher Responds to His Critics* (Nashville, Tenn./London: Vanderbilt University Press, 1995), 113.

6. Hegel's use of the term "pragmatic" does not provide clues for answering the question. Hegel uses the term in phrases such as "pragmatic reflections"—"pragmatische Reflexionen," in G. W. F. Hegel, *Vorlesungen über die Philosophie der Geschichte*, Theorie Werkausgabe, (Frankfurt a. M.: Suhrkamp Verlag, 1981), 12:17; English: *The Philosophy of History*, trans. J. Sibree (New York: P. F. Collier & Son, 1900)—in the context of the theory of writing history. This use reprises the sense of the Kantian differentiation between "pragmatic" and "practical" and comprehends the pragmatic, like Kant, as pertaining to considerations of utility and intelligence. This stands in contrast to the faculty of practical reason, which itself determines purpose. Neither classical pragmatism nor neopragmatism share this limited concept of "pragmatic."

7. McDowell's so-called nondogmatic empiricism should also be distinguished from this conception of experience, in that he stays within Kant's dualism of spontaneity and receptivity in an attempt to find "a conception of experiences as states or occurrences that are passive but reflect conceptual capacities, capacities that belong to spontaneity, in operation." John McDowell, *Mind and World* (Cambridge, Mass.: Harvard University Press, 1996), 23.

8. Arthur O. Lovejoy, "The Thirteen Pragmatisms," *The Journal of Philosophy, Psychology, and Scientific Methods* 5 (1908): 5–12, 29–39.

9. The linguistic turn in my view has added precision to the antirepresentationalism of classic American pragmatism, especially that of Dewey. For the characterization in this essay I limit myself to the basic idea, expressed equally well by Dewey and Rorty. Cf. Richard Rorty, "Pragmatism as Anti-Representationalism," in John P. Murphy, ed., *Pragmatism: From Peirce to Davidson* (Boulder, Colo.: Westview Press, 1990), 1–6.

10. Classic examples of the pragmatic critique of representationalism are John Dewey, *Quest for Certainty* and Richard Rorty, *Philosophy and the Mirror of Nature* (Princeton, N.J.: Princeton UP, 1979).

11. Dewey, *Quest*.

12. Michael Williams, *Unnatural Doubts. Epistemological Realism and the Basis of Skepticism* (Princeton, N.J.: Princeton University Press, 1996).

13. Cf. Rorty who highlights "how the difference between realistic epistemology and nonrealistic epistemology becomes negligible when metaphilosophical problems are posed in this purely practical context." Rorty, "Realism, Categories, and the Linguistic Turn," *International Philosophical Quarterly* 2 (1962): 313.

14. Dewey, *Quest*, 175.

15. Ibid., 9.

64   *Antje Gimmler*

16. Dewey, *Experience and Nature*, in *Later Works*, ed. Jo Ann Boydston (Carbondale: Southern Illinois University Press, 1988), 4: 28.

17. Ibid., 134.

18. Robert Brandom, "Pragmatik und Pragmatismus," in Mike Sandbothe, ed., *Die Renaissance des Pragmatismus. Aktuelle Verflechtungen zwischen analytischer und kontinentaler Philosophie* (Weilersvist: Velbrück Wissenschaft, 2000), 29–58.

19. Robert Brandom, *Making it Explicit* (Cambridge, Mass.: Harvard University Press, 1994).

20. John Dewey, "The Pragmatic Movement of Contemporary Thought," in *Middle Works*, ed. Jo Ann Boydston (Carbondale: Southern Illinois University Press, 1983), 4: 257.

21. I agree with Barry Allen's criticism of the development from classic pragmatism to neopragmatism, which is characterized by a devaluation of classic pragmatism in favor of logical positivism, as well as by the renewed linking of analytical philosophy with motifs of classic pragmatism without the latter's practical aims. Allen also criticizes this narrowing of neopragmatism and suggests that it does not value the achievements of knowledge any more, and is losing its sense of the relevance of philosophical contributions to questions in technology, science, or society. Cf. Barry Allen, "Is it Pragmatism? Rorty and the American Tradition," in John Pettegrew ed., *A Pragmatist's Progress? Richard Rorty and American Intellectual History* (Lanham,Md./ Boulder, Colo./New York/Oxford: Rowman & Littlefield, 2000), 135–149.

22. Richard Rorty, "Dewey between Hegel and Darwin," in *Truth and Progress: Philosophical Papers Volume 3* (Cambridge: Cambridge University Press, 1998), 302.

23. Rorty labels this way of interpreting Hegel that had been productivly undertaken by Dewey as a "de-absolutized Hegel." Ibid., 304.

24. Richard Rorty, "Introduction: Pragmatism and Philosophy," in *Consequences of Pragmatism* (Minneapolis: University of Minnesota Press, 1982), xli.

25. "[S]o ist auch die Philosophie ihre Zeit in Gedanken gefasst." G. W. F. Hegel, *Grundlinien der Philosophie des Rechts*, in *Theorie Werkausgabe* (Frankfurt a. M.: Suhrkamp Verlag, 1981), 7: 26. Cf. Rorty, "Dewey between Hegel and Darwin," 302.

26. Rorty, "Dewey between Hegel and Darwin," 302.

27. Robert Brandom, "Some Pragmatist Themes in Hegel's Idealism," in *European Journal of Philosophy* 7, no. 2 (1999): 164–189.

28. Ibid., 164.

29. Ibid., 164.

30. Ibid., 173.

31. G. W. F. Hegel, *Phenomenology of Spirit*, trans. A. V. Miller (New York: Oxford University Press, 1977), 112.

32. Brandom, "Some Pragmatist," 175

33. Cf. Alexandre Kojeve, *Hegel. Eine Vergegenwärtigung seines Denkens. Kommentar zur Phänomenologie des Geistes* (Frankfurt a. M.: Suhrkamp Verlag, 1975) and Manfred Riedel, *Theorie und Praxis im Denken Hegels* (Frankfurt a. M.: Ullstein Verlag, 1976).

34. Hans-Georg Gadamer, "The Idea of Hegel's Logic" in *Hegel's Dialectic. 5 Hermeneutical Studies*. (P. Christopher Smith, trans. New Haven, Conn.: Yale University Press, 1976), 75–100.

35. Rolf-Peter Horstmann, "What is Hegel's Legacy and What Should We Do With It?" *European Journal of Philosophy* 7 (1999): 284.

36. Jürgen Habermas has pointed to the pragmatic aspects of the *Jenaer Systementwürfe* from the perspective of a theory of intersubjectivity, picking up from his argument in the early text "Arbeit und Interaktion. Bemerkungen zu Hegels Jenenser Philosophie des Geistes," and continuing in "Wege der Detranszendentalisierung. Von Kant zu Hegel und zurück." Jürgen Habermas, "Arbeit und Interaktion" in *Technik und Wissenschaft als "Ideologie"* (Frankfurt a. M.: Suhrkamp, 1969), 7-47; Jürgen Habermas, "Wege der Detranszendentalisierung," in *Wahrheit und Rechtfertigung* (Frankfurt a. M.: Suhrkamp, 1999), 186–229.

37. G. W. F. Hegel, *Phenomenology of Spirit*, 46.

38. Ibid., 46.

39. Martin Heidegger, *Hegel's Concept of Experience* (New York: Harper & Row, 1970).

40. G. W. F. Hegel, *Phenomenology of Spirit*, 47.

41. John Dewey, "The Present Position of Logical Theory," in *Early Works* (Carbondale: Southern Illinois University Press, 1975), 3:135. Dewey points to the problems of Kant's transcendental logic in regard to its fruitfulness for the sciences and arrives at the, for some, surprising conclusion: "As against the usual opinion of the possibility of some compromise between science and Kant, while the scientific spirit and Hegel are at antipodes, it appears to me it is Kant who does violence to science, while Hegel (I speak of his essential method and not of any particular result) is the quintessence of the scientific spirit." Ibid., 134.

42. G. W. F. Hegel, *The Encyclopaedia Logic (with the Zusätze): Part I of the Encyclopaedia of Philosophical Sciences with the Zusätze*, trans. T. F. Geraets, W. A. Suchting, and H. S. Harris (Indianapolis/Cambridge: Hackett Publishing Co., 1991), 34 (§10). Cf. Tom Rockmore's instructive and detailed presentation of Hegel's critique of Kant's epistemology and Hegel's own theory of epistemology. Tom Rockmore, *Hegel's Circular Epistemology*, (Bloomington: Indiana University Press, 1986).

43. John Dewey, *Experience and Nature*, 18.

44. Cf. Ibid., 38. On Dewey's pragmatic-experimental method see: Antje Gimmler, "Pragmatische Heuristik oder: Don't block the road of inquiry!" in ed. Jürgen

Mittelstraß, *Die Zukunft des Wissens, XVII. Deutscher Kongreß für Philosophie* (Konstanz: Universitätsverlag Konstanz, 1999) 493–499.

45. G. W. F. Hegel, *Phenomenology of Spirit*, 54.

46. Michael Theunissen, "Begriff und Realität. Hegels Aufhebung des metaphysischen Wahrheitsbegriffs," in ed. Rolf-Peter Horstmann, *Seminar: Dialektik in der Philosophie Hegels* (Frankfurt a. M.: Suhrkamp Verlag, 1978), 333.

47. G. W. F. Hegel, *Encyclopaedia*, 48 (§19).

48. Cf. John Dewey, *Experience and Nature*, 107–108.

49. The translation of the German words "Herrschaft" and "Knechtschaft" which Hegel uses in the discussed chapter "Selbständigkeit und Unselbständigkeit des Selbstbewußtseins; Herrschaft und Knechtschaft" into English is difficult. The phrase "master and slave" that is used in this text is not the proper translation of the title of the chapter, but takes the dramatis personae as catchword.

50. G. W. F. Hegel, *Phenomenology of Spirit* , 113.

51. Ibid., 112.

52. Cf. the critique by Karen Gloy of what she refers to as the thesis of intersubjectivity in the *master and slave* chapter. She interprets Hegel's dialectic of self-consciousness as a variant of the theorem of self-identification in which internal distinction creates self-consciousness. But she neglects to note that Hegel decides against deducting the recognizing relationship of empirical self-consciousness in favor of a reconstruction of this structure in such a way that, as far as the constitution of self-consciousness is concerned, one has to assume the same origin for internal and external relations. Cf. Karen Gloy, "Bemerkungen zum Kapitel >Herrschaft und Knechtschaft< in Hegels Phänomenologie des Geistes," *Zeitschrift für philosophische Forschung*, 39 (1985): 187–213.

53. G. W. F. Hegel, *Phenomenology of Spirit*, 118.

54. Ibid., 110–111.

4

MIKE SANDBOTHE

The Pragmatic Twist
of the Linguistic Turn[1]

Translated by Lowell Vizenor

Modern academic philosophy currently finds itself in a transitional pe-riod marked by the increase in alternative, pragmatic approaches to philosophy.[2] Those approaches have come to stand alongside the long-dominating theoreticist conception of academic Philosophy. In the theoreticist approach the central question is the conditions under which human knowl-edge is possible. The mentioned alternative approaches suggest that we no longer place the emphasis of philosophy's self-understanding on the theoreticist question of the conditions under which the knowledge of reality is made possible, but rather on the intelligent collaboration in the shaping of prag-matic ways to alter human reality. The institutional propensity of the aca-demic field of philosophy toward the theoreticist approach appeared in the nineteenth century.[3] It has been—within the framework of the linguistic turn that came to pass in modern philosophy in the twentieth century—not simply continued, but at the same time problematized.

The following reflections attempt to lay bare the tense relationship between the pragmatic and the theoreticist understanding of philosophy that permeates the linguistic turn. This takes place in recourse to histori-cal-systematic considerations, which Richard Rorty sketched out in the

"Introduction" to his collection *The Linguistic Turn* (1967) and has further worked out in his later writings.[4] It has often been overlooked that Rorty already foregrounds the inner ambivalences of the linguistic turn in his "Introduction" from 1967. This is in part due to the fact that Rorty had not explicitly characterized these as ambivalences. In order to indicate the inner tensions that permeate the linguistic turn across their entire spectrum, I give here by way of introduction a brief outline of the three, in my view, crucial ambivalences of the linguistic turn.[5] I will refer back to these ambivalences in the continuation of my considerations, albeit placing greater emphasis on the third, as it is the deciding one as regards the pragmatic twist of the linguistic turn.

The first ambivalence relates to the *status* of the linguistic method. While the logical empiricists (Russell, Carnap I, Ayer I, among others), hold fast to the philosophically neutral value of logical syntax as the kernel of language in general, the representatives of ideal language philosophy (Carnap II, Ayer II, Bergmann, among others), as well as the champions of ordinary language philosophy (Ryle, Austin, Strawson, among others), relativize the claims of the linguistic method with respect to meaning criteria that are, respectively, relative to ideal languages or dependent on languages-in-use.

The second ambivalence relates to the *goal-determination* of the linguistic method and permeates both the school of ideal and ordinary language philosophy. The goal of a linguistic reformulation of philosophical problems is seen by different representatives of the two schools, on the one side, as a constructive solution to the problems, and on the other as their therapeutic dissolution.

Finally, the third ambivalence relates to the *metaphilosophical presuppositions* that generally underlie the search for a linguistic method, and with it the theoreticist conception of method, of ideal and ordinary language philosophy.

While both schools hold fast to the notion that the linguistic method places at their disposal a reliable set of tools for the analysis of philosophical problems, within the surrounding field of the linguistic turn positions have emerged at the same time that put in question exactly this presupposition and its connected dogmas. My explorations concentrate on the reconstruction of these positions, still not thematized in Rorty's "Introduction" of 1967, but which step into the foreground in his later work under the title of the so-called "Wittgenstein-Sellars-Quine-Davidson attack on distinctions between different classes of sentences."[6]

My considerations proceed in two parts. In the first part I will illustrate the pragmatic twist of the linguistic turn by way of the pragmatization movement that has been realized in analytic philosophy in the second half of the twentieth century. In the second part I show, by way of Rorty's confron-

tation with John McDowell and Robert Brandom, what sociopolitical implications could result from the current debate between representationalism and
antirepresentationalism.

THE PRAGMATIZATION OF ANALYTIC PHILOSOPHY

Against the background of the attacks that Wittgenstein, Sellars, Quine, and
Davidson have led against the residual dogmatism of linguistic philosophy,
Rorty suggests in the *Introduction* to *Consequences of Pragmatism* (1982), "that
what Gustav Bergmann called 'the linguistic turn' should not be seen as the
logical positivists saw it—as enabling us to ask Kantian questions without
having to trespass on the psychologists' turf by talking, with Kant, about
'experience' or 'consciousness'."[7] Rorty continues in the same vein: "That was,
indeed, the initial motive for the 'turn', but (thanks to the holism and pragmatism of the authors I have cited) analytic philosophy of language was able
to transcend this Kantian motive and adopt a naturalistic, behavioristic attitude toward language."[8] Through the naturalistic and behavioristic perspective on language opened up by Wittgenstein, Sellars, Quine, and Davidson,
the dialectic that permeates analytic philosophy and its underlying linguistic
turn, receives a positive meaning. Rorty sees the deciding point of this meaning in the so-called "pragmaticization of analytic philosophy."[9]

In order to avoid terminological vagueness, it is important in this context to separate out Rorty's affirmative use of the concepts pragmatism,
pragmaticization, pragmatic, etc., from the ways of using these terms that are
associated with the conception of a formal, or rather quasi-transcendental,
pragmatics, as has been developed in the framework of ordinary language
philosophy. The pragmatism represented by Rorty in *Philosophy and the Mirror of Nature* and in *Consequences of Pragmatism* aims to underscore the linguistic differentiation between "semantic" and "pragmatic," insofar as it
presupposes the difference, problematized by Wittgenstein, Sellars, Quine,
and Davidson, between "necessary" and "contingent."

In the place of this twofold difference, Rorty backs in a use of "pragmatic" that aims at reconnecting linguistic utterances to a naturalistic context
of nonlinguistic behavioral practices, which are to be investigated by empirical means. This use of "pragmatic" in the sense of "naturalistic" or "behavioristic" is made explicit in *Philosophy and the Mirror of Nature*. Rorty writes:
"Epistemological behaviorism (which might be called simply 'pragmatism,'
were this term not a bit overladen) . . . is the claim that philosophy will have
no more to offer than common sense (supplemented by biology, history, etc.)
about knowledge and truth."[10]

Rorty's interpretation of the "pragmaticization of analytic philosophy"[11]
initiated by Wittgenstein, Sellars, Quine, and Davidson has frequently been

misunderstood as saying that nothing remains of philosophy in view of its pragmatic naturalization other than its self-dissolution. Nonetheless, Rorty clearly stresses in the concluding passages of *Philosophy and the Mirror of Nature* that "There is no danger of philosophy's 'coming to an end'."[12] What in Rorty's view can and should come to an end, in view of the pragmaticization movement, is the regressive persistence of academic philosophy in the theoreticist disciplinary matrix of the "traditional problems of modern philosophy."[13]

This persistence is broken through, following Rorty in reference to the "Wittgenstein-Sellars-Quine-Davidson attack,"[14] by a transformative self-understanding of philosophical thinking. Through this it becomes possible for philosophy to work in close cooperation with the sciences, arts, and technology to develop a pragmatic vocabulary. This new vocabulary of philosophy no longer attempts to analyze or give reasons for the foundations of the sciences, arts, and technology. On the contrary, it is a "new way of describing knowledge and inquiry"[15] that puts the emphasis (from the external perspective) on causal links and (from the internal perspective) on those useful aspects of knowledge that feed back normatively and can be described by the social sciences, the humanities, and literature.

With this new way of describing knowledge and inquiry a second aspect of Rorty's usage of "pragmatic" comes into play. This usage connects "pragmatic" with "transformative" in the sense of "abnormal," "innovative," and "changing." It is closely connected with the opposition central to the third ambivalence of the linguistic turn. The pragmatic vocabulary of philosophy recommended by Rorty does not regressively aim to solve or dissolve the old philosophical problems with new means. Rorty's "new way" is, on the contrary, characterized by the fact that under the description of a pragmatic vocabulary the theoreticist textbook problems of philosophy step into the background and new questions and problems take their place.

The pragmatic twist of the linguistic turn can be understood as transformative in three different ways. First, it can be understood as transformative in the *weak* sense of a transition that comes to pass within the continuing tradition of philosophical research from an old to a new disciplinary matrix. Second, it can be understood in the *strong* sense of a typological change that affects the activity of philosophical research itself in its fundamental determinations. And thirdly it can be understood as transformative in the *strongest* sense, according to which philosophical activity undergoes a redefinition that makes transformation as such the main purpose of philosophical inquiry. Philosophy is then no longer understood as the methodological analysis of present states of affairs or existing linguistic structures. Instead, it is comprehended and carried out as a transformative activity that experimentally works toward changes in common sense in order to develop new knowledge practices.

In *Philosophy and the Mirror of Nature* and *Consequences of Pragmatism*, Rorty reconstructs the genealogy of the pragmatic "new way" of philosophy such that deciding impulses for the development of a pragmatic vocabulary arise from the immanent dialectic of the linguistic turn itself. To this end he distinguishes three types of authors within the "Wittgenstein-Sellars-Quine-Davidson attack."[16]

The first group of authors move within the second ambivalence of the linguistic turn. Sellars and Quine are authors of this type. They negatively prepare the "pragmaticization of analytic philosophy"[17] through its therapeutic de-transcendentalization.

Wittgenstein appears against these as a mixed type. On the one hand, his thinking still moves very strongly within the second ambivalence of the linguistic turn. On the other hand, however, we already find in his thinking transitions to the problem level of the third ambivalence.

The third type of author distinguished by Rorty is represented by Donald Davidson. In Davidson, the passage from the second to the third ambivalence is carried out in a more radical way than in Wittgenstein. From Rorty's perspective it is thus Davidson who, within the "Wittgenstein-Sellars-Quine-Davidson attack,"[18] made the central contribution to the pragmatic twist of the linguistic turn.

It remains to be shown that on the basis of the commonalities set forth by Rorty, residual differences nevertheless persist between Davidson and him. But before I go more closely into Davidson and the third ambivalence of the linguistic turn, I would like to call attention to how the second ambivalence of the linguistic turn determines the thinking of Wittgenstein, Sellars, and Quine.

a) Wittgenstein, Quine, and Sellars

The second ambivalence of the linguistic turn results from the tensions existing between a constructive problem-solving and a therapeutic problem-dissolving way of dealing with the fundamental problems that have been passed on by modern philosophy. For Wittgenstein, this tense relationship is to be diagnosed in two ways. First, his thinking diverges into two philosophical positions: the logicist position, which the early Wittgenstein represented in the *Tractatus*; and the use-theoretic view, which the late Wittgenstein developed in the *Philosophical Investigations* (posthumous 1953).[19]

The constructive claim formulated in the "Preface" of Wittgenstein's early major work, the *Tractatus*, consists in the claim "that the problems [of philosophy] have in essentials been finally solved."[20] Against this, the therapeutic claim of the *Philosophical Investigations* is not so much directed at the solution of the theoretical textbook problems of modern philosophy, but rather at their dissolution.

Secondly, the perspective of the *Philosophical Investigations* is itself ambivalent. On the one hand, Wittgenstein is ironic regarding the program, defended by him in the *Tractatus,* of a linguistic philosophy based on logic, and still concedes to philosophy only the negative task of unmasking the false claims of purity. On the other hand he falls back (as in the weak meaning of transformative philosopher) on the idea, which he first ridiculed, of the difference between the empirical and the grammatical, or between the nonphilosophical and philosophical investigation, in order to develop on its basis a "Theory of Philosophy as Oversight."[21]

The second ambivalence of the linguistic turn also determines to a large extent the thinking of Sellars and Quine. As opposed to Wittgenstein, who at the same time (in the strong sense of a transformative philosopher) made important contributions toward the development of a pragmatic vocabulary of philosophy,[22] it is the case with Quine and Sellars that their achievements are to be described as above all therapeutic or destructive. In this sense, Rorty observes: "Neither Quine nor Sellars . . . has developed a new conception of philosophy in any detail."[23] Rather, the historically significant achievements of both authors consist in the problematization of the fundamental dogmas that, from Kant to the major representatives of both schools of the linguistic turn, have served as the unquestioned fundaments of the theoreticist conception of modern philosophy (as an autonomous discipline over and against the sciences).

Sellars put into question the difference between the empirically given and the conceptually postulated. Quine destroyed the synthetic-contingent/analytic-necessary distinction as well as the separation between the sciences and philosophy that went along with it. The specific ambivalence of Sellars's and Quine's positions is shown by the fact that each failed to recognize as problematic the distinctions problematized by the other and presupposed more or less without question his own constructive program: "It is as if Quine, having renounced the conceptual-empirical, analytic-synthetic, and language-fact distinctions, is still not quite able to renounce that between the given and the postulated. Conversely, Sellars, having triumphed over the latter, could not quite renounce the former cluster."[24]

With a view to Sellars as well as to Quine it should be noted that the constructive elements of their thinking at the same time make clear the transformative traits. Nevertheless it is a question of transformative traits only in the *weak* sense made explicit above, because both thinkers conceive their transition to a naturalistic discourse as a change in the disciplinary matrix of academic philosophy, which is carried out within a continually presupposed categorization of philosophical activity.

Hence Sellars sets forth, albeit critically, "that the atomistic conception of philosophy is a snare and a delusion,"[25] and that the hierarchical and separatist structuring of the disciplinary matrix is problematic. But at the same time he holds fast to the dogmatic division between the empirical sciences, which engage in synthetic-contingent truths, and nonempirical philosophy, which should be about analytic-necessary truths, when he takes as self-evident "that philosophy is not a science."[26]

The transformative aspects of Sellars's thinking are expressed in his critique of the atomistic understanding of the academic discourse: "As long as discourse was viewed as a map, subdivided into a side-by-side of sub-maps, each representing a sub-region in a side-by-side of regions making up the total subject matter of discourse, . . . one could view with equanimity the existence of philosophical specialists . . ."[27] As a consequence of this understanding, philosophy supplies the conceptual definitions and logical analyses, while the sciences, resting on the foundation of a terminology clarified by philosophy, work on empirical questions. Against this, Sellars describes the emerging new configuration of the analytic work of philosophy as follows: "For 'analysis' no longer connotes the definition of terms, but rather the clarification of the logical structure—in the broadest sense—of discourse, and discourse no longer appears as one plane parallel to another, but as a tangle of intersecting dimensions whose relations with one another and with extra-linguistic fact conform to no single or simple pattern."[28]

With this a new structure of the disciplinary matrix of philosophy steps into view, one that no longer is hierarchically centered on a fundamental discipline, but rather operates in the fashion of a network. In this sense Sellars emphasizes: "No longer can the philosopher interested in perception say 'let him who is interested in prescriptive discourse analyze its concepts and leave me in peace.' Most if not all philosophically interesting concepts are caught up in more than one dimension of discourse . . ."[29]

Against this background, the relation of philosophy and science also changes for Sellars. When philosophy is no longer only responsible for the atomistic analyses and definitions of individual scientific terms, but rather aims collectively at the holistic analysis of the relational inner-dependencies of everyday, scientific, and philosophical discourse—that is, when it is to be understood as a "discourse-about-man-in-all-discourse"[30]—then "familiarity with the trend of scientific thought is essential to the *appraisal* of the framework categories of the common-sense picture of the world."[31]

But at the same it remains certain for Sellars that a holistic philosophy that aims "toward that articulated and integrated vision of man-in-the-universe"[32] remains structurally separated from the sciences. This is the case insofar as it makes this vision its object in a specifically philosophic way. Philosophical activity as such remains for Sellars—as opposed to Quine, Davidson, and Rorty—methodologically separated from the research practices of science. This becomes clear when one views the above-quoted passage in its context. It reads: "The procedures of philosophical analysis as such may make no use of the methods or results of the sciences. But familiarity with the trend of scientific thought is essential to the *appraisal* of the framework categories of the common-sense picture of the world."[33] And in the same context Sellars makes clear: "I am not saying that in order to discern the logic—the polydimensional logic—of ordinary discourse, it is necessary to make use of the results or methods of the sciences."[34]

It is otherwise for Quine. In *Word and Object*, Quine simply remarks: "And philosophy . . . , as an effort to get clearer on things, is not to be distinguished in essential points of purpose and method from good and bad science."[35] Common sense, science, and philosophy form for Quine only a gradually—but not in principle—separated whole, which he described in his earlier essay "Two Dogmas of Empiricism" as a "total field,"[36] in which it is a question of "a man-made fabric which impinges on experience only along the edges."[37] Whereas Quine's residual dogmatisms of an empirical foundation of our "web of belief"[38] in a holistically-thought dimension of immediate experience has been problematized by Sellars (and later especially by Davidson and Rorty), Quine's naturalistic description of the inner state of the network of human beliefs goes beyond Sellars's holding fast to a deep-structural separation between philosophical and scientific discourse.

Thus Quine describes the program, developed in his main work *Word and Object*, of a "naturalized epistemology"[39] as an undertaking that not only dislodges "epistemology from its old status of first philosophy,"[40] but also brings it about that "epistemology merges with psychology, as well as with linguistics."[41] This "rubbing out of boundaries"[42] between philosophy and science emerges naturally from Quine's critique of the dogmatic pair of opposites of analytic-synthetic and necessary-contingent, with whose help the theoretical demarcation of modern academic philosophy from the empirical sciences has been realized, both within the framework of logical empiricism as well as by the two schools of linguistic philosophy.

At the same time, it is important to see that the dissolution defended by Quine of the border between philosophy and science does not aim at a new determination of philosophical activity as such. In Quine's view the disciplinary matrix of philosophy can be entwined with the empirical sciences like psychology or linguistics, without the original purpose of epistemology thereby running into danger. This purpose is, according to Quine, not only not betrayed by the naturalization movement he promotes, but on the contrary cured of its traditional aporiae and thus for the first time made realizable in a progressive way.

Quine's Self-assessment becomes especially clear in his demarcation of the late Wittgenstein and the therapeutic current running through linguistic philosophy. Quine writes: "Wittgenstein and his followers, mainly at Oxford, found a residual philosophical vocation in therapy: in curing philosophers of the delusion that there were epistemological problems. But I think that at this point it may be more useful to say rather that epistemology still goes on, though in a new setting and a clarified status. Epistemology, or something like it, simply falls into place as a chapter of psychology and hence of natural science."[43] Now, as Quine continues, "it studies a natural phenomenon, viz., a physical human subject."[44] And at the same time the naturalized epistemology devotes its attention to a thematic, "we are prompted to study for somewhat the same reasons that always prompted epistemology; namely, in order to see how evidence relates to theory, and in what ways one's theory of nature transcends any available evidence."[45]

Holding fast to the presupposition of continually writing off the theoreticist conception of philosophical activity—supported at different times by Quine and Sellars respectively—refers back again to the fact that their thought moves within the framework of the second ambivalence. The behavioristic naturalism that Quine and Sellars developed as a new paradigm of philosophical research is related back by them to the fundamental questions of modern academic tradition, i.e., is placed in the regressive horizon of the question concerning the problem-solving or problem-dissolving potential of the new (naturalistic) research matrix. They boast of it in different ways: Sellars, in that he newly structures the disciplinary matrix of philosophy, thereby securing the discipline in its academic identity from outside; and Quine, in that he brings the borders of the disciplines into a transdisciplinary movement, all the while adhering to the basic epistemological alignment of philosophical activity and placing the sciences in the service of this theoretical alignment.

In this respect Donald Davidson's situation is different than Sellars' and Quine's. Davidson overcomes the second ambivalence of the linguistic turn, in that he conceives the task of philosophy neither as problem-solving nor as problem-dissolving, but rather starts out from an understanding of philosophy that is transformative in the *strong* sense, i.e., newly defining philosophical activity itself. That connects with Rorty, who also stands for a transformative understanding of philosophy in the *strongest* sense, according to which philosophical activity is itself to be determined as transformative.

b) Davidson and Rorty

In his influential essay "On the Very Idea of a Conceptual Scheme" (1974), Davidson developed, on the basis of his critique of the "dualism of scheme and content,"[46] the twisting point within the linguistic turn for Rorty's suggestions for the development of a pragmatic vocabulary of philosophy.[47] Davidson's reflections focus on the critique of an understanding of philosophy, at the center of which stands the question—which he characterizes as "empirical"—of the schematizing relations of language to reality. The original scene of this questioning is for Davidson a result of the simple idea "of [an] organizing system and something waiting to be organized."[48] This idea,

Davidson continues, lies at the base of a large part of contemporary philosophy as "the third dogma . . . of empiricism."[49]

The dogmatic determination of philosophical achievement as a reflex-
ive scheme analysis is juxtaposed by Davidson against his own position of a
holistic coherence theory: "What distinguishes a coherence theory is simply
the claim that nothing can count as a reason for holding a belief except
another belief. Its partisan rejects as unintelligible the request for a ground of
source of justification of another ilk."[50] In this way, the recourse to an immediate given (the uninterpreted content) and the reference to conceptual schemes
(linguistic categories, logical forms, formal-pragmatic universals) are excluded.

As a consequence of dismissing the scheme-content dualism, Davidson
limits himself to the behavioristic perspective of the linguistic field researcher,
which Quine had already introduced in *Word and Object*. By doing this, he
brings about at the same time definite alterations in the way Quine models
the activity of the field linguist. For Davidson, what are from the ethnocentric
perspective of the linguist to be described as physical objects, and to which
the natives acting as test-subjects are linguistically conditioned, take the place
of the nervous stimuli claimed by Quine as neutral reference points.[51] The
question for the linguistic scheme of the interpretation of the given "irrita-
tions of all the far-flung surfaces"[52] is replaced by Davidson with the hermeneutic naturalism of his theory of "radical interpretation,"[53] in which it is a
question—as Rorty pointedly formulated—of the field linguist "going around
and around the hermeneutic circle until he begins to feel at home."[54]

Davidson's radical interpretation theory aims, from the external perspective of the field linguist, at external causes, i.e., at the causal mechanism
of conditioning that leads to a specific sign being used in a specific situation
in a specific way. In this way it is clear to Davidson's linguistic ethnologist
that there is no neutral procedure at his or her disposal for the description of
these causes. The linguistic ethnologist can only attempt to fit, as best as
possible, the convictions that he or she assumes the speakers he is investigating with those convictions he or she brings to the situation him or herself.
The linguistic field researcher is thus at the same time conscious that radical
interpretation begins at home. He or she knows that, as far as the relation
existing between his or her own beliefs and the world is concerned, "there is
nothing more to be known . . . than what we learn from an empirical study
of causal transactions between organisms and their environment."[55]

The situation of so called "triangulation"[56] is, according to Davidson,
characteristic of both the field linguist's going out into the unknown as well
as of the acquisition of his or her mother tongue, which comes about as a
child at home. This is because in both cases it holds that "[the] identification
of the objects of thought rests, then, on a social basis,"[57] i.e., it occurs in a
"simple triangular arrangement of the two agents and a commonly observed
object."[58] The first foundations of linguistic instruction, in whose framework

"one person learns from another how to speak and think of ordinary things,"[59] Davidson describes as follows: "the learner is rewarded, whether deliberately or not, when the learner makes sounds or otherwise responds in ways the teacher finds appropriate in situations the teacher classes together. . . . Success at the first level is achieved to the extent that the learner responds with sounds the teacher finds similar to situations the teacher finds similar. The teacher is responding to two things: the external situation and the responses of the learner. The learner is responding to two things: the external situation and the responses of the teacher."[60] In conclusion, Davidson reveals that "[a]ll these relations are causal. Thus the essential triangle is formed that makes communication about shared objects and events possible."[61] In this way, the conception of an "externalized epistemology"[62] connected with social-pragmatic triangulation replaces, for Davidson, the introspective-Cartesian perspective of traditional epistemology, which is (up to and including Quine) "essentially first person."[63]

Under the conditions of a linguistic turn that remains under the spell of the scheme-content dualism, linguistic competence (in part still with Wittgenstein, but especially with Quine and Sellars) was understood as the introspectively-investigating capacity to form contents inside a differentially-structured or holistically-conceived scheme, and thereby to make something distinguishable and identifiable as something. This view is juxtaposed by Davidson against the provocative thesis "that there is no such thing as a language."[64] This is a consequence of the dismissal of the fundamental premises of the philosophical tradition, elaborated by Davidson as "the third dogma of empiricism,"[65] which can be traced back to Kant[66] and lies at the basis of the various versions of the linguistic turn from Carnap and Bergmann to Quine and Sellars.

Against this, Davidson suggests that we "think of linguistic competence as a kind of know-how,"[67] i.e., as a pragmatic set of tools that allows us to interact with other humans and the nonhuman environment. It is this aspect of the way he uses "pragmatic" that Rorty first highlights in his interpretation of Davidson. This emphasis is made explicit in Davidson's suggestion that we should remove "the boundary between knowing a language and knowing our way around in the world generally."[68]

According to Davidson, a new typological determination of philosophical activity becomes possible under the conditions of a pragmatized understanding of language, which makes Davidson a transformative philosopher in the strong sense. While Quine takes the empirical work of the field linguist to be oriented toward the philosophical service of a pre-given epistemological questioning, Davidson understands philosophical activity as an activity that does not already have its goal determined from outside, but rather attains this determination in new ways in the midst of the work of the field linguist.

Philosophy can thus, from Davidson's perspective, bring into the field linguist's research context logical tools that spring from Davidson's application of the Tarskian theory of truth to natural languages. Nevertheless—so Davidson believes—no second, possibly genuine philosophical perspective is added to or propped up on the perspective of the field linguist. On the contrary, the typological transformation of philosophical activity, which Davidson supports on the basis of the situation of triangulation that he moves to the foreground, consists precisely in the fact that the philosophical perspective is dissolved in the contingent external perspective of the field linguist, who works empirically with the formal set of tools and thereby determines anew and in nonreductionistic ways scientific activity itself.

Davidson and Rorty share the opinion that the pragmatic naturalization of philosophy of language and epistemology is to be radicalized beyond Wittgenstein, Sellars, and Quine. Also common to both is the diagnosis and the affirmative realization of a "sea change in contemporary philosophical thought,"[69] connected with the establishment of the pragmatic vocabulary in philosophy. Nevertheless, different from Davidson, the pragmatic naturalization of Rorty leads to a transformative conception of philosophical activity in the strongest sense. According to this conception, philosophy becomes an epistemological experiment aimed at making possible future changes in common sense.

Against this, Davidson understands himself as a champion of a typological change that is less radical than the suggestions of Rorty. His hermeneutic naturalism aims at establishing a philosophical-linguistic type of inquiry that for all its naturalistic embeddedness is nevertheless to be designated as genuinely theoretical in the sense of descriptive observation. This is because, in Davidson's view, the inquiries of the philosophically versed field linguist do not aim at the *change* of the linguistic reality. Rather, Davidson's work is concerned with the empirically founded and hermeneutically relativized *description* of various natural languages, which are grasped as pragmatic tools of interaction.

Against this backdrop, Davidson's *analytic antirepresentationalism*, which aims at the formal-logical reconstruction of natural languages' truth theories without recurring thereby introspectively to representational tertia, allows itself to be differentiated by Rorty's pronounced *transformative pragmatism*. The latter renounces the instruments of symbolic logic, because it does not aim at the descriptive analysis of existing forms of interaction, but rather at the politically and socially motivated transformation of future rules of action. In contrast to Davidson, Rorty does not base his approach on the model of science, but rather on models that he takes from the cultural domains of literature and art and transfers over to science.

The related sociopolitical perspectivization of Rorty's recommended pragmatic vocabulary is still not contained in *Philosophy and the Mirror of*

Nature or in *Consequences of Pragmatism*. Rorty first develops it in the later works, published in the nineties, which grew out of his late major work *Contingency, Irony, and Solidarity* (1989). Rorty has described the basic strategic idea of these works as follows: "In short, my strategy . . . is to move everything over from epistemology and metaphysics to cultural politics, from claims to knowledge and appeals to self-evidence to suggestions about what we should try."[70]

The humanistic embeddedness of philosophical activity that is expressed in this strategy stands at the center of Rorty's transformative pragmatism (in the strongest sense). It marks a usage of "pragmatic" according to which the adjective means something like "oriented toward the socio-political realization of the ideals of democratic enlightenment." I will now turn to this usage and to its resulting perspective on the current debate between representationalism and antirepresentationalism.

THE SOCIOPOLITICAL IMPLICATIONS OF THE DEBATE OVER REPRESENTATIONALISM VS. ANTIREPRESENTATIONALISM

The opposition introduced by Rorty between representationalism and antirepresentationalism is to be distinguished from the difference, originating with Michael Dummett, between realism and antirealism.[71] In the current debate over the self-understanding of contemporary philosophy, many misunderstandings have emerged as a result of the first opposition being equated straightforwardly with the latter one. In Rorty's use, the difference between realistic picture-theories of knowledge and antirealistic construction-theories of knowledge serves not as a synonym for the opposition between representationalism and antirepresentationalism, but rather as an inner difference in which this distinction gets worked out within the area of representationalist positions. Rorty explicitly emphasizes this when he writes: "I claim that the representationalism-vs.-antirepresentationalism issue is distinct from the realism-vs.-antirealism one, because the latter issue arises only for representationalists."[72]

In his more recent publications, Rorty uses the correspondence theory of truth in both its underlying variants as the central characteristic of representationalism: "There is no point to debates between realism and anti-realism, for such debates presuppose the empty and misleading idea of beliefs 'being made true'."[73] The idea that human knowledge aims primarily at giving an adequate representation of reality determines both picture-theoretic as well as constructionist epistemologies. Even though realistic picture-theories and antirealistic constructionisms apply different criteria of adequation and presuppose different concepts of reality, both remain within the paradigm of a representationalism that aims at correspondence. While the adequacy of a

representation is determined picture-theoretically by its relation to a represented transcendent object, the constructionist correspondence criterion is
defined as immanent to the process of representation. The deciding question
here is whether the representation of a state-of-affairs formally corresponds
to the rules of the construction of something as something, understood as the
conditions of the possibility of representation in general.[74]

According to Rorty, the underlying presupposition in the realistic and
the antirealistic concepts of correspondence is the acceptance of an "ontological homogeneity"[75] between beliefs and nonbeliefs. The physicalistically arguing realist "thinks that nothing can correspond to a bit of spatio-temporal
reality except by being another bit linked to the first by appropriate causal
relationships."[76] On the other hand, the idealistically arguing antirealist maintains that "nothing can correspond to a representation except a representation."[77] This contention is then propped up by the interpretation "that there
was an intermediary 'scheme' which 'shaped' the non-beliefs before they became talkable-about."[78]

Advanced representationalists like John McDowell attempt to reconcile
realistic and antirealistic thinkers in a linguistically-reflected realism. Rorty
describes McDowell's position in relation to the linguistic turn in the following way: "In McDowell's picture, the linguistic turn in philosophy helped us
see that nothing is part of the process of justification which does not have a
linguistic shape. It did not, however, take away the need to 'make sense of the
world-directedness of empirical thinking.'"[79] Rorty summarizes McDowell's
strategy of connecting both aspects together when he continues in reference
to McDowell: "He thinks of a perceptual appearance as a request to you by
the world to make a judgment, but as not yet itself a judgment, even though
it has the conceptual form of a judgment."[80]

In fact, McDowell's fundamental idea is that the space of experience
guarantees "a constraint from outside exercises of spontaneity"[81] that suceeds,
"though not from outside what is thinkable, so not from outside the space of
concepts."[82] On the basis of his Hegel-inspired reading of Kant,[83] McDowell
assumes that the relation to nonlinguistic facts is not to be understood as an
immediate certainty, but rather as a reflexively-won determination of language
itself. The realistic intuition of the independence of the facts, to which our
linguistic statements relate, becomes in this way a determination capable of
being made explicit as something that is itself linguistically composed and has
the character of interpretation on its side. If one understands the realistic manner
of speaking with McDowell *cum grano salis*, i.e., in linguistically reflected form,
then it says that we have no immediate certainty of nonlinguistic entities, but
rather we rightly refer within language to objects in such a manner that we
interpret them as nonlinguistic and independent of interpretation.

From Rorty's perspective the linguistically difficult rehabilitation of
empiricism that McDowell performs is "brilliantly original and completely

successful."[84] But at the same time it is—and this is the deciding point for Rorty—either politically irrelevant, because it cannot be effected by common sense, or instead politically contraindicated, if it should in the long run sediment into everyday epistemology against all expectations. So, according to Rorty, not only the empirical dogmatism criticized by Davidson, but also McDowell's reflective concept of experience, aim, in the last instance, at "the figure of 'the world' as a nonhuman authority to whom we owe some sort of respect."[85]

The sublime authority of an interpretation-independent instance of reference for our linguistic statements is understood by McDowell as itself being an interpretation, and insofar as this is the case is relativized a bit further. But at the same time this relativized interpretation still takes place with the goal of carrying out a legitimation of the realistic intuition of transsubjective instances of reference, which transcends the space of intersubjective understanding from within.

Even if, going beyond McDowell, one understands with Robert Brandom the objectivity of reference as an intersubjective obligation, in which we have implicitly committed ourselves in the context of a linguistic use that is well established in social practices,[86] the question, according to Rorty, is whether it is desirable to hold fast to this intersubjectively-established language game of transubjectivity or reference.[87] Rorty gives two arguments that move him to answer this question in the negative. Both arguments, in Rorty's view, hold true even in the unlikely case that the social signature of the reference-language-game is able to make itself explicit not only for philosophers but also for the common man. The first argument Rorty names is already found with Davidson. It says that through the establishment of a transsubjective frame of reference the actual use of language as a pragmatic tool of communication, which serves thereby to make possible the coordination of behavior, comes out of view.

Following Brandom, it can be responded against this argument that the realistic frame of reference with its associated representationalist terminology is not to be understood as an inner determination of language itself (as with McDowell), but rather as a social tool that serves the coordination of behavior. Rorty anticipates this response when he argues "that Brandom and Davidson pretty much agree on all the issues and are simply employing different rhetorical strategies to make essentially the same points."[88]

While Davidson gives the linguistic turn a pragmatic twist by describing natural languages as instruments of interaction in an antirepresentationalist terminology, Brandom's strategy consists in adhering to the representationalist terminology in order to redefine it pragmatically into a (in Brandom's sense) "normative" fundamental vocabulary.[89] What appears on the surface as merely a strategic difference shows itself instead to be a deep underlying difference in philosophical understanding. Rorty makes this clear with the following remark: "But rhetoric matters, especially if one sees, as I do, the pragmatic tradition not just as clearing up little messes left behind by the great philosophers, but as contributing to a world-historical change in humanity's self-image."[90]

The second argument that Rorty brings against Brandom's representation-alist pragmatism results from the background of Rorty's transformative pragma-tism (in the strongest sense), according to which the task of philosophy consists in contributing to the development of human societies organized along secular, liberal-democratic lines. This is what Rorty means when he understands the pragmatic tradition as a tradition of thought that, since William James[91] and John Dewey,[92] attempts to perform philosophy not above all as a professionalized specialty, but rather transdisciplinarily as democratically-engaged thought, which in the context of the political project of the enlightenment actively cooperates in a "world-historical change in humanity's self-image."[93]

It is this sociopolitical background that gives the already-mentioned rhetorical difference for Rorty its meaning: "The choice is between dropping the notions of 'answering' and 'representing' . . . and keeping them. My argu-ment for dropping them is that they preserve an image of the relation be-tween people and nonpeople that might be called 'authoritarian'—the image of human beings being subject to a judgment other than that of a consensus of other human beings."[94] And in direct reference to Brandom, Rorty puts forward: ". . . I see Brandom's persistence in using the terms 'getting right', 'really is', and 'making true' as tools that will fall into authoritarian hands and be used for reactionary purposes."[95]

By reactionary purposes Rorty means purposes that still get expressed in McDowell's linguistically-reflected representationalism, which McDowell describes as a "relaxed Platonism."[96] The Platonic heritage of representation-alist epistemologies consists, according to Rorty, in the continued attempt to legitimate the agency of a sublime authority to which we have to show respect. In his book *Hoffnung statt Erkenntnis*, Rorty describes the desire for an internal or external legitimating agency that transcends the intersubjective consensus as the desire for a theoretically-aligned culture in whose center stands the determination of humans as knowing beings.

Actually, knowledge has been understood since the ancients as an ac-tivity, removed from the burden of performing practical deeds, that has its goal in itself.[97] Rorty points out, with reference to Dewey, the politically motivated signature of this separation, and the determination of humans as essentially knowing beings supported by it, when he writes: "In Dewey's view, all the noxious dualisms handed over by philosophy were the flotsam and jetsam of the social separation between observing and doing, between a class of *flâneurs* and one of producers."[98]

From Rorty's perspective McDowell's thought, which in a curious way claims for itself to represent a pragmatism "less half-baked than Rorty achieves,"[99] remains beholden to the theoreticist signature that connects the philosophical self-understanding of modern academic philosophy with that of the ancients. Rorty opposes this signature to his alternative design for philosophical activity: "Pragmatists do not think inquiry can put us more in touch with non-human reality than we have always been, for the only sense of 'being in touch' they recognize is causal interaction (as opposed to accurate representation). So in their view the only question is: will human life be better in the future if we adopt this belief, this practice, or that institution?"[100]

Rorty confronts the theoretical orientation toward the sublime authority of an externally pre-given or internally constituted frame of reference, to which we have to show respect in our thought and knowledge, with an alternative understanding of philosophy. The latter goes back to Dewey and is currently being pursued by politically minded philosophers like Habermas, Rawls, and Rorty himself. With regard to Habermas's thought, Rorty writes: "Such a philosophy politicizes epistemology, in the sense that it takes what matters to the search for truth to be the social (and in particular the political) conditions under which that search is conducted, rather than the deep inner nature of the subjects doing the searching."[101]

Rorty has further explicated, in the three volumes of his *Philosophical Papers* (1991–1998), the sociopolitical signature of the antirepresentationalist pragmatism, which he suggests as a model for determining new types of philosophical activity. And in his books *Achieving Our Country* (1998) and *Philosophy and Social Hope* (1999) he attempts to shift the philosophical practice a bit further. Succinctly, the central thought that links the philosophical antirepresentationalism (as it is represented by Rorty in connection to Davidson) with political pragmatism (as it was developed in the first half of the century by James and Dewey) reads as follows: "The pragmatists' antirepresentationalist account of belief is . . . a protest against the idea that human beings must humble themselves before something non-human."[102] And in a more positive manner: "I . . . think that a world of pragmatic atheists— people who thought realism versus antirealism is as little worth thinking about as Catholicism versus Protestantism—would be a better, happier world than our present one."[103]

Here the politicization that Rorty adds to Davidson's antirepresentationalism becomes explicit. Davidson is not interested in the political implications of his antirepresentationalism (or—as he calls it—his "new antisubjectivism"[104]). But he develops a naturalistic description of knowledge and language by which these get released from the representational relation to a realistic pre-given or antirealistic construed authority. What interests Rorty in this description is not the question, itself under the spell of representationalism, of whether it is in agreement with our established intuitions, but on the contrary the question of what contribution it could make to the political project of enlightenment, if it sometimes became the signature of common sense.

The "priority of democracy to philosophy"[105] defended by Rorty gets expressed in this sociopolitical perspectivization of epistemological questioning. At the same time it is setting his thinking apart from the motives of philosophical foundation, characteristic of the transcendentally-grounded pragmatism of Habermas.[106] According to Rorty, philosophy as a transformative activity (in the strongest sense) under the conditions—to be recognized as contingent and thus as presupposing normative frames of action and valuation—of the grand sociopolitical experiment of modern enlightenment, does not serve to ground the political form of government of democracy. Philosophical thinking works much more actively within an interdisciplinary academic environment to perform a contribution to the working out, realization, and optimizing of democratic forms of human coexistence.

A pragmatic philosophy—in an exacting sense—also subjects this project from a theoretical perspective to the traditional questions that investigate the relation of mind and world, of the structure of knowledge and language, of the inner constitution of sense and meaning. The theoretical reflection on the conditions of the possibility of our realistic or antirealistic understandings of reality is replaced by a pragmatic experiment with various common sense epistemologies.

It is a central vision of Rorty's pragmatic conception of philosophy to transform the representationally impressed common sense, which is directed at external or internal authorities, into an antirepresentationalist or antiauthoritarian common sense by which the goals of the democratic culture of political enlightenment could be further advanced. This vision is articulated in Rorty's thought as the "romantic hope of substituting new common sense for old common sense."[107]

The weak point of Rorty's romantic pragmatism consists in the fact that he does not attempt to name any concrete instruments that could serve as the means for the realization of his vision of an antirepresentationlist transformation of common sense.[108] Instead he hopes for a lucky turn of history as a result of which some idiosyncratic mutations of philosophical thought might at least once in a while seep down into common sense, a sedimentation so selected that "the spin-offs from private projects of purification turn out to have enormous social utility."[109]

NOTES

1. This text originates in an essay that appeared under the title "Die pragmatische Wende des linguistic turns" in the volume I edited, *Die Renaissance des Pragmatismus. Aktuelle Verflechtungen zwischen analytischer and kontinentaler Philosophie* (Weilerweist: Velbrück Wissenschaft, 2000), 96–126. The first part of the present essay comprises a reduced version of the original. The second develops further considerations that are not to be found in the German version.

2. For examples of this, see Hilary Putnam, *Renewing Philosophy* (Cambridge, Mass., and London: Harvard UP, 1992), and Richard Rorty, *Philosophy and Social Hope* (London and New York: Penguin, 1999).

3. Cf. Klaus Ch. Köhnke, *Entstehung und Aufstieg des Neukantianismus. Die deutsche Universitätsphilosophie zwischen Idealismus und Positivismus* (Frankfurt a. M.: Suhrkamp, 1993).

4. *The Linguistic Turn. Essays in Philosophical Method*, ed. Richard Rorty (Chicago: The University of Chicago Press, 1992 [1967]).

5. For a detailed exposition, cf. Sandbothe, ibid., 97–105.

6. Rorty, "Introduction: Pragmatism and Philosophy," in *Consequences of Pragmatism: Essays: 1972–1980* (Minneapolis: University of Minnesota Press, 1982), xiii–xlvii, xix.

7. Ibid., xxi.

8. Ibid.

9. Ibid.

10. Rorty, *Philosophy and the Mirror of Nature*, 2nd printing, with corrections (Princeton, N.J.: Princeton UP, 1980), 176.

11. "Introduction," xxi.

12. *Mirror*, 394. Cf. also Rorty, "Hilary Putnam and the Relativist Menace," in *Truth and Progress*, Philosophical Papers, vol. 3, (Cambridge and New York: Cambridge UP, 1998), 43–62, 47, see note 16 ; first appeared: *The Journal of Philosophy*, 90, no. 9 (September 1993), 443–461. For a critical confrontation with what he calls the "demonizing approaches" within Rorty reception, cf. Bjørn Ramberg, "Rorty und die Werkzeuge der Philosophie," in *Renaissance*, 127–166.

13. Ibid.

14. "Introduction," xix.

15. Rorty, "Twenty-Five Years Later," in *The Linguistic Turn*, 371–374, 373.

16. "Introduction," xix.

17. Ibid., xxi.

18. Ibid., xix.

19. The difference between the early and late Wittgenstein may also be described with reference to the first ambivalence of the linguistic turn. Similarly, the inner tension that permeates the thought of the late Wittgenstein implies a relation to the third ambivalence.

20. Ludwig Wittgenstein, *Tractatus Logico-Philosophicus*, trans. C. K. Ogden (London: Routledge and Kegan Paul, 1981), preface.

21. Anthony Kenny, "Wittgenstein über Philosophie," in Ludwig Wittgenstein, *Schriften, Beiheft 3: Wittgensteins geistige Erscheinung* (Frankfurt a. M.: Suhrkamp, 1979), 17.

22. Cf. Mike Sandbothe, "Pragmatismus und philosophische Medientheorie," in *Repräsentation und Interpretation*, ed. Evelyn Dölling, *Reihe: Arbeitspapiere zur Linguistik* (Berlin: TU Berlin, 1998), 99–124, esp. 113–122.

23. Rorty, "Epistemological Behaviorism and the De-Transcendentalization of Analytic Philosophy," in *Hermeneutics and Praxis*, ed. Robert Hollinger (Notre Dame, IN: University of Notre Dame Press, 1985), 89–121, 96.

24. Ibid.

25. Wilfrid Sellars, *Empiricism and the Philosophy of Mind*, second printing (Cambridge, Mass. and London: Harvard University Press, 1997), 80.

26. Ibid.

27. Ibid.

28. Ibid.

29. Ibid., 80–81.

30. Ibid., 81.

31. Ibid.

32. Ibid.

33. Ibid.

34. Ibid.

35. Willard Van Orman Quine, *Word and Object* (New York and London: The Technology Press of The Massachusetts Institute of Technology, 1960), 3–4.

36. Quine, "Two Dogmas of Empiricism," in *From a Logical Point of View*, second edition, revised (Cambridge, Mass.: Harvard UP, 1964), 42.

37. Ibid.

38. Thus reads the title of a book that Quine published together with Joseph S. Ullian, (New York: Random House, 1978).

39. Quine, "Epistemology Naturalized," in *Ontological Relativity and Other Essays* (New York and London: Columbia UP, 1969), 69–90.

40. Ibid., 87.

41. Ibid., 89–90.

42. Ibid., 90.

43. Ibid., 82.

44. Ibid.

45. Ibid., 83.

46. Donald Davidson, *Inquiries into Truth and Interpretation* (Oxford/ New York: Oxford UP, 1984), 189; first appeared in *Proceedings and Addresses of the American Philosophical Association* 47 (1974): 5–20.

47. In his retrospective on the path of his own thought, which is to be found in the essay "Davidson between Wittgenstein and Tarski," (*Crítica. Revista Hispanoamericana de Filosofía* 30, no. 88 [April 1998]: 49–71), Rorty writes: "In 1971 my philosophical views were shaken up, and began to be transformed. That was the year in which Davidson let me see the text of his 1970 Locke Lectures, which included an early draft of his *On the Very Idea of a Conceptual Scheme*" (51). Cf. also Davidson's commentary: "I have always been grateful to Richard Rorty for his response to my thoughts about conceptual schemes. For a time it seemed to me almost no one else understood what I was getting at in *On the Very Idea of a Conceptual Scheme*, and it mattered a good deal to me that Rorty not only grasped the main point but also endorsed it" (Davidson, "Reply to Rorty," *The Philosophy of Donald Davidson*, ed. Lewis Edwin Hahn, *The Library of Living Philosophers*, vol. XXVII [Chicago and La Salle, Illinois: Open Court, 2000], 595–600, 595). A documetation of the ongoing debate between Davidson and Rorty may be found in *Wozu Wahrheit? Schlüsseltexte der Davidson-Rorty-Debatte*, ed. Mike Sandbothe, *forthcoming* (Frankfurt aM.: Suhrkamp, 2004). For a summary see Sandbothe, in *Analytic/Continental: A Fresh Look*, ed. Carlos G. Prado, forthcoming, 2002.

48. Davidson, ibid., 189. "Reshaping Analytic Philosophy for a Transcontinental Conversation" (Amherst, NY: Humanities Press, 2003), 235–258.

49. Ibid.

50. Davidson, "A Coherence Theory of Truth and Knowledge," in *Kant oder Hegel? Über Formen der Begründung in der Philosophie*, ed. Dieter Henrich (Stuttgart: Klett-Cotta, 1983), 423–438, 426. Cf. also Davidson's more precise (or rather corrective) formulation in "Afterthoughts, 1987": "My emphasis on coherence was probably just a way of making a negative point, that 'all that counts as evidence or justification for a belief must come from the same totality of belief to which it belongs'" (Davidson, "A Coherence Theory of Truth and Knowledge: Afterthoughts, 1987," in *Reading Rorty: Critical Responses to 'Philosophy and the Mirror of Nature' (and Beyond)*, ed. Alan Malachowski [Oxford and Cambridge, Mass.: Blackwell, 1990], 120–138, 135).

51. Cf. Quine, *Word and Object*, chapter 2. On the distinction between the "distal theory" represented by Davidson and the "proximal theory" favored by Quine, see Davidson, "Meaning, Truth, and Evidence," in *Perspectives on Quine*, ed. Robert Barrett and Roger Gibson (Oxford and Cambridge, Mass.: Blackwell, 1990), 68–79.

52. *Word and Object*, 22.

53. "Radical Interpretation," in *Inquiries into Truth and Interpretation*, 125–139.

54. Rorty, "Pragmatism, Davidson and Truth," in *Objectivity, Relativism, and Truth, Philosophical Papers: Vol. 1*, (Cambridge/New York: Cambridge UP, 1991), 126–150, 133; first appeared in *Truth and Interpretation. Perspectives on the Philosophy of Donald Davidson*, ed. Ernest LePore (Oxford/New York: Blackwell, 1986), 333–355.

55. Ibid., 135.

56. "Epistemology Externalized," *Dialectica* 45 (1991):191–202, 201.

57. Ibid.

58. "Meaning, Truth, and Evidence," 70.

59. "Epistemology Externalized," 201.

60. Ibid.

61. Ibid.

62. Ibid., 191.

63. Ibid., 193.

64. Davidson, "A Nice Derangement of Epitaphs," in *Truth and Interpretation*, 433–446, 446.

65. "On the Very Idea," 189.

66. Davidson, "The Myth of the Subjective," in *Relativism: Interpretation and Confrontation*, ed. Michael Krausz (Notre Dame, IN: University of Notre Dame Press, 1989), 159–172, 160.

67. Rorty, "Sind Aussagen universelle Geltungsansprüche?," in *Deutsche Zeitschrift für Philosophie*, 42, no. 6 (1994): 975–988, 976.

68. "A Nice Derangement," 445–446.

69. "The Myth of the Subjective," 159.

70. Rorty, "Relativist Menace," 57. Cf. as well *Contingency, Irony*, 68; and "Pragmatism," in the *Routledge Encyclopedia of Philosophy*, ed. Edward Craig (London and New York: Routledge, 1998), 7: 633–640: "The naturalist strain in pragmatism . . . is . . . important mainly as a strategy for shifting philosophers' attention from the problems of metaphysics and epistemology to the needs of democratic politics" (638).

71. Michael Dummet, "Realism," in *Truth and Other Enigmas* (Camridge, Mass./ London: Harvard UP, 1978), 145–165. On the realism/antirealism debate, cf. also *Realism/Antirealism and Epistemology*, ed. Christopher B. Kulp (Lanham, Md.: Rowman & Littlefield Publishers, 1997). On Rorty's opposition between representationalism and antirepresentationalism, see Rorty, "Pragmatism as Anti-Representationalism," in *Pragmatism. From Peirce to Davidson*, ed. John P. Murphy (Boulder, Colo.: Westview Press, 1990); Rorty, "Introduction: Antirepresentationalism, Ethnocentrism, and Liberalism," in *Objectivity, Relativism, and Truth*, 1–17; Rorty, "Representation, Social Practice, and Truth," ibid., 151–161, first appeared in *Philosophical Studies* 54 (1988): 215–228.

72. Rorty, "Introduction: Antirepresentationalism, Ethnocentrism, and Liberalism," in *Objectivity*, 2. Elsewhere Rorty writes: ". . . on my view the futile metaphysical struggle between idealism and physicalism was superseded, in the early years of this

century, by a metaphilosophical struggle between the pragmatists . . . and the anti-pragmatists . . . The latter struggle is *beyond* realism and anti-realism." Rorty, "Pragmatism, Davidson, and Truth," 149. Cf. also Rorty, "Beyond Realism and Anti-Realism", in *Wo steht die Analytische Philosophie heute?*, eds. Ludwig Nagl and Richard Heinrich (Wien/München: Oldenbourg, 1986), 103–115.

73. Rorty, "Pragmatism, Davidson, and Truth," 128.

74. Martin Heidegger has already pointed out, as regards the state-of-affairs, that "the old concept of truth in the sense of the 'correspondence' (adaequatio) of knowledge to the being is so little shaken that it [the Copernican Revolution] actually presupposes it [the old concept of truth], indeed even grounds it for the first time." Martin Heidegger, *Kant and the Problem of Metaphysics*, trans. Richard Taft (Indianapolis: Indiana UP, 1990), 8. His reconstruction of the Kantian arguments goes as follows: "Ontic knowledge can only correspond to beings ('objects') if this being as being is already first apparent [offenbar], i.e., is already first known in the constitution of its Being. Apparentness of beings (ontic truth) revolves around the unveiledness of the constitution of the Being of beings (ontological truth); at no time, however, can ontic knowledge itself conform 'to' the objects because, without the ontological, it cannot even have a possible 'to what'" (ibid).

75. Rorty, "Pragmatism, Davidson, and Truth," 131.

76. Ibid.

77. Ibid.

78. Ibid., 136.

79. Rorty, "The Very Idea of Human Answerability to the World: John McDowell's Version of Empiricism," in *Truth and Progress*, 138–152, 142. Rorty's own positive assessment of the linguistic turn differs from McDowell's in the following way: "I take the linguistic turn in philosophy . . . to be a turn away from the very idea of human answerability to the world."

80. Ibid., 148.

81. John McDowell, *Mind and World* (Cambridge, Mass./London: Harvard UP, 1996), 144.

82. Ibid.

83. Cf. John McDowell, "Having the World in View: Sellars, Kant, and Intentionality," in *Journal of Philosophy*, XCV, n. 9 (September 1998): 431–491, esp. 466ff and 490ff.

84. "The Very Idea of Human Answerability," 150.

85. Ibid.

86. Robert Brandom, *Making it Explicit: Reasoning, Representing, and Discursive Commitment* (Cambridge, Mass./London: Harvard UP, 1994), esp. chapt. 8, 495–613.

87. Rorty, "Robert Brandom on Social Practices and Representations," in *Truth and Progress*, 122–137, esp. 130ff.

88. Ibid., 132.

89. "Normative" means, for Brandom—who designates his own thought as "normative-pragmatic"—not "moral-practical," but rather touching on intersubjective relations of obligation. See Brandom, *Making It Explicit*, 3–66.

90. Rorty, "Robert Brandom on Social Practices," 132.

91. Cf., for example, William James, "The Moral Philosopher and the Moral Life," in *The Will to Believe, and Other Essays in Popular Philosophy* (New York: Longmans, Green & Co, 1897).

92. Cf., for example, John Dewey, *Democracy and Education. An Introduction to the Philosophy of Education* (New York: Macmillan, 1916); *Reconstruction in Philosophy* (New York: Henry Holt, 1920); *Human Nature and Conduct. An Introduction to Social Psychology* (New York: Henry Holt, 1922); *The Public and Its Problems* (New York: Henry Holt, 1927); *The Quest for Certainty. A Study of the Relation of Knowledge and Action* (New York: Minton, Balch & Co., 1929).

93. Rorty, "Robert Brandom on Social Practices," 132.

94. Ibid., 135.

95. Ibid. Cf. also "What Do You Do When They Call You a Relativist?", in *Philosophy and Phenomenological Research*, LVII, n. 1 (March 1997):173–177: "My hunch is that Brandom would do well ... to situate his philosophy of language within an immodest metaphilosophical framework, according to which philosophical reflection can reject the intuitions of the vulgar as well as the metaphors of the learned" (177).

96. *Mind and World*, 178.

97. On the recontruction of the "spectator theory of knowledge" based on the model of the gaze, which goes back to Plato and Aristotle, see Dewey, *The Quest for Certainty*, esp. chapts. 1, 2, and 4, as well as *Reconstruction in Philosophy*, esp. chapt. 1.

98. Rorty, *Hoffnung statt Erkenntnis. Eine Einführung in die pragmatische Philosophie* (Wien: Passagen, 1994), 18. Cf. Dewey, *The Quest for Certainty*, esp. chapts. 1 and 2; as well as *Reconstuction in Philosophy*, esp. chapt. 1.

99. *Mind and World*, 156.

100. Rorty, "Pragmatism as Anti-Authoritarianism," in *Revue Internationale de Philosophie*, 207, n. 1 (1999): 7–20, 16.

101. Rorty, "Habermas, Derrida, and the Functions of Philosophy," in *Truth and Progress*, 307–326, 309. For Rorty's critique of Habermas's attempt to universalize the procedural aspects of language, cf. Rorty, "Sind Aussagen universelle Geltungsansprüche?"

102. "Anti-Authoritarianism," 7.

103. Rorty, "Response to Frank Farrell," in *Rorty & Pragmatism. The Philosopher Responds to His Critics*, Herman J. Saatkamp ed. (Nashville, Tenn./London: Vanderbilt UP, 1995), 189–195, 195.

104. Davidson, "The Myth of the Subjective," 168.

105. "The Priority of Democracy to Philosophy," in *The Virginia Statute of Religious Freedom*, Merrill Peterson and Robert Vaughan eds. (Cambridge/New York: Cambridge UP, 1988), 257–288.

106. In contrast to Davidson and Brandom, and in alliance with Rorty, Habermas configures philosophy in a decidedly sociopolitical way. But unlike Rorty, Habermas is of the opinion that the political ideals of modern democracy cannot be realized without an intersubjectively-founded representationalism. Habermas configures this as "pragmatic knowledge-realism" (Habermas, "Einleitung: Realismus nach der sprachpragmatischen Wende," in *Wahrheit und Rechtfertigung. Philosophische Aufsätze* (Frankfurt a. M.: Suhrkamp, 1999, 7–64, 14) or rather as a "Kantian pragmatism, supported on the transcendental fact that subjects capable of speech and action who allow themselves to be affected by reasons, can learn—in the long run even, cannot not learn" (ibid.). Cf. as well Thomas McCarthy's critique of Rorty (*Ideals and Illusions. On Reconstruction and Deconstruction in Contemporary Critical Theory* [Cambridge, Mass.: MIT Press, 1991]), which Habermas cites for support.

107. Rorty, "On Moral Obligation, Truth, and Common Sense," in *Debating the State of Philosophy. Habermas, Rorty, and Kolakowski*, Józef Niznik and John T. Sanders, eds. (Westport, Conn./London: Praeger, 1996), 48–52, 52.

108. I make a suggestion as to how this weak point might be greatly compensated for by means of media-philosophy in my book, *Pragmatische Medienphilosophie* (Weilerswist: Velbrück Wissenschaft, 2001). Cf. as well "Pragmatic Media Philosophy and Media Education in the Age of the Internet," in *Enquiries at the Interface: Philosophical Problems of On-line Education*, Paul Standish and Nigel Blake, eds. (Oxford: Blackwell, 2000), 59–77 (also in *The Journal of Philosophy of Education*, 34, n. 1 (February 2000), 53–69), as well as "Media Temporalities of the Internet: Philosophy of Time and Media in Derrida and Rorty," in *Cultural Attitudes Towards Technology and Communication*, Special issue of *AI & Society*, Charles Ess and Fay Sudweeks, eds., 14, n. 1 (London: Springer, 2000).

109. Rorty, "Heidegger, Kundera and Dickens," in *Essays on Heidegger and Others. Philosophical Papers. Volume 2* (Cambridge/New York: Cambridge University Press, 1991), 66–82, 72.

5

ALBRECHT WELLMER

The Debate about Truth: Pragmatism without Regulative Ideas[1]

*Translated by William Egginton**

1.

The classical definition of truth that has largely determined the understanding of the concept in the history of European philosophy comes, as is well known, from Aristotle. Aristotle says: "To say of what is that it is not, or of what is not that it is, is false, while to say of what is that it is, and of what is not that it is not, is true."[2] This formulation of Aristotle's has been understood, to a large extent, in the history of European philosophy in the sense of an "agreement," "adequation," or finally also a "correspondence theory" of truth. The medieval formulation according to which truth is an "adequatio rei et intellectus" is only one version of this basic idea. Even Kant, in *The Critique of Pure Reason*, plainly presupposed a corresponding understanding of the concept of truth: "The old and famous question with which the logicians were to be driven into a corner . . . is this: *What is truth?* The nominal definition of truth namely, that it is the agreement of cognition with its object, is here granted and presupposed."[3]

2.

If one wanted to reformulate what Aristotle and Kant said in an easier and somewhat schematic format, one could do so as follows:

> (T) the assertion, (statement or conviction), that p, is true if and only if p.

And this biconditional is then in formal semantics reduced to the following schema:

> (T¹) "p" is true if and only if p.

The problem that concerns us emerges in both formulations: *on the one hand*, in both cases the "truth condition"—whether the assertion that p, or of the sentence "p"—is formulated with the help of the same sentence for which or for whose assertion the necessary and sufficient condition for being true is sought—such that we, so it seems, don't at all go beyond the sentence "p," or rather the assertion that p. But *on the other hand*, both biconditionals should explain truth as a relation of *agreement* between a statement (a conviction) and reality, such that the expression "p" would thus have to emerge on the left and right sides as differentiated functions: on the left side it is a question of the statement (assertion, conviction) that p; on the right side, juxtaposed to this, is the "state of affairs" that p. Nevertheless, it is of course no coincidence that we can *specify* the "fact" with which the statement (conviction) that p should "agree," again, only with the help of the same sentence "p" with whose help the statement was also made (or the conviction formulated).

Next we ask: how can we ascertain whether such an agreement exists between an assertion and a "thing"—a state of affairs, reality?

Let us assume that someone claims "both doors are closed." I turn around and determine that no, both doors are not closed. It is *not* the case, as it was asserted. Or in another situation, I determine yes, both doors are closed. It is the case, as was asserted. In both cases, therefore, I determine *whether* the assertion agrees with reality by determining *whether* it is *the case, as* was asserted. The precondition for this is that I understand the sentence "both doors are closed," that I know to what the expression "both doors" refers in this case, and that I can correctly use the predicate "is closed." If these preconditions are given, I can determine, as a rule—if I find myself in an adequate position—*whether* the doors are closed. My ability to determine *whether* the two doors are closed is my ability to determine whether the assertion that both doors are closed agrees with reality (whether it is the case *as* asserted)—and this means: whether the assertion is *true*.

What "agreement" between a statement and reality *means* can thus only be clarified when we reflect on our ability to find out in many cases—for instance, through perception—whether things are as asserted. And if we have learned a language, we can do this in many elementary cases.

Naturally, things are much more complicated when speaking of logically-complex moral, aesthetic, mathematical, historical, or philosophical judgments (or statements or convictions). In such cases we cannot persuade ourselves, as a rule, merely by "looking into it," whether it is the case *as* asserted: here, as a rule, the idea of a direct comparison between a statement and reality makes no sense. In order to find out whether it is the case *as* asserted, we are, on the contrary, dependent on "indirect" procedures, namely, on ways of reasoning that so and so is the case—whereas the possible ways of reasoning for statements pertaining to the past, for aesthetic or moral judgments, or for mathematical or scientific assertions or convictions are completely different. We try to decide the question whether something is *so*, *as* one says it is, with *reasons* (where in many cases the reasons that are at our disposal are not sufficient for bringing about such a decision). At this point it becomes clear that the idea of a "correspondence" between a statement and reality (or between a statement and a fact) suggests a misleading picture: namely, it suggests the picture of a relation of agreement—ascertainable from some standpoint (which cannot be ours, but perhaps that of God)—between statements or beliefs and a piece of reality or the things themselves. If, however, one detaches the idea of agreement between what one says and what is (really) the case from the way we justify or deny assertions or beliefs with reasons—or by calling on perceptions—then this idea becomes something completely incomprehensible. For how then should one think such an agreement between statements (thoughts, convictions, etc.) and reality—two totally incommensurable *relata*: how and what should be tested here as agreement—and *who* should carry out such a test? A correspondence concept of truth, such as seems to be suggested by Aristotle's formulation, becomes either incomprehensible or metaphysical, or both at the same time, if we seek to think of the idea of "just like," i.e. "agreement," independently of our justificatory praxis.

3.

Let us now return to our biconditional (T): the assertion that p is true if and only if (really) p. The intuition that this sentence expresses could also be reformulated as such: an assertion is true if and only if it is the case as was asserted. We can now think what *place* such an explanation of the concept of truth can have in our practice of making assertions. This practice is of a *normative* kind: assertions are moves in a language game that are "justified" or "unjustified." We are entitled to assertions if we have good reasons to assert that p, or if we have convinced ourselves through our perceptions that p—or also if Someone whom we have good reason to trust has said to us that p (i.e., reason for the assumption that this Someone could provide good reasons). What we learn when we learn a language is—among other things—to judge in a reasoned way and to distinguish between justified and unjustified assertions (convictions). This suggests a new interpretation of the biconditional (T), which no longer frames it as an attempt to interpret truth as an agreement between statements and states of affairs, but rather as an attempt to determine the place the word "true" has in our assertive and justificatory praxis. Accordingly, we could now read the biconditional as such: someone is justified in asserting that p is true precisely when he or she is justified in asserting that p. And this could now be further interpreted as saying: to say that an assertion is true is nothing other than to say that the assertion is legitimate (grounded, justified). Truth would then become no more than "warranted assertability" or "rational acceptability." The concept of truth would consequently be drawn back onto justification.

4.

Of course, upon closer examination it appears that something in this reduction—or equation—cannot be correct. Nevertheless, the new interpretation of the biconditional (T) makes clear an internal relation between truth and justification—which in its correspondence-theoretical interpretation is lost from view—and which I would like once again to clarify differently. In Ludwig Wittgenstein's *Tractatus Logico-Philosophicus* one finds the famous sentence: "to understand a sentence means to know what is the case if it is true."[4] This sentence denotes the fundamental idea of truth-conditional semantics. Wittgenstein's sentence says: we understand a sentence if we know its truth conditions. For example, we understand the proposition "both doors are closed" if we know under which conditions a corresponding assertion is true. Now, it is clear that the knowledge of the truth conditions of a sentence p cannot be anything other than the knowledge of the conditions under which I am entitled to assert that p. If I have learned a language, and so long as I understand the sentences of the language, I know, as a rule, when the conditions are present under which I am entitled (or not entitled) to assert that p. This knowledge is only in part a *propositional* knowledge. To a considerable degree it is *practical* knowledge—a *knowing how*—as the *later* Wittgenstein always emphasized (I *can* ascertain, e.g., through perception, whether the predicate "is closed" applies to both doors). My knowledge of the truth conditions is, in practical terms, a knowledge of *assertability* conditions. Since the conditions under which I am entitled to assert that p are precisely the conditions under which I am entitled to assert that p is *true*, and in that sense the knowledge of the conditions of assertability is the same as the knowledge of the conditions of truth, it would appear that truth *is* warranted assertability. Truth would thus become, as one says, an *"epistemic"* concept, which should mean: a concept that can be traced back to "justification." Upon closer inspection, however, something about this conclusions appears to be false.

5.

Putnam has made clear that the words "true" and "justifiable" (referring to assertions or convictions) cannot be equated by reference to the grammar of these words: one is entitled (has good reasons) under certain conditions to believe or to assert that p—and such reasons can later be revealed to be insufficient. "Justification can be lost"[5]—justification is relative to time or circumstances and also to people, whereas truth "cannot be lost"—i.e., a conviction or an assertion cannot today or for me be true and tomorrow or for you not be. Truth is transsubjective and timeless. This points to a grammatical difference between the predicates "is true" and "is justified,"[6] which certainly remains to be clarified. A corresponding attempt at clarification has been undertaken, in particular, by Putnam, Habermas, and Apel. The basic idea common to all three philosophers is as follows: if truth is internally connected with justification and nevertheless not the same as justification (here and now), then further conditions must be stated in such a way that an assertion or conviction justified under such conditions would be *necessarily* true. Truth would, therefore, be maintained as an "epistemic" concept—internally connected with the concept of justification—and nevertheless the simple equation of the predicates "is true" and "is justified" would be avoided. The conditions in question would have to be *ideal* conditions, and the basic idea is that an assertion or conviction justified under such ideal conditions would be necessarily true—whereas the "necessarily" should give expression to a conceptual necessity. Putnam, Habermas, and Apel want to say that this is how we *understand* the concept of truth (or this is how we *ought to* understand it).

Let us first make clear the point of the basic argumentation strategy: if one eliminated the *difference* between truth and justification, there would be *relativistic* consequences, because it is easy to see that in the vertical dimension of historical time, as well as in the horizontal dimension of a plurality of cultures, situations, and contexts, many mutually *incompatible* convictions are held to be true by different people, in different cultures, etc., and all with—prima facie—good reasons. This even goes for the history of science—it is not only a problem for cultural pluralism. (It would be absurd to assert, for example, that not one scientist in the past had good reasons for theories he was convinced of, even though *we* might *today* hold these theories to be *false*).

The consequence of an equation of truth and justification would be relativism, because with such an equation the contextual index that belongs to the concept of justification (*someone at a specific time* is convinced, with good reasons that . . .) would be transferred to the idea of truth: truth would be tantamount to what, according to the respective prevailing standards of justification for someone or some group, is justified to be held as true. Such a relativistic dissolution of the idea of truth appears, however, to be incoherent.

6.

For Putnam, Habermas, and Apel, the problem to solve is how the "absoluteness"—in the sense of timelessness and nonindexicality—of the concept of truth can be reconciled with the conceptual connection between truth and justification. The answer from all three authors is that an opinion can be called "true" when it would be accepted as justified under ideal conditions—conditions that have to be further specified. Characteristic of all three versions of this answer is the following: the idealization upon which the explanation of the concept of truth seems to depend must already be operative, as pragmatically effective, on the level of everyday communication and argumentative discourse, be it as "necessary presuppositions" or as "regulative ideas."[7]

Putnam has sought to define truth as rational acceptability under epistemically-ideal conditions.[8] Against this, Habermas and Apel have rightly insisted that the idealization contained in the concept of truth should refer not merely to ideal cognitive conditions (i.e., to scientific progress), but should be understood in a more comprehensive way. Namely, if one considers the different dimensions of truth and validity with reference to which we can speak of validity claims and their justifications, and if one considers further the social dimension of our justification practices and thereby the internal relation between giving reasons and the attempt to bring about a consensus, then the idealization implicit to the concept of truth must refer to ideal epistemic, moral, and communicative conditions all at the same time. I restrict myself here to Apel because I believe that Apel has worked out this idea in the most conclusive way. The idea of truth for Apel is the idea of an ultimate and infinite consensus of an ideal communication community.[9] Truth becomes a regulative idea. Here, in fact, the idea of an *absolute* truth appears to be reconciled with the insight into the internal connection between truth and justification. Whereas the concept of truth in metaphysical realism severs this connection and thereby implies fundamentally the fiction of a "God's eye view" outside of our practice of justification, one could label Apel's position as the attempt to inscribe something analogous to such a "God's eye view" into our practices of justification as a regulative idea. And thus Apel claims that this idea is a *constitutive* regulative idea for linguistic communication and the justification practices attached to it. The idea of truth is at once "constitutive" and "regulative" in that, on one hand, the truth-orientation of linguistic communication is unavoidable, while, on the other hand, thanks to the unavoidable truth-orientation of linguistic communication, we know ourselves to be obliged in our discursive practice to approximate ever more the rational consensus of an ideal communication community.

7.

If one now attempts to spell out the implications of Apel's explanation of the concept of truth, it becomes clear that in it the idea of a final, complete, and absolute truth is short-circuited with that of a morally perfect order and that of a completely transparent communicative situation. But this idea is, I believe, metaphysical. It is the idea of a communication community that would have escaped, to put it in Derrida's words, "play and the order of signs";[10] it is the idea of a state of full transparency, absolute knowledge, and moral perfection—in short: of a communicative situation that has left behind the constraints, the opacity, the fragility, the temporality, and the materiality of finite, human forms of communication. Derrida has correctly pointed out that, in such idealizations, the conditions of possibility of what is being idealized are negated. Ideal communication would be communication beyond the conditions of "différance"—to speak with Derrida—and thus communication outside of and beyond the conditions of possibility of communication. However, insofar as the idea of an ideal communication community includes the negation of the conditions of finite human communication, it also implies the negation of the natural and historical conditions of human life, of finite, human existence. The idea of an ideal communication community remains paradoxical, even if it is only understood as a regulative idea to which nothing real in the world can ever correspond; because it belongs to the meaning of this idea, it commits us to work toward its realization. The paradox in this is that we would be committed to strive toward the realization of an ideal whose realization would be the end of human history. The goal is the end; ideal communication would be the death of communication. This paradoxical structure reveals that the idea of an ideal communication community still contains a *metaphysical* explication of the concept of truth, which finally does not distinguish itself from that of metaphysical realism structurally, except through its greater subtlety. I will return to this theme.

8.

The result thus far is that the concept of truth cannot be explained with the help of the idea (or even the "regulative idea") of justification—or of consensus—under ideal conditions. From this circumstance, Rorty has drawn the conclusion that "truth" and "justification" are two *different* concepts that have nothing to do with one another. What matters for us in our discursive practices—everyday practices and scholarly research—is, according to Rorty, not truth but justification. "Truth," in contrast, would be a *semantic* concept, useful for formal semantics or theories à la Davidson. In this way, Rorty wants to cut through the internal connection between truth and justification, not in the sense of metaphysical realism—which is the actual object of his critique—but rather in that he, as it were, lets the air out of the concept of truth. This corresponds to the strategy that has come to be known as that of a "deflationary theory" of truth. One could also speak of a "deflationary" interpretation of Aristotle's explanation of the concept of truth, which takes the semantic equivalence of "'p' is true if and only if p" as its starting point. One can interpret this equivalence—as I did at the outset—such that I am entitled to assert that "p" is true to exactly the same extent that I am entitled to assert that p. Rorty, however, does *not* draw the conclusion that I had suggested earlier: namely, that truth could be drawn back onto justification— a conclusion that, in the end, leads to the untenable idealization theses of Putnam, Apel, and Habermas. Rorty would on the contrary say that because the assertion that "p" is true brings nothing to the assertion that p, because both assertions have the same content, the semantic concept of truth has nothing to do with the pragmatic concept of justification. Accordingly, the concept of truth would have primarily theoretical (for instance, formal semantic) functions and, in addition, only some rather trivial pragmatic functions regarding the expression of agreement or disagreement[11]—as when one says "that is true" or "that is not true"—but the concept of truth would have in this way lost all weight and substance. What our discursive practices are about—and the only thing they can be about—according to Rorty, is the justification of our assertions and beliefs: not truth but justification is the goal of inquiry.

I believe that Rorty's considerations signify a step in the right direction compared to those of the "idealization theoreticians"; I wish to interpret this step, however, in a somewhat different manner than Rorty himself does.[12] To this end I would like to stick, for the time being, to the basic intuition of Putnam, Habermas, and Apel that in order to understand the role the concept of truth plays for our discursive practices, one must understand not only the difference but also the internal connection between "truth" and "justification." Later on I will return to Rorty's thesis.

9.

First I would like to show why regulative ideas are not *necessary* in order to explicate a normatively meaningful concept of truth, *and* that the search for such an explication runs up against a "grammatical error." Herein I proceed from an internal connection between truth and ways of reasoning (justification), which could be explained by the following two theses: (a) The *truth* conditions of statements are only *given* to us as conditions of justifiability and assertability, respectively. (b) Assertions (and in general, convictions) are, according to their meaning—as validity claims—internally related to justification in a *normative* sense. Assertions are only rightfully raised—convictions are only rightfully held—if one can justify them. Nevertheless, to justify them means to justify them *as true*. To justify the assertion (or conviction) that 'p' is the same as to justify the assertion that 'p' is true (and with this thesis we need not yet distinguish between the different kinds of truth claims—empirical, evaluative, aesthetic, hermeneutic, and moral—that we raise while speaking). That to justify an assertion, that p, means to justify it as true, is the pragmatic explanation of the semantic equivalence, 'p' is true = if p. As soon as we explain the Tarskian equivalence pragmatically in this way, it becomes clear at once that, in order to completely explain it, we must take into account the difference between the perspective a first person (a speaker) has of him or herself and the first person's perspective on *another* speaker. In fact, it is valid for me, as for any other, that to justify an assertion (a conviction) means to justify it as *true*. *Reciprocally*, however, we do not recognize justifications necessarily as *valid*, such that in the difference in perspective between two speakers there emerges the difference between something "held to be true" (held as justified) and *being* true (*being* justified).[13] And as soon as this difference emerges, without which a concept of truth is not possible, it of course also emerges for each speaker with reference to him or herself. Thus it appears that a gap remains between "justified" and "true"—that between *apparent* and *real* justification. And now one can attempt to make explicit under which conditions a justification would *really* be a justification, thus guaranteeing the truth of the so-justified—for instance, by saying that the justification of an assertion guarantees truth if it occurs under epistemically-ideal conditions or under conditions of an ideal communication community. Justification as such does not guarantee truth, rather only justification under ideal conditions; that—so goes the misleading and already criticized conclusion—is what we mean by *truth*. The *error* of all considerations of this kind lies in the fact that they do not take seriously the constitutive difference between a first person's perspective on herself and her perspective (as that of a "second person" or interpreter) on *other speakers*, and instead attempt to take on a "metaperspective"; that is precisely what I called "metaphysical." Let me try to show next how the normative force of the concept of truth becomes operative through the difference between first and second person perspectives, as it plays itself out for each individual speaker.

If I make an assertion—hold a belief—with reasons—then I understand it, with reasons, *as* true. That is the internal connection between truth and justification. If, however, another makes an assertion—holds a belief—then I can only *understand* this as the assertion or conviction it is, in that I understand it with its—factual or possible—reasons. I can only ascribe convictions to another insofar as I can understand them as rationally tied together with reasons, evidences, and other convictions. But here to understand beliefs or assertions as being based on reasons does not necessarily mean to understand them as *true*. To ascribe reasons to another does not necessarily imply *recognizing* these reasons as sound. *My* reasons—whatever I accept as good reasons—are eo ipso *good* reasons (that is a comment on the grammar of "good reasons"); this should mean that for me the justified beliefs are necessarily the *true* beliefs. With reference to another person, however, his or her ways of reasoning are not necessarily sound from my perspective, and the corresponding convictions not necessarily *true*. This should not mean that I exclude myself from the sphere of fallible beings, because the same goes for every other speaker in the I-perspective. That *my* reasons are eo ipso good reasons, that my reasoned convictions are necessarily true convictions, should only mean that what makes sense as a persuasive reason to me *is* precisely for that reason a persuasive reason *for me*.[14] I cannot place myself outside of my convictions, reasons, and evidences; if I doubt, that only means that I do not feel myself persuaded by the reasons available to me, that they are, for me, (still) not persuasive reasons. And of course I know not only—by understanding myself as, so to speak, the other of another—that the justifications that I give to another will not necessarily be recognized by him or her as sound; rather, I also know that what I hold as a reasoned truth may appear to me at some later time—perhaps on the basis of new experiences or counterarguments that I am confronted with—as not (really) justified. This knowledge, however, alters nothing of the fact that what is true for me is[15] what I take to be as justified belief.

What I hold as reasoned truth *deserves* agreement: truth is transsubjective. And if I argue for my conviction, I wish to bring about, with reasons, such an agreement. In *this* sense a rational consensus is the telos of argumentation. But "rational" here means precisely reasoned, and that means: *similarly* reasoned for all those taking part. We can offer no criteria for rational consensus other than this: that precisely all those taking part are similarly persuaded by good reasons. Since, however, what "good reasons" are can only be shown in that they *compel* us towards an agreement, a consensus can never be the criterion that what we have before us are good reasons. The concept of a "good reason" is attached, in an irreducible way, to the perspective of the one "persuaded" by good reasons. One cannot describe from a metaperspective which "qualities" reasons must have in order to be *really* good reasons. To call reasons "good" is not the ascription of an "objective" quality, rather it is the adoption of an attitude with normative consequences. These reasons compel *me* to accept that p as true. And naturally these are often the reasons that another brings up; in this sense, linguistic communication is, among other things, also a medium for progress in knowledge.

10.

The answer to the question "why do you believe that?" or "by what right do you assert that?" is the giving of reasons or evidence. This shows that "asserting" and "believing" are internally geared to the giving and asking for reasons. And to show that an assertion—a conviction—is justified means to show that it is *true*. Since for every speaker, however, there exists a difference between the first person's perspective on him or herself and the first person's perspective on another, there *also* exists a difference between "justified" and "true." What another holds as true, with reasons, may not be true (i.e., I may not recognize it as true if their reasons do not convince me or if I have good opposing reasons myself). What I myself, however, hold with reasons as true, I recognize eo ipso as true. I cannot position myself between my (good) reasons and my affirmation of something as true. But if it is correct that a transsubjective space of truth can only be constituted by way of an irreducible difference between the perspectives of different speakers, this also means that consensus and dissent are equiprimordial: just as every controversy about truth claims has its telos in an uncoerced consensus, so does every consensus carry in itself the seed of new disagreements. And this now means that truth, as *encompassing* various perspectives is essentially controversial. That truth is transsubjective means that truth is, at the same time, contested. The debate about truth is the element in which truth has its being, a being that compels us ever further to rediscover truth, to take a position in the space of truth, to give and accept reasons. Only against the background of a cooperative debate about truth are shared convictions possible that are taken to be justified by all those who share them. In this context, the idea of a final, ultimate consensus makes no sense: because it would be the idea of a cessation of that dialogue and dispute in which truth has its being, it would be the idea of an end of truth.

11.

I now return to Rorty's thesis that the disquotation theory of truth contains everything elucidating that can be said about the concept of truth. I wish to explain in what sense I believe this thesis to be prima facie plausible, and in what sense I believe it to be false. It is plausible insofar as "truth" cannot mean a property of assertions or convictions like "agreement with a reality existing in itself" or "the possible content of a rational consensus under ideal conditions." Actually, it does not designate, as Brandom has convincingly shown, a "*property*" of assertions or convictions at all. On the contrary we call "true" those assertions or convictions that we take to be justified: taking-to-be-true is a taking-a-position in a social space of reasons and not the ascription of a mysterious property. This is exactly what appears to speak for Rorty's thesis that the concept of truth plays (or should play) absolutely no role in our justificatory practice. Since we call "true" precisely the *justified* assertions or convictions—and one could be of the opinion that my reflections (directed against the "idealization theorists") on the constitutive connection between a transsubjective space of truth and a plurality of social perspectives can be just as well formulated with the help of the concept of justification—then the "recognizing-as-(really)-justified" would precisely move into the place of the "recognizing-as-true." Nevertheless, Rorty's thesis appears false to me. I would now like to show that the concept of truth is significant for our discursive practices in that it makes explicit a central trait of these practices.[16] If this demonstration is successful, this means that the concepts of truth and of justification *mutually* point to and demand one another.

What is it about our discursive practices that is made explicit by the concept of truth? The key to answering this question is, I believe, the fact, emphasized by Rorty *and* Putnam, that "justification" has a time and person index that does not hold for the concept of truth. Whereas Rorty, however, seeks to trivialize the "nonindexicality" of the concept of truth, I see in it a clue that in the concept of truth a constitutive trait of our assertion and justification praxis is revealed: namely, that the timelessness and nonindexicality of the concept of truth reveals what the implicit meaning of asserting and justifying is. Even though justification always has a time and person index— which is easily made clear by reflection on our justification practices—nevertheless the justification of assertions or convictions from the perspective of those who bring forth such justifications is in no way meant as having a time or person index: where they argue for assertions or convictions, they raise— as one can say with the help of the concept of truth—context-transcending and transsubjective *truth* claims. To express a conviction would not be what it is were it not at least implicitly already the expression of a context-transcending truth claim. And this is exactly what is made explicit by the nonindexicality of the concept of truth.

Rorty once said that he himself has never raised a context-transcending truth claim.[17] This is of course a meaning-critical [*sinnkritische*], not an empirical, thesis. It expresses in another way what Rorty also explains as the "cautionary" use of "true" when he says "that the entire force of the cautionary use of 'true' is to point out that justification is relative to an audience and that we can never exclude the possibility that some better audience might exist, or come to exist, to whom a belief that is justifiable to us would not be justifiable."[18] This is Rorty's version of fallibilism; and a great deal, it seems to me, hangs on it. Namely, if it were correct, then one could say: because taking-to-be-true itself is plainly context-relative, even the nonindexicality of the concept of truth cannot help us to get beyond particular justification contexts (as it certainly cannot), and therefore the idea of a context-transcending truth claim could look like a piece of empty rhetoric. However, I believe that Rorty's version of fallibilism is false. I will return to this shortly.

First, though, back to my thesis that the disquotation schema of truth in no way shows us everything there is to say about the place of the concept of truth in our assertion and justification praxis. In an initial step I argued that we ourselves only understand this schema correctly when we relate the concept of truth as "making explicit"[19] back to our assertion and justification practices. If we do this, however, we can also show that we only then correctly understand the role of the concept of truth when we make clear to ourselves in what way the truth-value of statements is dependent on—and varies with—a "truth-enabling" conceptual background or "vocabulary." This interdependence may be spelled out in two ways: (1) *On the one hand*, vocabularies and conceptualizations are always-already potentially at stake in the debate about the truth of propositions, and hence can also, at any time—in spectacular or in inconspicuous forms—become the object of the debate about truth. Rorty's own reflections on the difference between "inferential" and "dialectical" forms of argumentation[20] point, in my opinion—despite Rorty's intentions—to a corresponding connection—which means, however, that they also point to the necessity of a broadened understanding of propositional truth. I have tried elsewhere[21] to show in more detail that "inferential" and "dialectical" forms of argumentation in Rorty's sense designate only two extreme poles of argumentation, which in all interesting forms of argumentation are always already tied up together. This means, however, that we only correctly understand the debate about the truth of propositions when we recognize that it is potentially always already tied together with a debate about the appropriateness of the vocabularies in which assertions and convictions are formulated. Turned around, this means that what is at stake in the debate about the appropriateness of language is always also the truth of our beliefs, such that we thus do not correctly understand the role of the concept of truth when we understand truth values as being ultimately determined by a specific vocabulary.[22] (2) *On the other hand*—as Wittgenstein in my opinion showed in *On Certainty*—"paradigms" of doubt-free assertions and beliefs are also always already given in every language or, to speak with Heidegger, every form of "disclosure," beliefs that require no justification, but which rather define the elementary conditions of possible justification. Some of these beliefs may not be situation-specific, like "the earth already existed long before my birth"[23]; others may be beliefs, like "there's a hand there,"[24] about which one can quite easily be mistaken—"only," as Wittgenstein says, "not in particular circumstances"—in circumstances, to be sure, which cannot exactly, as Wittgenstein adds—in the sense of a rule—be specified in advance.[25] "The *truth* of my statements," says Wittgenstein, "is the test of my *understanding* of these statements."[26] And "the *truth* of certain empirical propositions belongs to our frame of reference."[27] If I have until now assumed that we call "true" those beliefs that we take to be justified or recognize as justified, then I have spoken above all about beliefs that are the possible object of a controversy. Wittgenstein, in contrast, is concerned with beliefs about which we cannot say what the *meaning* of a controversy (a doubt) should be. We assume them to be justified, without really being able to justify them. And that means that they are truth "paradigms."

Granted, the linguistic "frame of reference" is also, as has already been emphasized above, never safe from revision—"The mythology may change back into a state of flux, the river-bed of thoughts may shift"[28]; nevertheless— and this seems to me the point of Wittgenstein's considerations—nothing about the "structural" trait of our truth praxis is changed by any of this: namely, that certain paradigmatic truths that we presuppose without justification as certain define the elementary conditions of a possible justification of beliefs. This means, however, that without such "truth paradigms" standards of justification are not thinkable. And this further means that the concept of justification is not explainable independently of those of truth and certainty.[29] Granted, this presupposes that the ever-present possibility of a revision of vocabulary also does not justify a general, fallibilistic reservation, as Rorty expresses it when he speaks of a "cautionary" use of the concept of truth. The "contextualistic" aspect of our use of the concept of truth in no way makes it a victim of a fallibilistic devaluation. If Rorty believes that each one of our beliefs may turn out to be unjustified, this also means—despite Rorty's Davidsonian protest, according to which most of our beliefs must be true— that *all* of our beliefs (not all at once, but certainly successively) could turn out to be unjustified. If one wants to avoid this consequence—which is certainly incompatible with Rorty's Davidsonianism—then one must admit that the "truth paradigms" of which I have spoken cannot in any case be revisable in the *same* sense as all those (possibly) controversial beliefs that one actually means when one formulates a fallibilism principle. If we, for instance, take the conviction that the Earth existed long before my birth—of which Wittgenstein says that to put it in question means to put in question the possibility of historical or natural-historical research (and we must ask ourselves how we should ever do *that*)—it would still be thinkable that our concept of "Earth" and the network of inferential relations with which it is tied up could change. But the practically relevant kernel of that (common) conviction would in no way be put into question—which is in *some ways* comparable to the case of Newtonian physics, which in the limited domain in which it had proven itself a thousandfold was in no way put in question by the scientific revolution of quantum physics or of the theory of relativity, but rather remained valid as their limiting case (cf. Bohr's "correspondence principle"). Precisely from a pragmatist perspective, one should not *equate* "false" (in the sense of a problematic vocabulary) with "false" (in the sense of "untrue"). But if this is correct, then one should not say that each one of our convictions could turn out to be unjustified, but rather—if one wants to say something general—that every vocabulary, every network of convictions, may reveal itself to be in need of revision (and in fact constantly does). If there were no paradigmatic certainties = truths in Wittgenstein's sense, then there would also be no linguistic praxis with its accompanying possibility of revision. If one takes what was said under (1) and (2) together, however, then it becomes clear, as I believe, that a deflationist interpretation of the concept of truth conceals constitutive traits of our justification practices or, rather, makes them inaccessible to an appropriate thematization.

12.

In closing, I wish to explain my thesis, directed against Karl-Otto Apel, that the attempt to anchor truth in the idea of an ideal communication community is structurally analogous to the strategy of the metaphysical realists. After all, one could object that that idea has its place in the context of an already admitted *internal* relationship between truth and justification, and consequently attempts merely to explain the barely doubtful difference between "justified" and "true" in another way than I have attempted to here. My argument for the thesis that the explanation of that difference with help of the idea of an infinite consensus of an ideal communication community still structurally participates in the weakness of metaphysical realism has two parts: the *first* part is of a meaning-critical kind; the ideal communication community is the Nirvana of linguistic communication, therefore it makes no sense (just like the idea of a world in itself, portrayed as escaping our epistemic capabilities, makes no sense). The *second* part of my argument is that the consensus of an ideal communication community defines a *measure* of absolute truth that is not available to any finite being as a measure of his or her judgments. It is located beyond those standards toward which we are factically always-already oriented when we call convictions true or false and reasons sound or not. So the measure defined by Apel's explication of truth is a measure against which, in principle, no one can measure his or her judgments and reasons. It is a measure beyond the human capacity for knowledge and judgment, and is in this way comparable to the measure of a world-in-itself,

of which we can not know whether our convictions and judgments are appropriate to it. What I have attempted to show is that we don't need such a
measure in order to understand our differentiation between "justified" and
"true"; a measure beyond our actual judging and reasoning praxis helps us
neither to better understand this judging and reasoning praxis, *nor* to better
orient ourselves in it. In Wittgesteinian terms, it is like a wheel in a machine
that spins alone. To ignore it or to remove it does not threaten our practice
of raising and criticizing context-transcending truth claims. For that it is
enough that we understand ourselves as beings who, in a social "space of
reasons" (Brandom), and from a respectively "subjective" perspective, are com-
pelled to take a position whose *meaning* can only be explained with the help
of an interperspectival and context-transcending concept of truth. But in
order to understand how the latter can be coherently thought, we would only
have to bid farewell to metaphysical understandings of such an absolute truth;
and that is exactly what I think is possible when we understand the connection between truth and justification as I have explained it.

13.

My conclusion thus runs: truth is not a regulative idea. The attempt to
replace a metaphysical correspondence theory of truth with an epistemic
concept of truth—with the expectation that truth and justification (or truth
and consensus) will coincide, not here and now but rather under ideal conditions—will not lead us out of metaphysics. Truth and justification coincide
with reference to the making of judgments and the holding of beliefs, but not
in reference to the ascription of judgments and beliefs to others. From this
"grammatical" difference result both the normativity and *trans*subjectivity of
truth, as well as the "contested" aspect of truth.

Apel has always believed that the only alternative to "truth-absolut-
ism"—as he sought to explain it through the idea of an ideal communication
community—is a relativistic-historicist dissolution of the concept of truth.
But I believe this is an optical illusion. What is common to Apel's and the
relativistic position is the attempt to look at our truth practices from a standpoint outside these practices. The relativist tries to step out of the truth game
while playing it at the same time—at the cost, of course, of a performative
contradiction. Against this, Apel would like to make it clear to the relativist
that he or she absolutely cannot coherently do this, because one must always
already stake a claim to a nonrelativistic concept of truth in order to deny it.
And this argument appears correct to me. The problem lies in Apel's next
step: when he attempts to prove to the relativist that he or she must always
already have recognized a concept of absolute truth—which Apel explains
with the help of the concept of an idealized communication community—he

opens up for the relativist a breathing space for a metacritique: namely, if the ideal communication community turns out to be a metaphysical fiction, then this means—presupposing that the relativist accepts Apel's proof—that the idea of an absolute truth is merely the expression of a transcendental illusion that surrounds our discursive practices. And *this* was in fact exactly what the relativist wanted to say. Perhaps at this point I could be allowed to cite myself: as I said in "Ethics and Dialogue," it is likely "that the problem of relativism is merely the abiding shadow of an absolutism which would like to anchor the truth in some Archimedean point lying outside the world of our actual discourse. Relativism in this connection, would be the reminder that there can be no such Archimedean point. But if it is true that we can hold fast to the idea of truth *without* the aid of such an Archimedean point, then at the same time as we take our leave of absolutism, we can also bid farewell to its shadow, relativism."[30]

What I have tried to show is that we in fact need no such Archimedean point in order to save the normative power of truth.

NOTES

* The translator would like to thank Eric Little for a first version of this translation. My gratitude as well to Bernadette Wegenstein for her invaluable help with the final version.

1. This is the revised and greatly expanded version of a lecture I first held in 1995 at a conference on "Pragmatism Without Regulative Ideas?" at the Institute for Cultural Science in Essen, Germany. This occasion explains the strong and originally central reference to Karl-Otto Apel—who was present at the conference and whose seventy-fifth birthday marked the occasion of this event—as well as the title of the essay. Later workings over have somewhat shifted the weight, but the conclusion of the essay, in which I summarize my critique of Apel, remains unchanged. Since the German publication of Mike Sandbothe's volume *Die Renaissance des Pragmatismus* (Weilerswist: Velbrück, 2000), I have once more revised my article, prompted in large part by a criticism of Richard Rorty's (see notes 15 and 18). Several notes, and section 11, are newly written.

2. Aristotle, *Metaphysics*, in *The Basic Works of Aristotle*, Richard McKeon, ed. (New York: Random House, 1941) IV, 7, 1011b.

3. Immanuel Kant, *Critique of Pure Reason* (Paul Guyer and Allen W. Wood, trans. New York: Cambridge University Press, 1997), B83/A58.

4. Wittgenstein, *Tractatus Logico-Philosophicus*, C. K. Ogden, trans. (London: Routledge, 1981), 4.024; translation modified.

5. Hilary Putnam, "Reference and Truth," in *Realism and Reason: Philosophical Papers Vol. 3* (Cambridge, Mass.: Harvard UP, 1983), 84.

6. Here I employ the concept of justification in a broad sense. An assertion can be justified in a narrower sense by reasons that stand in an inferential connection with the propositional content of an assertion. In the broader sense, it can also be justified through reference to perceptions (or, indirectly, to the reliability or believability of another speaker). Cf. the analogous differentiation by Robert Brandom in *Making It Explicit* (Cambridge, Mass.: Harvard UP, 1994), chs. 3 & 4. Incidentally, I concur with McDowell—differently than Brandom, Rorty, or Davidson—that convictions are also justified through recourse to perceptions (although I also have some reservations about the details McDowell's argument). Rorty's (Sellars's, Davidson's, and Brandom's) causal interpretation (i.e., elimination) of the concept of experience is, in my opinion, only convincing insofar as it is directed against the empirical "myth of the given": namely, against the idea that "sense data" or "sensory feelings" could play an epistemic role in the formation of our empirical convictions. A remainder of this idea is still found in Quine's concept of "stimulus meaning." Now Rorty rightly points out, for instance, that Davidson—to whom, among others, he himself refers with regard to his own causalistic elimination of the concept of experience—has long since dismissed the Quinean version of empiricism. "Davidson substitutes a 'distal' theory of meaning formulated in terms of public external objects; he allows no intermediate terrain of philosophical inquiry between linguistically formulated beliefs and physiology." (Richard Rorty, "Dewey Between Hegel and Darwin," in *Truth and Progress. Philosophical Papers Volume 3* [Cambridge: Cambridge UP, 1998]). If the causal interpretation of the concept of experience refers to "public external objects" as the causes of noninferentially received convictions, then—against Davidson's and Rorty's opinion—there exists absolutely no further objection to an epistemic role for (linguistically impregnated) experience (i.e., perceptions). If I justify my assertion that the corner window on the second floor of the house across the street is open, with the indication that I see it (or have seen it), then here, in my opinion, it clearly concerns an *epistemic* relationship between my perception and my conviction. Granted I can also *causally* interpret the same relationship, as Davidson does in the context of his theory of interpretation. (It is the rabbit hopping by that causally brings about the conviction "Gavagai" in my foreign-speaking interlocutor). But now it appears to me that, in this case, the epistemic interpretation is to have conceptual precedence over its interpretation as a causal relation, for the following reason: to interpret a relation as causal means to assume that we could discover something empirical about the asserted causal relation. Of course, this is possible in the case of radical interpretation, because the interpreter could discover that it is not the rabbit hopping past, but rather something else that (the interpreter presumes) caused the foreign speaker's conviction expressed by his uttering "Gavagai." But *what* is here empirically clarified is nothing of the sort that under these or those circumstances certain objects of the public world cause this or that noninferential conviction. What is clarified is, on the contrary, the question, *which* is the conviction that the foreign speaker expresses (i.e., what "Gavagai" means). But what about the *interpreter's* conviction (that there is a rabbit hopping past), which is clearly already implied by his interpretation of the foreign speaker? As to what concerns *its* cause, as a rule the interpreter has no choice (because most of *his*—noninferential—convictions must also be true): it is the rabbit hopping past (that he *sees* hopping past). But the "principle of charity" now says that, as a rule, the same objects will effect the same noninferential convictions in speaker and interpreter. The

interpreter, as noted, has no choice as to what affects him: the cause of his non-inferential conviction is that thing he—in an ordinary way of speaking— *sees* (that of which he sees that it is the case). And insofar as "seeing that" is an "achievement" word, he can also occasionally be mistaken. What I am driving at is that we can only *identify* the causes of our noninferential beliefs in Davidson's scenario (which Rorty makes his own), in that we say what we *see*. And that must be—still in Davidson's scenario—as a rule the *correct* identification. Accordingly, another method of identifying the causes of our noninferential beliefs can in principle not be at our disposal (except if one would cross over again into "physiology"). But then there can be nothing disreputable in the (justifying) appeal to (linguistically impregnated) perceptions; on the contrary, the implication of a causal interpretation of noninferential convictions leads us back to the possibility of justifying such convictions through recourse to perceptions. In reality, however, the praxis of such justification has conceptual priority over a causal interpretation of noninferential beliefs (as far as the possible *identification* of the corresponding causes is concerned). The causal interpretation is not *false*, but *first* it is compatible throughout with an epistemic interpretation, and because we must now give the epistemic interpretation an epistemic priority over the causal interpretation, *second*, the causal interpretation of the concept of experience reveals itself to be an empty piece of rhetoric that at best can remind us that we are, even in perception and cognition, still (linguistically skilled) natural beings.

7. For the following criticism of the "Idealization Theory" of truth see Albrecht Wellmer, "Ethics and Dialogue," in *The Persistence of Modernity*, trans. David Midgley (Cambridge, Mass: The MIT Press, 1991), especially 175–182, as well as Wellmer, "Truth, Contingency and Modernity", in *Endgames: The Irreconcilable Nature of Modernity*, David Midgley, trans. (Cambridge, Mass.: The MIT Press, 1998), 137 ff.

8. For example in Hillary Putnam, *Reason, Truth, and History* (New York: Cambridge University Press, 1981). I think that, in the meantime, Putnam's position has changed (cf. his criticism of consensus theory in "Philosophy as a Reconstructive Activity: William James on Moral Philosophy," in this volume). For the sake of a clear presentation of my argument, I refer nevertheless to Putnam's old formulation.

9. Cf. Karl-Otto Apel, "Fallibilismus, Konsenstheorie der Wahrheit und Letztbegründung," in *Philosophie und Begründung* (Forum für Philosophie Bad Homburg, ed.) (Frankfurt a. M.: 1986), IV.1: 139–150; IV.3: 151–163.

10. Cf. Jacques Derrida, "Structure, Sign, and Play in the Discourse of the Human Sciences," in *Writing and Difference*, Alan Bass, trans. (Chicago: Chicago University Press, 1978), 292.

11. I will come back to Rorty's "cautionary" use of "true."

12. Rorty objected, in response to an earlier version of this work (in a personal communication), that I could not (in what follows in the next two sections) simultaneously call upon Brandom *and* argue against a deflationist concept of truth. I will attend to this objection further on (see section 11).

13. I have worked out the meaning of this difference in perspective from a somewhat different point of view in my article "Verstehen und Interpretieren," *Deutsche*

Zeitschrift für Philosophie 3 (1997). Robert Brandom has shown that it is precisely thanks to this difference in perspective that a transsubjective space of truth can be constituted—(cf. "Knowledge and the Social Articulation of the Space of Reasons," *Philosophy and Phenomenological Research*, LV, no. 4 [1995]: 903 ff). Brandom has worked out this idea in *Making it Explicit*, especially in Ch. 8. Nevertheless, I have reservations concerning the reductive theory-design in whose framework Brandom develops this idea. For a brilliant exposition of the same idea, cf. also Sebastian Rödl, *Selbstbezug und Normativität* (Paderborn: mentis, 1998), especially 182 ff.

14. For the connection between "justification" and the "I-perspective," cf. Sebastian Rödl, ibid., 96 ff.

15. One could take offense at the formulation "true for me," after I claimed that the grammar of "true" does not allow such a formulation. My answer to this (possible) objection has two parts: (1) in the present context it is a question of there always being certain speakers who recognize something as true (or justified). Thus one could also say that the differentiation between justification as context-relative and truth as noncontext-relative is misleading insofar as, of course, the "taking-to-be-true" is just as context relative as the "taking-to-be-justified." This is also the reason, if I see it correctly, why Rorty holds the concept of truth in the pragmatic context of our justification practices to be dispensable. Against this I will try to show to what extent the concept of truth nevertheless plays a constitutive role in this context (see section 11). (2) As long as I have not shown this, the above-mentioned objection must be taken seriously, because my arguments up to now leave open the possibility of a general fallibilistic reservation. Such a *general* fallibilistic reservation would have as a consequence, however, that the only choice we would have left would be between Apel and Rorty.

16. Michael Williams, in an article on "Meaning and Deflationary Truth" (*The Journal of Philosophy* XCVI, no. 11 [1999]), has argued for an *expressive* role of the concept of truth: "For a disquotationalist, 'true' offers a way of replacing talk about the world with logically equivalent talk about words. This move to the level of talk about words ("semantic ascent") gives us new things to generalize over—that is, linguistic objects, sentences—thereby enabling us to express agreement and disagreement with sentences that we cannot specify: for example because we do not know what they are ('What the president said is true') or because there are too many of them ('Every sentence of the form "P or not P" is true')" (547). This, I believe, corresponds to Rorty's position. Against this I would like to point to an "explicitating" (Brandom's term) role of the concept of truth, which is not reducible to an "expressive" role in Williams's sense.

17. Nevertheless, he says such things as these: "Large-scale astrophysical descriptions of [the solar system, A.W.] are, if true at all, always true. So if Kepler's description is right now, it was right before Kepler thought it up." ("Charles Taylor on Truth", in *Truth and Progress*, 90.) And, "It was, of course, *true* in earlier times that women should not have been oppressed, just as it was *true* before Newton said so that gravitational attraction accounted for the movements of the planets." ("Feminism and Pragmatism," ibid., 225.) One need only reverse the temporal direction of these sentences to see what a "context-transcending truth-claim" is: it is the kind of truth-

"claim," like Kepler and Newton raised in *their* time, as they formulated and justified their theses (namely, as true).

18. Richard Rorty, "Is Truth a Goal of Inquiry?", ibid., 22.

19. If I use an expression of Brandom's here, I am doing so—as already indicated—not exactly in Brandom's sense, because my intention is to make clear a mutual relation of explication between "truth" and "justification." This is incompatible with a reductive theory-design. In fact, I should say: I (as a philosopher) try to make explicit how the concept of truth is built into our discursive practices. However, I believe that what I here say about the concept of truth as "context-transcending" corresponds in some way to what Brandom says about the concept of objectivity as one of "perspectival form": "What is shared by all discursive perspectives is that there is a difference between what is objectively correct in the way of correct concept application and what is merely taken to be so, not *what* it is—the structure, not the content." (*Making It Explicit*, 600.)

20. Cf. For instance Rorty, *Contingency, Irony, and Solidarity* (Cambridge: Cambridge UP, 1989), 12, 78: "the ironist's preferred form of argument is dialectical in the sense that she takes the unit of persuasion to be a vocabulary rather than a proposition" (78).

21. In a piece entitled "Gibt es eine Wahrheit jenseits der Aussagenwahrheit?" in Klaus Günther and Lutz Wingert, eds., *Die Öffentlichkeit der Vernunft und die Vernunft der Öffentlichkeit.Festschrit für Jürgen Habermas*, (Frankfurt am Main: Suhrkamp 2001).

22. From this it follows, of course, that the inferential concept of justification, which I have invoked in the preceding considerations, is too narrow in reality to help us to an appropriate concept of possible argumentation.

23. Ludwig Wittgenstein, *On Certainty*, trans. Denis Paul and G. E. M. Ascombe (New York: Harper & Row, 1969), § 203. ". . . we are interested in the fact that about certain empirical propositions no doubt can exist if making judgments is to be possible at all" (§ 308). And: "What stands fast does so, not because it is intrinsically obvious or convincing, it is rather held fast by what lies around it" (§ 144).

24. Ibid., §32.

25. Ibid., § 25, § 27.

26. Ibid., § 80.

27. Ibid., § 83.

28. Ibid., § 97.

29. One could object that what was said under (1) does not go together with what was said under (2): Wittgenstein speaks of changes in language like changes in nature ("the river-bed of thoughts may shift"), so he can thus also easily say: "When language-games change, then there is a change in the concepts, and with the concepts the meanings of words change" (Ibid., § 65). But that means: in all language games

something is undoubtably certain and something else is not, and what is certain and what is not changes with the changing of the language game. Against this I have spoken, with Rorty, of another kind of changing of language games, one in which the invention of new vocabularies is critically related to problems, incoherences, or dead ends—which an established vocabulary has led to. Here, then, the language change is of the sort that relates critically to the respective established language. Only from such a perspective a problem emerges that in Wittgenstein's description of language changes cannot emerge at all: I mean the problem of a generalized fallibilistic reservation, which both Apel and Rorty—the latter with the idea of a "cautionary" use of the concept of truth—postulate as necessary. For Apel this reservation holds for all convictions with the exception of those that are "ultimately grounded"; for Rorty it holds—just as for Davidson—in the sense that although not all of our convictions can be false, any one taken individually may turn out to be false. Were a general fallibilistic reservation—be it in Rorty's or in Apel's version—justified, it would have to also incorporate Wittgenstein's doubtless "certainties," and my references to Wittgenstein could appear to be somehow displaced. Against this I believe that Wittgenstein's considerations contain the arguments against both versions of a generalized fallibilism that I have mentioned. I don't want to speak here of Apel's theses concerning an "ultimate grounding of certain necessary presuppositions of rational discourse," which I have elsewhere criticized ("Ethics and Dialogue," 182 ff.); in what follows I will refer only to Rorty's version. What Wittgenstein's considerations show, in my opinion, is that *not* any one of our convictions taken individually can be false. As far as a particular, relatively stable system of reference is concerned, this appears to be trivial, because—as Wittgenstein shows—it can still only ever turn on an axis of nondoubtable convictions. Everything depends, therefore, on what happens when "vocabularies" are revised or new vocabularies invented—when, hence, the "river-bed of thoughts" shifts not merely in a natural sense but rather in the context of a controversy about truth. In this way, certainly, as I assumed above, many truths believed to be certain may be put in question; but for the "empirical" certainties discussed by Wittgenstein as paradigmatic this cannot hold in the same sense as it does for common errors or hypotheses, which can be revealed to be false. This is what I am arguing for in the main text, and this is also what, in my opinion, makes an unqualified fallibilism incoherent. The problem with a generally formulated fallibilism principle with reference to the truth of statements is, in my opinion, that it tosses together into one pot completely different cases of a possible revision of concepts and convictions without differentiating among them. If one does not do so, then one cannot, as Rorty does, say *in general*: "that we can never exclude the possibility that some better audience might exist, or come to exist, to whom a belief that is justifiable to us would not be justified."

    30. "Ethics and Dialogue," 180 f.

6

∾

ARTHUR FINE

The Viewpoint of
No One in Particular

"The whole of science is nothing more than a refinement of everyday thinking."[1]

My title is drawn from the little book *(Space, Time and Gravitation)* written in 1920 by the physicist Arthur Eddington.[2] I am grateful to Thomas Ryckman, who has been working on Eddington, for bringing him and his delightful book to my attention. I hope that Eddington's "point of view of no-one in particular" may call to mind some more recent notions: Thomas Nagel's "view from nowhere,"[3] or Bernard Williams "absolute conception,"[4] expressions that are supposed to single out the domain of natural science. It is these conceptions, especially as they relate to the issue of objectivity, that I want to talk about here today.

1. EDDINGTON

But first Eddington. Arthur Eddington was the leader of the British expedition of 1919 that verified the first dramatic prediction of Einstein's theory, the bending of light rays around the sun. He was also an outstanding theoretical physicist. His book is a lovely treatment of the general theory of relativity and of the program for a unified field theory where, finally, Eddington believes, we fully achieve the point of view of no one in particular. According to Eddington we come to this view in stages. We first eliminate individual standpoints by taking into account the various spatial positions from which an object can be observed or described. This results in an instantaneous three-dimensional Newtonian worldview. It is truly a view from nowhere-in-particular. Eddington describes it as the viewpoint of a superobserver, where one "sees" things from all locations all at once. (Putnam would call this a "God's eye" point of view, the perspective he associates with metaphysical realism and warns us against.[5]) After positions are accounted for, the next step is to take account of motion—all conceivable motion. We accomplish this by integrating time with space. The result is the four-dimensional manifold of relativity. Finally, and speculatively, Eddington suggests we also take into account the gauge or magnitude involved in our observations or descriptions. This is a step he attributes to Herman Weyl in Weyl's (1918) field theory that unifies electromagnetism with gravity. In Weyl's construction that unification depends critically on transformations of gauge. Although many now consider Weyl's efforts at unification mistaken, as Einstein did at the time, Weyl's ideas are also recognized as important heuristically in opening the path to contemporary quantum gauge field theory. Eddington, however, regards Weyl's work as the culmination of the program we have been tracking, that of defining physical reality as the synthesis of all possible physical aspects of things: their position, their motion, and their magnitude. Anticipating Williams and Nagel, Eddington acknowledges that more personal points of view may be needed to describe "ultimate reality." But they are not required, he thinks, for the real world of physics.

2. The View from Nowhere and The Absolute Conception

Nagel's view from nowhere and Williams's absolute conception seek to mark out a point of view, or a way of knowing, that is distinctive of the natural sciences, and appropriate there, but a way not to be imported to other areas, especially not when we turn to thinking about people and their lives. Nor when we think philosophically either. The idea seems to be that science involves a special mode of thought, a distinctively scientific way of thinking about the world. This is an idea that may appeal to those who want to see science as something especially valuable and privileged. It may also appeal to those who want to see science restrained and limited in its claims. Actually, Nagel and Williams share both desires. They see science as a good thing, in its place, and they see their way of marking out science as a win-win strategy, one that does not undervalue science but that does not overvalue it either. Here are some of the elements that go into that strategy.

The style of thought that leads to a viewpoint of no one in particular combines the impersonal with the unbiased. Impersonal goes with nonperspectival, perhaps detached and disinterested. Unbiased goes with impartial and neutral. The style could also be abstract or disengaged. No doubt Sherlock Holmes employed this combination of the impersonal with the unbiased.[6] In literature it can be the style of the omniscient narrator. In anthropology, it corresponds to the observer's pose of "strangeness," and in sociology it is the style of thought employed by what Kathryn Pyne Addelson calls the "judging observer" (as opposed to the participant observer).[7] Its legal form is that of blind justice with her balanced scale. Notwithstanding Williams's reservations, John Rawls has made the style famous in ethics by featuring judgments that occur behind a veil of ignorance.[8] Notice, however, that these illustrations, which come readily to mind, are drawn from arenas where it was presumed that an impersonal and nonperspectival stance would be inappropriate. I think we begin to see here a certain confusion of thought and distinctions that will need to be sorted. What then of that stance in the natural sciences?

In natural science we recognize the viewpoint of no one in particular right away in the peculiar literary genre known as the scientific paper or report. Just as Eddington proceeds by making salient particulars (position, motion, magnitude) disappear, so in the contemporary scientific paper the author herself disappears along with time and place. Moreover, in the experimental report particular circumstances are described so as to be reproducible by anyone—which is to say, precisely by no one in particular. The scientific paper is frequently regarded as the public face of the scientific method and, I believe, it is not to literary form but to the demands of scientific practice that the idea of a distinctively scientific mode of thought is meant to attach.

3. SCIENTIFIC METHOD

The idea of method, whether with Bacon's roughly inductive spin or with Descartes roughly deductive one, is a way of drawing a line between common sense or everyday thinking, and scientific thought. Bacon warns of a whole tribe of idols, or pitfalls, in everyday thinking. Notoriously, Descartes is obsessed with the avoidance of error. The idea of method, then, comes with a charge and a claim. The charge is that everyday thinking is flawed and easily liable to lead us astray. The claim is that in science we have a better way, a way more rigorous and more accurate than that of common sense. To do better than everyday thinking we need to be detached, impartial, disinterested, unbiased. We need to abstract from our everyday concerns and disengage from common habits and private perspectives. We need to consider things from an impersonal and neutral point of view. In short, the ideal of method requires us to be no one in particular.

One might think that feminists would be delighted with this ideal. It is certainly gender neutral. It treats masculine perspectives and feminine perspectives equally—like the authors of scientific reports, it disappears them. On the whole, however, feminists have not been delighted; indeed, they have not been amused. The ideal of method, we are told, is a masculine ideal that functions to exclude specifically feminist perspectives from science. In so doing, it degrades the openness and democracy of science. This is not a good thing especially because, as Helen Longino and others argue, democracy in science has epistemological weight and is not just an abstract ideal.[9] For evidence only emerges against background beliefs. So, to the extent to which different voices and points of view are not active in the background, the range of hypotheses that can be challenged or confirmed is restricted, and knowledge itself becomes impoverished. That is a strong line of argument, but against what?

In Paul Feyerabend's hands it appeared to be an argument against method.[10] However, contrary to the impression that Feyerabend conveyed (and, mostly, was pleased to convey) the actual lesson to be learned from his writing was not deconstructive; it was not that anything goes. It was the Hegelian attitude embodied in John Stuart Mill's lesson that good scientific practice involves many (and competing) voices. Despite the image that Feyerabend cultivated as philosophy's anarchist bad boy, his argument was actually standard libertarian pleading on behalf of open, democratic, Millian ideals. Indeed, what Feyerabend's arguments support, and what recent feminist writings underscore, is an openness to many methods. The lesson was that many things go.

4. PROCEDURAL OBJECTIVITY

That lesson concerns objectivity, where objectivity is conceived as procedural. In this conception objectivity has to do with the process of inquiry which, when objective, can be thought of as impersonal and impartial, unbiased and neutral, and the like. The view from nowhere, or of no one in particular, thus levels the playing field. This procedural conception of objectivity derives from Kant. It was taken up by logical positivism, and in recent years it has been deepened and developed by Habermas and critical theory. It regards objectivity as a form of intersubjectivity. By imposing conditions on the process of inquiry, including not only checks and balances but also requirements of publicity and responsiveness, this conception allows for more or less objectivity. In connection with the view from nowhere, Nagel endorses such a grading system even for the outcome of inquiry. He puts it this way: "A view or form of thought is more objective than another if it relies less on the specifics of the individual's makeup and position in the world, or on the character of the particular type of creature he is."[11]

Contemporary critiques of scientific method, and related suggestions regarding public responsiveness and a plurality of methods in many voices, are sometimes taken as criticism of objectivity itself, criticism raised by those who oppose it. It would be better to see the issue as one about the character of objectivity, with the critics claiming that inquiry will be more objective (not less) the more it is open and democratic. Where objectivity is procedural and embodied in forms of intersubjective action, that certainly seems like a viable claim.[12] It is, moreover, a claim of some practical importance. For example, due in large part to the political protests of AIDS activists and the killer nature of that disease, the Federal Drug Administration (FDA) has modified its long entrenched guidelines for placebo-controlled, double-blind experiments. In certain cases the guidelines now open the process (somewhat) by requiring a supervisory panel, including a medical ethicist. The panel is charged with monitoring the clinical trials expressly to determine at what point (if any) the drug should be offered to all the participants. This was the procedure followed in the important recent study of Tamoxifen in the prevention of breast cancer.[13]

5. THE LIBERTARIAN CRITIQUE

The libertarian critique of scientific method, however, involves an internal difficulty. If more voices need to be brought into the process, then how many more, whose voices, how responded to, and who is to determine where (or whether) boundaries are to be drawn? In the political arena questions of this sort are addressed by means of the several devices available for resolving political disputes. In a liberal democracy one looks to voting and lobbying, to forms of public conversation and education. Various organizations weigh in and eventually compromises are achieved that one expects to be negotiated and renegotiated over time. Similar processes are at work in the scientific arena. Those processes involve specialists, who act as consultants and advisors to the agencies that fund and promote scientific research. Sociologically and historically this is old news. Science is a social institution, like others, and it has a history. One can trace shifting conceptions of objectivity from the seventeenth century onwards.[14] One can look at the professionalization of science and the development of scientific elites. One can track the institutionalization of procedures that secure objectivity, the introduction of quantitative methods such as cost-benefit analysis, and examine how they are shaped, for example by the pressure to resolve political disputes over such things as rivers and the building of bridges.[15]

Still, the difficulty for the libertarian critique remains. The question is whether the social history of objectivity is constrained by general norms built into the very conception of objective inquiry, or whether nothing more than local practice (some would say, mob rule) governs. The worry is that unless there are universal principles governing the procedures that make for objectivity, or at least some very general principles, then. . . . Well, I don't know how to finish that sentence, but I know that unless there are universal constraints, something very bad is supposed to follow, probably something that involves relativism and irrationalism.

How did we get to relativism and irrationalism? We began by exploring the viewpoint of no one in particular as characterizing a distinctively scientific way of thinking. What appeared to distinguish that way from everyday thinking was a matter of process; it was the scientific method. It seems, however, that scientific method, which marks a procedural conception of objectivity, needs to be reconfigured. What counts as objective inquiry needs to be opened and made more flexible. How open? How flexible? More generally, how do we go about determining the boundaries of objectivity? Do we proceed on the basis of universal or general principles, or do we go local and political? Are there general standards to which we can appeal, or do we just adopt the customs of the natives? That is how we got to relativism and irrationalism.

I hope everyone can see one big, false step along the way. It is in the alternative between proceeding on the basis of perfectly general principles (or standards) or of no principles (or standards) at all. Much of the fervor in contemporary discussions of objectivity derives from this false alternative. It is false because there is middle ground, and lots of it. There are intermediate standards of all sorts that one can explore as we examine answers. Depending on subject and context, we can propose temporary rules for the discussion. As a principle, we can agree to accommodate some local customs. We can set up feedback procedures. (We can, for example, put an ethicist on a scientific panel and see how that works.) We can encourage the equivalent of what Mill called experiments in living and see who prospers. In a large variety of ways we can negotiate compromises that are stable enough for a while, and then renegotiate. There is no relativism in working out procedures that are neither absolutely universal nor specifically local. Looking for intermediate standards is not irrational either. To the contrary, it would be irrational to suppose that we need general procedural rules a priori; that is, that we need them even before we can begin to sort out in different areas which procedural rules might be good ones to adopt. Correspondingly, it would be relativist to take the need that some feel for general principles constitutive of objectivity as making it true (or even plausible) that there really are such constitutive principles. We can do better than irrationalism and relativism. We do do better—even the FDA does better!

What I am supporting here is an experimental point of view. It is basically John Dewey's. The idea is that we learn in inquiry how better to conduct it. Thus I am urging that we move beyond heated debates over objectivity by trying out different conceptions of what counts as an objective process, that we learn from those trials and that we use this knowledge to move toward temporary equilibria about the characteristics of objectivity. Nothing guarantees that we will achieve acceptable equilibria, but nothing shows the contrary either.

6. OBJECTIVITY AS PRODUCT

I have been focusing on procedural objectivity, objectivity as process. That is the conception that drew us to Sherlock Holmes, to the omniscient narrator, to the anthropological pose of strangeness, to the judging observer, and to Rawls's judgments behind a veil of ignorance. Aspects of practically any subject matter can be approached this way, which is one reason why the attempts by Nagel and Williams to use objectivity as a criterion that marks a special way of knowing characteristic of the natural sciences fails straight-away. Their discussions of objectivity take processes that are impersonal and nonperspectival and runs them together with procedures that are impartial and unbiased. Impersonal ways of interacting may indeed threaten to treat people as means and not as ends or to substitute sympathy for empathy. To forsake a personal perspective may make it impossible for us to understand what it is like to be another, much less to be a bat. But impersonal does not imply unbiased, nor conversely.

Whoever has suffered from the bias of an impersonal bureaucrat and whoever has had the frustration of trying to get beyond the prejudices of orthodox medicine with their "personal" physician knows that, unfortunately, bias and the impersonal are quite happy companions. Conversely, what Daniel Dennett calls the "intentional stance,"[16] which is about relating personally, is the stance that many scientists adopt toward the subjects of their investigation precisely in order to get beyond bias and to the heart of their subject. And not just in the human sciences. Look in the physics laboratory any day and you will see them talking with atoms and communing with the quarks. Moreover the interplay among scientists who are each personally involved with their pet hypotheses is one of the best ways that we have found to get beyond bias and partiality.[17] Thus being unbiased and interacting personally are quite compatible, too. The objectivity that Nagel and Williams try to mark out is a hodgepodge and not a natural kind. Their attempts to demarcate a specifically scientific way of knowing fails for another reason as well, and that is because they do not separate process from product.

Objectivity certainly relates to both. The way inquiry is conducted can be objective, but so can the results of inquiry. The information, the data, the truths, the understanding, the theories, or the knowledge that we produce, they too can be objective. Eddington's central image, the viewpoint of no one in particular, displays this double edge nicely. When Eddington traces the historical development of an impersonal point of view in physics, he traces how we came to carry out physical investigations in a way that abstracts from the particulars of place, motion, and magnitude, but he shows as well how a synthesis of all those particulars is embedded in the physical theories themselves. It is not just that physicists investigate nature as though they were no one in particular (process), it is also that physical theories somehow represent nature that way (product). Williams describes his "absolute conception" as one that seeks "to represent the world in a way to the maximum degree independent of our perspective and its peculiarities." The payoff for achieving such an absolute conception of the world, according to Williams, is "that the natural sciences, at least, are capable of objective truth."[18]

Here lies an issue not only for Nagel and Williams but also for the libertarian critique of objectivity. That project, I believe, hoped to show that, when properly reconfigured in the direction of more open and democratic processes, objectivity attaches to a domain wider than that sanctioned by the old conception of scientific method—and properly so. The hope, thus, was to enlarge the scope of objectivity, to make more things objective. What things? Well, things in the category of the products of inquiry. Like Williams's absolute conception, the libertarian project is after objective knowledge, objective truth, objective understanding, and the like. But now it looks as though we may have an instance of the classical process-product fallacy. Even if we bridge the gap between the impersonal and the unbiased and also agree that considerable openness and democracy in the conduct of inquiry is part and parcel of what makes for an objective process, how does it follow that the outcome of that process will be objective?

One line of response would be to claim that "objective truth" or "objective knowledge" simply designate truth or knowledge obtained by means of an objective procedure. The claim would be that the quality of the process attaches to the product. Bernard Williams believes something like that. He thinks that a conception of the world that could be arrived at by any investigators, however different from us, must be an absolute conception.[19] But there are safe processes for producing bombs, and bombs are not safe products. Similarly there can be inquiries that embody the highest ideals of procedural objectivity but whose outcomes are not objective. For example, the outcome may consist in information about precisely those perspectival particulars that objectivity was supposed to abstract from, information about places and motions and magnitudes—as well as about colors and sounds, or about attitudes and feelings. An outcome of inquiry may be objective in the sense of having been obtained by objective means, but it does not follow that the outcome is objective in the sense that the outcome represents the viewpoint of no one in particular. Procedural objectivity, no matter how liberally reconfigured, is not objective enough. Not even nineteenth-century models of scientific method, such as those proposed by Mill or Whewell or Herschel, could guarantee that objective procedures produce products whose contents are part of an absolute conception of the world.

7. OBJECTIVITY AND TRUTH

Williams and Nagel believe that the content of scientific knowledge needs to be nonperspectival. The libertarian critique of objectivity does not share that belief (quite sensibly!), and so it is not especially worried about the fact that a liberalization of objectivity as process is not enough to guarantee that the products of objective procedures represent a view from nowhere. There is a concern, however, as to whether a liberal conception of objective inquiry will guarantee objectivity in yet another sense: namely, in the sense in which to say that something is objective is to say that it really is true of the object. In her discussion of what she now calls "the secret life of objectivity," Lisa Lloyd dubs this the conception of the objective as the "really real."[20] In these terms the worry about liberalizing procedural objectivity is that it may break the traditional connection between objective inquiry and the really real.

Before we examine concerns over what connections are broken, however, let us look at what connections there are. If we first confine ourselves to the products of inquiry, we can ask how "objective" in the sense of *nonperspectival* relates to "objective" in the sense of the *really real*. It is easy to see that what is really real does not need to be nonperspectival. For example, even though, as Williams notes, "green" and probably "grass" too are concepts that would not be part of an absolute conception, our knowledge that grass is green will be objective, in the *really real* sense, just in case grass really is green. So the really real does not imply the nonperspectival. What of the converse?

Certainly Williams thinks that the absolute conception guarantees at least that the natural sciences *can* be objectively true. Nagel echoes similar sentiments in his view from nowhere. Taking an image from Aristotle's cosmology, Nagel writes, "We may think of reality as a set of concentric spheres, progressively revealed as we detach gradually from the contingencies of the self."[21] Despite these bold claims, I see no entailment between a view of the world that is nonperspectival and what is really real. Consider relativity. Both Nagel and Williams share with Eddington the idea that relativistic physics embodies an absolute conception of the world. Maybe so. Still, we do not know whether the world really is relativistic, and long-standing difficulties in building an account of gravity—one that would unify relativity with the quantum theory—may even make us wonder whether the world *can* be relativistic. In his last years Einstein had this worry. Moreover in a treatment of the quantum theory that derives from Louis de Broglie and David Bohm, the "absolute" view of relativity turns out to be phenomenal, a phenomenon whose viability depends on contingencies early in the universe.[22] In the de Broglie-Bohm treatment the relativistic merger of space and time is only apparent, and relativity is not really real at all. So the viewpoint of no one in particular, in this case the relativistic viewpoint, does not tell us what *is* really real, not even what *can be* really real. Among the products of inquiry there is simply no logical connection between being objective in these two senses.

What about the really real and procedural objectivity in general? Could procedural objectivity guarantee the really real? Here, surely, the connections are very tenuous, for method is always fallible, any method is. Retreating to probability will not help either. That is, we should not hope that some special advance in methodology will guarantee access to the truth with a high probability. To be sure we sometimes learn special, one-off procedures that produce certain goods with high reliability. That is what quality control engineers are good at, as are the manufacturers of interchangeable widgets. However, there is no magic method that is reliable all around. Science proceeds on the basis of trial and error, and what happens in most laboratories and in most centers of calculation on most days in most years is the methodical, procedurally objective production of errors. The whole conception of method, moreover, suffers from an incommensurability of ends. We want to maximize the attainment of truth, and for that purpose we need to take risks in the generation of hypotheses. We also want to minimize error, and for that purpose we need to avoid risk and flights of fancy. Sometimes we can strike a balance between risk taking and risk avoidance, but not always and not according to any general scheme. Procedural objectivity is terrific, but it scarcely guarantees overall reliability, much less access to what is really real.

We can now put to rest the worry that the libertarian critique of objectivity may break the traditional connection between objective inquiry and the really real. Indeed, a liberal version of procedural objectivity cannot ensure that objective investigations will produce what is really real. That is no special problem for the liberal version, however, since it is true of procedural objectivity in general, whether liberalized or not. The "traditional connection" turns out to be no connection at all, and so there is no connection for the libertarians to break.

There remains a worry that may be triggered by the libertarian critique. It is that going public, opening the door to many voices, allowing in different methodologies, making the investigation respond to several competing interests, and the like would actually diminish the overall reliability of the investigation. The liberal response to this criticism would be to invoke suitable variations of Mill's classic argument that in the marketplace of ideas open competition works to weed out the bad and promote the good. Despite its pedigree, I do not see how that response can be valid in general. Think of Kuhn. While I do not defend Thomas Kuhn's overall dynamic for scientific change, he saw something important in his emphasis on "normal science." What he saw was the importance of consolidation and of articulation on the basis of limited techniques against a relatively stable background. This is important for the development of experimental practice as well as for the development of theory. When it comes to instrumentation, that sort of stability can be essential. Indeed, no social enterprise can flourish in the face of relentless critical disruption. On the other hand, no social enterprise will continue to grow and move forward with its windows closed and its wagons circled. The earlier example of a shifting paradigm for double-blind experiments would be a case in point. There will certainly be many investigations where opening the doors would be just what is needed to get the investigation on the right track. Who can possibly say in general what policy will always be best? What we need here are good, local judgments about particulars.

8. WHAT GOOD IS PROCEDURAL OBJECTIVITY?

Procedural objectivity does not guarantee objectivity for the products of inquiry. It does not guarantee that the contents of those products are nonperspectival nor that the products themselves are really real. Procedural objectivity does not ensure that such objectivity among the products will be likely either. So what good is it? My suggestion is that procedural objectivity speaks to our attitude toward the products of inquiry rather than to traits of those products themselves. The operative attitude is that of trust. Where the process of inquiry has certain built-in procedural features ("safeguards," we sometimes call them), we are inclined to trust it more than we would a procedure that fails to have those features. That is why the libertarian critique is important. In suggesting openness, publicity, responsiveness, and democratization, it is pointing to features that may enhance public trust. These are features we already value in the political context, even though we certainly do not believe that the best candidates necessarily win in fair elections. Electoral fairness, however, helps to bind the electorate together in a political community because it promotes mutual trust. Objectivity in inquiry promotes a similar faith in the process, even though we do not believe that we will necessarily get things right in an objective investigation.

Suppose this is correct, suppose that the virtue of objectivity is that it promotes trust in the process. What about the product? Does trust in the process make for trust in the product? Curiously, in this instance, it does. We know perfectly well that, however objective it is, inquiry can turn out the wrong answers. Indeed, from the history of the natural sciences, we know that over the long run the best scientific practices turn out wrong answer after wrong answer. The history of science shows the repeated overthrow of scientific theories, the revision of so-called facts, the removal of "things" from the supposed ontology of the world. Often science even discards the best tools and instruments of the preceding generations as no longer reliable. Still, as though defying induction, we continue to place considerable trust in science.

That trust is not generated by counterinduction. Rather, it arises in conformity with what I call the Fundamental Axiom of Inquiry. That axiom (actually a schema for producing axioms) simply states that the proper sort of inquiry is the best way to get things right. When the process of inquiry is objective, in a way that is suitably tailored to its subject matter, we trust the process because, in conformity with the Fundamental Axiom, we believe it is the best way to get things right. Recall Churchill's remark about democracy: "the worst form of government except all those other forms that have been tried from time to time."[23] According to the Fundamental Axiom, the same is true of objective inquiry.

9. Concluding Thoughts

Eddington's image of the viewpoint of no one in particular brings together several aspects of objectivity that I have tried to separate. It cuts across both the process of inquiry and the product. Within the process it assimilates unbiased inquiry to impersonal inquiry. Within the product, those whose contents are not perspectival are lumped together with those that correspond to what is objectively real. I have tried to show that the objectivity of the process does not in fact attach to the products. I have also tried to show both with respect to process and product that neither aspect singled out is logically connected to the other.

Eddington's lessons for physics are not damaged very much by crossover effects, for in the end he is not fooled into taking the world of physics as the real world. Rather he thinks "the mind's search for permanence has created the world of physics."[24] Eddington is after an understanding of natural necessity, which he locates in the mind. The crossover effects of treating the many aspects of objectivity as one are more pernicious for those whose aim is a form of realism. Nagel and Williams use their framework to this end. They support a realist attitude toward natural science as the realm of the truly objective, and they want to say that elsewhere, in dealing with mind and human affairs, objectivity would be misplaced. Their considerations are riddled with crossover effects, the false assimilation to one another of independent aspects of objectivity. What is important to learn from this is that realism and objectivity are not logically tied together. Unless objectivity is simply defined as real-making, irrealism can be objective and realism can fail to be.

If we rely on the Fundamental Axiom, we can fashion a better conception of objectivity: namely, as that which in the process of inquiry makes for trust in the outcome of inquiry.[25] Here objectivity is fundamentally trust-making, not real-making. In this conception there is no special provenance for objectivity. It is not special to the natural sciences, nor excluded when we inquire into the mind or human affairs. Similarly, in this conception, there is no list of attributes of inquiry that necessarily make it objective. What counts as an objective procedure is something that needs to be tailored to the subject matter under consideration in a way that generates trust. It follows that attributes like "unbiased" or "impersonal" may be objective here and not there. It also follows that other attributes, like the publicity and democracy that go into the libertarian model, need to be topically indexed as well. In every case the question is whether a process marked out as objective makes for trust in the product. According to my Deweyan experimentalism, that is among the things we learn by doing.

I want to draw a final lesson about science. It is that no distinctive mode of thought goes into its making. Insofar as its methods promote trust, science is objective. But its methods are many and varied, as varied as the laboratory manuals for the several special sciences. Perhaps the first false step in this whole area is the notion that science is special and that scientific thinking is unlike any other. The best antidote to that is contained in my epigram from Einstein, with which I will end,

"The whole of science is nothing more than a refinement of everyday thinking."

NOTES

* This article first appeared in *Proceedings and Addresses of the APA* 72.2 (1998): 9–20. The editors would like to express their thanks for the permission to reprint it here.

1. From Albert Einstein, "Physics and Reality" (1936) reprinted in *Ideas and Opinions* (New York: Crown Publishing Co., 1954), 290.

2. Arthur Eddington, *Space, Time and Gravitation* (Cambridge: Cambridge University Press, 1921).

3. Thomas Nagel, *The View From Nowhere* (Oxford: Oxford University Press, 1986).

4. Bernard Williams, *Ethics and The Limits of Philosophy* (Cambridge, Mass.: Harvard University Press, 1985).

5. Hilary Putnam, *Reason, Truth, and History* (Cambridge: Cambridge University Press, 1981).

6. It is interesting to contrast Holmes with Mrs. Peters and Mrs. Hale, the women detectives in Susan Glaspell's 1916 play, "Trifles." C. W. E. Bigsby, *Plays by Susan Glaspell* (Cambridge : Cambridge University Press, 1987), 35–45. Unlike Holmes, the Peters-Hale team is both biased and personal. Nevertheless, they wind up trusting that they have it right—and so do we. For the connection with objectivity, see sections 8 and 9 below. (Thanks to Alexandra Bradner for the reference.)

7. Kathryn Pyne Addelson, *Moral Passages* (New York: Routledge, 1994).

8. John Rawls, *A Theory of Justice* (Cambridge, Mass.: Harvard University Press, 1971).

9. See Helen Longino, *Science as Social Knowledge: Values and Objectivity in Scientific Inquiry* (Princeton, N.J.: Princeton University Press, 1989). Similar themes run through the essays in Louise M. Antony and Charlotte Witt (eds.), *A Mind of One's Own : Feminist Essays on Reason and Objectivity* (Boulder, Colo.: Westview Press, 1993).

10. Paul Feyerabend, *Against Method* (New York: New Left Books, 1977).

11. Nagel, 5.

12. The claim is developed and defended by Lisa M. Heldke and Stephen Kellert, "Objectivity as Responsibility," *Metaphilosophy* 26 (1995): 360–378.

13. "Breast Cancer Prevention Trial Shows Major Benefit, Some Risk," *National Cancer Institute*, Press Office, Washington, D.C., April 6, 1998.

14. Recent work along these lines by historians and sociologists include Lorraine J. Daston, "Objectivity and the Escape from Perspective," *Social Studies of Science* 22 (1992): 597–618; Lorraine J. Daston and Peter Galison, "The Image of Objectivity," *Representations* 40 (1992): 81–128; and Steven Shapin, *A Social History of Truth* (Chicago: University of Chicago Press, 1994).

15. See Theodore Porter, *Trust in Numbers: Objectivity in Science and Public Life* (Princeton, N.J.: Princeton University Press, 1995).

16. Daniel Dennett, *The Intentional Stance* (Cambridge, Mass.: MIT Press, 1987).

17. This is a central point in Hull's evolutionary approach to science. David Hull, *Science as a Process* (Chicago: University of Chicago Press, 1988).

18. Williams, 139, 198.

19. Ibid., 139.

20. Elizabeth A. Lloyd, "Objectivity and the Double Standard for Feminist Epistemologies," *Synthése* 104 (1995): 351–381.

21. Nagel, 5.

22. For the de Broglie-Bohm theory, see James T. Cushing, *Quantum Mechanics: Historical Contingency and The Copenhagen Hegemony* (Chicago: University of Chicago Press, 1994). Several essays among the following are also relevant, James T. Cushing,

Arthur Fine, and Sheldon Goldstein (eds.), *Bohmian Mechanics and Quantum Theory: An Appraisal* (Dordrecht : Kluwer Academic Publishers, 1996).

23. Angela Partington, *The Oxford Dictionary of Quotations*, 4th edition (Oxford: Oxford University Press, 1992), 202.

24. Eddington, 198.

25. Several people have suggested that "magic," or other sorts of "trust-making" gimmicks, are counterexamples to this way of connecting objectivity with trust. If we reflect on why we regard these procedures as flimflam, however, we can see that they are not counterexamples at all but, rather, provide support for the thesis.

7

Richard Rorty

A Pragmatist View of
Contemporary Analytic Philosophy

This paper has two parts. In the first I discuss the views of my favorite philosopher of science, Arthur Fine. Fine has become famous for his defense of a thesis whose discussion seems to me central to contemporary philosophy—namely, that we should be neither realists nor antirealists, that the entire realism-antirealism issue should be set aside. On this point he agrees with my favorite philosophers of language, Donald Davidson and Robert Brandom. I see the increasing consensus on this thesis as marking a breakthrough into a new philosophical world. In this new world, we shall no longer think of either thought or language as containing representations of reality. We shall be freed both from the subject-object problematic that has dominated philosophy since Descartes and from the appearance-reality problematic that has been with us since the Greeks. We shall no longer be tempted to practice either epistemology or ontology.

The second, shorter, portion of the paper consists of some curt, staccato, dogmatic theses about the need to abandon the intertwined notions of "philosophical method" and of "philosophical problems." I view the popularity of these notions as an unfortunate consequence of the overprofessionalizaton of philosophy that has disfigured this area of culture since the time of Kant. If one adopts a nonrepresenationalist view of thought and language, one will move away from Kant in the direction of Hegel's historicism.

Historicism has no use for the idea that there are recurrent philosophical problems that philosophers have employed various methods to solve. This description of the history of philosophy should, I think, be replaced by an account on which philosophers, like other intellectuals, make imaginative suggestions for a redescription of the human situation; they offer new ways of talking about our hopes and fears, our ambitions and our prospects. Philosophical progress is thus not a matter of problems being solved, but of descriptions being improved.

I

Arthur Fine's famous article "The Natural Ontological Attitude" begins with the sentence "Realism is dead." In a footnote to that article, Fine offers a pregnant analogy between realism and theism.

> In support of realism there seem to be only those 'reasons of the heart' which, as Pascal says, reason does not know. Indeed, I have long felt that belief in realism involves a profound leap of faith, not at all dissimilar from the faith that animates deep religious convictions. . . . The dialogue will proceed more fruitfully, I think, when the realists finally stop pretending to a rational support for their faith, which they do not have. Then we can all enjoy their intricate and sometimes beautiful philosophical constructions (of, e.g., knowledge, or reference, etc.) even though to us, the nonbelievers, they may seem only wonder-full castles in the air.[1]

In an article called "Pragmatism as Anti-authoritarianism,"[2] I tried to expand on Fine's analogy. I suggested that we see heartfelt devotion to realism as the Enlightenment's version of the religious urge to bow down before a nonhuman power. The term "Reality as it is in itself, apart from human needs and interests," is, in my view, just another of the obsequious Names of God. In that article, I suggested that we treat the idea that physics gets you closer to reality than morals as an updated version of the priests' claim to be in closer touch with God than the laity.

As I see contemporary philosophy, the great divide is between representationalists, the people who believe that there is an intrinsic nature of nonhuman reality that humans have a duty to grasp, and antirepresentationalists. I think F. C. S. Schiller was on the right track when he said that "Pragmatism . . . is in reality only the application of Humanism to the theory of knowledge."[3] I take Schiller's point to be that the humanists' claim that human beings have responsibilities only to one another entails giving up both representationalism and realism.

Representationalists are necessarily realists, and conversely. For realists believe both that there is one, and only one, Way the World Is In Itself, and that there are "hard" areas of culture in which this Way is revealed. In these areas, they say, there are "facts of the matter" to be discovered, though in softer areas there are not. By contrast, antirepresentationalists believe that scientific, like moral, progress is a matter of finding ever more effective ways to enrich human life. They make no distinction between hard and soft areas of culture, other than the sociological distinction between less and more controversial topics. Realists think of antirepresentationalists as antirealists, but in doing so they confuse discarding the hard-soft distinction with preaching universal softness.

Intellectuals cannot live without pathos. Theists find pathos in the distance between the human and the divine. Realists find it in the abyss separating human thought and language from reality as it is in itself. Pragmatists find it in the gap between contemporary humanity and a utopian human future in which the very idea of responsibility to anything except our fellow-humans has become unintelligible, resulting in the first truly humanistic culture.

If you do not like the term "pathos," the word "romance" would do as well. Or one might use Thomas Nagel's term: "the ambition of transcendence." The important point is simply that both sides in contemporary philosophy are trying to gratify one of the urges previously satisfied by religion. History suggests that we cannot decide which form of pathos is preferable by deploying arguments. Neither the realist nor her antirepresentationalist opponent will ever have anything remotely like a knockdown argument, any more than Enlightenment secularism had such an argument against theists. One's choice of pathos will be settled, as Fine rightly suggests, by the reasons of one's heart.

The realist conviction that there just must be a nonhuman authority to which humans can turn has been, for a very long time, woven into the common sense of the West. It is a conviction common to Socrates and to Luther, to atheistic natural scientists who say they love truth and fundamentalists who say they love Christ. I think it would be a good idea to reweave the network of shared beliefs and desires that makes up Western culture in order to get rid of this conviction. But doing so will take centuries, or perhaps millenia. This reweaving, if it ever occurs, will result in everybody becoming commonsensically verificationist—in being unable to pump up the intuitions to which present-day realists and theists appeal.

To grasp the need to fall back on reasons of the heart, consider the theist who is told that the term "God," as used in the conclusion of the cosmological argument, is merely a name for our ignorance. Then consider the realist who is told that his explanation for the success of science is no better than Molière's doctor's explanation of why opium puts people to sleep.

Then consider the pragmatist who is told, perhaps by John Searle, that his verificationism confuses epistemology and ontology. All three will probably be unfazed by these would-be knockdown arguments. Even if they admit that their opponents' point admits of no refutation, they will remark, complacently and correctly, that it produces no conviction.

It is often said that religion was refuted by showing the incoherence of the concept of God. It is said, almost as often, that realism has been refuted by showing the incoherence of the notions of "intrinsic nature of reality" and "correspondence," and that pragmatism is refuted by pointing out its habit of confusing knowing with being. But no one accustomed to employ a term like "the will of God" or "mind-independent World" in expressing views central to her sense of how things hang together is likely to be persuaded that the relevant concepts are incoherent. Nor is any pragmatist likely to be convinced that the notion of something real but indescribable in human language or unknowable by human minds can be made coherent. A concept, after all, is just the use of a word. Much-used and well-loved words and phrases are not abandoned merely because their users have been forced into tight dialectical corners.

To be sure words and uses of words do get discarded. But that is because more attractive words or uses have become available. Insofar as religion has been dying out among the intellectuals in recent centuries, it is because of the attractions of a humanist culture, not because of flaws internal to the discourse of theists. Insofar as Fine is right that realism is dying out among the philosophers, this is because of the attractions of a culture that is more deeply and unreservedly humanist than that offered by the arrogant scientism that was the least fortunate legacy of the Enlightenment.

For all these reasons, I do not want to echo Fine's charge that the realist, like the theist, lacks "rational support" for his beliefs. The notion of "rational support" is not apropos when it comes to proposals to retain, or to abandon, intuitions or hopes as deep-lying as those to which theists, realists, and antirepresentationalists appeal. Where argument seems always to fail, as James rightly says in "The will to believe," the reasons of the heart will and should have their way. But this does not mean that the human heart always has the same reasons, asks the same questions, and hopes for the same answers. The gradual growth of secularism—the gradual increase in the number of people who do not find theism what James called "a live, momentous and forced option"—is testimony to the heart's malleability.

Only when the sort of cultural change I optimistically envisage is complete will we be able to start doing what Fine suggests—enjoying such intricate intellectual displays as the *Summa Contra Gentiles* or *Naming and Necessity* as aesthetic spectacles. Someday realism may no longer be "a live, momentous and forced option" for us. If that day comes, we shall think of questions about the mind-independence of the real as having the quaint charm of questions about the consubstantiality of the Persons of the Trinity. In the sort of culture that I hope our remote descendants may inhabit, the philosophical literature about realism and antirealism will have been aestheticized in the way that we moderns have aestheticized the medieval disputations about the ontological status of universals.

Michael Dummett has suggested that many traditional philosophical problems boil down to questions about which true sentences are made true by "facts" and which are not. This suggestion capitalizes on one of Plato's worst ideas: the idea that we can divide up the culture into the hard areas, where the nonhuman is encountered and acknowledged, and the softer areas in which we are on our own. The attempt to divide culture into harder and softer areas is the most familiar contemporary expression of the hope that there may be something to which human beings are responsible other than their fellow humans. The idea of a hard area of culture is the idea of an area in which this responsibility is salient. Dummett's suggestion that many philosophical debates have been, and should continue to be, about which sentences are bivalent amounts to the claim that philosophers have a special responsibility to figure out where the hard stops and the soft begins.

A great deal of Fine's work is devoted to casting doubt on the need to draw any such line. Among philosophers of science, he has done the most to deflate Quine's arrogant quip that philosophy of science is philosophy enough. His view that science is not special, not different from the rest of culture in any philosophically interesting way, chimes with Davidson's and Brandom's attempt to put all true sentences on a referential par, and thereby to erase further the line between the hard and the soft. Fine, Davidson, and Brandom have helped us understand how to stop thinking of intellectual progress as a matter of increasing tightness of fit with the nonhuman world. They help us picture it instead as our being forced by that world to reweave our networks of belief and desire in ways that make us better able to get what we want. A fully humanist culture, of the sort I envisage, will emerge only when we discard the question "Do I know the real object, or only one of its appearances?" and replace it with the question "Am I using the best possible description of the situation in which I find myself, or can I cobble together a better one?"

Fine's "NOA papers"[4] fit together nicely with Davidson's claim that we can make no good use of the notion of "mind-independent reality" and with Brandom's Sellarsian attempt to interpret both meaning and reference as functions of the rights and responsibilities of participants in a social practice. The writings of these three philosophers blend together, in my imagination, to form a sort of manifesto for the kind of antirepresentationalist movement in philosophy whose humanistic aspirations I have outlined.

Occasionally, however, I come across passages, or lines of thought, in Fine's work that are obstacles to my syncretic efforts. The following passage in Fine's "The Natural Ontological Attitude" gives me pause: "When NOA counsels us to accept the results of science as true, I take it that we are to treat truth in the usual referential way, so that a sentence (or statement) is true just in case the entities referred to stand in the referred-to relations. Thus NOA sanctions ordinary referential semantics and commits us, via truth, to the existence of the individuals, properties, relations, processes, and so forth referred to by the scientific statements that we accept as true."[5] Reading this passage leaves me uncertain of whether Fine wants to read *all* the sentences we accept as true—the ones accepted after reading works of literary criticism as well as after reading scientific textbooks—as true "just in case the entities referred to stand in the referred-to relations." Davidson is clearer on this point. He thinks that the sentence "Perseverance keeps honor bright" is true in this way, the same way that "The cat is on the mat," "F=MA," and every other true sentence is true. But Davidson thinks this in part because he does not think that reference has anything to do with ontological commitment. The latter is a notion for which he has no use, just as he has no use for the distinction between sentences made true by the world and those made true by us.

Fine, alas, does seem to have a use for ontological commitment. Indeed, I suspect he drags in "ordinary referential semantics" because he thinks that the deployment of such a semantics might help one decide what ontological commitments to have. But it would accord better with the overall drift of Fine's thinking if he were to discard that unfortunate Quinean idea rather than attempting to rehabilitate it. NOA, Fine says, "tries to let science speak for itself, and it trusts in our native ability to get the message without having to rely on metaphysical or epistemological hearing aids."[6] So why, I am tempted to ask Fine, would you want to drag in a semiotic hearing aid such as "ordinary referential semantics"? Fine recommends that we stop trying to "conceive of truth as a substantial something," something that can "act as limit for legitimate human aspirations."[7] But if we accept this recommendation, will we still want to say, as Fine does, that we are "committed, via truth, to the existence" of this or that?

As support for my suggestion that the notion of ontological commitment is one Fine could get along nicely without, let me cite another of his instructive remarks about the analogy between religion and realism. Fine's answer to the question "Do you believe in X?," for such X's as electrons and dinosaurs and DNA, is "I take the question of belief to be whether to accept the entities or instead to question the science that backs them up."[8] Then, in response to the objection "But does not 'believe in' mean that they really and truly exist out there in the world?," Fine says that he is not sure it does. He points out that "those who believe in the existence of God do not think that is the meaning [they attach to their claim] at least not in any ordinary sense of 'really and truly out there in the world.'"

I take the point of the analogy to be that unquestioningly and unphilosophically religious people need not distinguish between talking about God as they do and believing in God. To say that they believe in God and that they habitually and seriously talk the talk are two ways of saying the same thing. Similarly, for a physicist to assert that to say that she believes in electrons and to say that she does not question the science behind electron-talk are two ways of asserting the same thing. The belief cannot count as a reason for the unquestioning attitude, nor conversely.

When Kant or Tillich ask the pious whether they are perhaps really talking about a regulative ideal or a symbol of ultimate concern rather than about the existence of a being, the pious are quite right to be annoyed and unresponsive. Physicists should be equally irritated when asked whether they think that statements about electrons are true or merely empirically adequate. The theist sees no reason why he need resort to natural theology, or analyses of the meaning of "is," or distinctions between the symbolic-existential and the factual-empirical. For he takes God-talk into his life in exactly the way in which a physicist takes electron-talk into hers—the same way we all take dollars-and-cents talk into ours.

It accords with the overall humanist position I outlined earlier to say there are no acts called 'assent' or 'commitment' we can perform that will put us in a relation to an object different than that of simply talking about that object in sentences whose truth we have taken into our lives.

The idea of ontological commitment epitomizes a confusion between existential commitment on the one hand and a profession of satisfaction with a way of speaking or a social practice on the other. An existential commitment, as Brandom nicely says in *Making It Explicit*, is a claim to be able to provide an address for a certain singular term within the "structured space provided mapped out by certain canonical designators."[9] To deny the existence of Pegasus, for example, is to deny that "a continuous spatiotemporal trajectory can be traced out connecting the region of space-time occupied by the speaker to one occupied by Pegasus." To deny that Sherlock Holmes's Aunt Fanny exists is to deny that she can be related to the canonical designators in Conan Doyle's text in the way that Moriarty and Mycroft can. And so on for other addresses for singular terms, such as those provided for the complex numbers by the structured space of the integers.

Putting the matter Brandom's way highlights the fact that metaphysical discourse, the discourse of ontological commitment, does not provide us with a such a structured space. For no relevant designators are agreed upon to be canonical. This discourse is, instead, one in which we express our like or dislike, our patience or impatience with, various linguistic practices.

As a safeguard against linking up referential semantics with ontological commitment, it is useful to bear in mind Davidson's insistence that we should not treat reference as "a concept to be given an independent analysis or interpretation in terms of non-linguistic concepts."[10] Reference is rather, he says, a "posit we need to implement a theory of truth."[11] For Davidson, a theory of truth for a natural language "does not explain reference, at least in this sense: it assigns no empirical content directly to relations between names or predicates and objects. These relations are given a content indirectly when the T-sentences are."[12] If one assumes that a theory that permits the deduction of all the T-sentences is all we need in the way of what Fine calls "ordinary referential semantics," then reference no longer bears on ontological commitment. The later notion will seem otiose to anyone who takes the results of both physics and literary criticism in (as Fine puts it) "the same way as we accept the evidence of our senses."

Perhaps, however, Fine would agree both with Davidson about the nature of the notion of reference and with me about the need to treat literary criticism and physics as producing truth—and reference—of exactly the same sort. That he would is suggested by his saying that those who accept NOA are "being asked not to distinguish between kinds of truth or modes of existence or the like, but only among truths themselves in terms of centrality, degrees of belief, and the like."[13]

This last quotation chimes with Fine's remark that "NOA is basically at odds with the temperament that looks for definite boundaries demarcating science from pseudo-science, or that is inclined to award the title 'scientific' like a blue ribbon on a prize goat."[14] It chimes also with the last paragraph of his recent Presidential Address to the APA, in which he says that "the first false step in this whole area is the notion that science is special and that scientific thinking is unlike any other."[15] If we carry through on these remarks by saying that there is no more point in using notions like "reference" and "ontological attitude" in connection with physics than in connection with literary criticism, then we shall think that nobody should ever worry about having more things in her ontology than there are in heaven and earth. To stop dividing culture into the hard and the soft areas would be to cease to draw up two lists: the longer containing nominalizations of every term used as the subject of a sentence, and the shorter containing all the things there are on heaven and earth.

Before leaving the topics of reference and ontological commitment, let me remark that the passage I quoted about "ordinary referential semantics" has been seized upon by Alan Musgrave to ridicule Fine's claim to have a position distinct from that of the realist.[16] Musgrave would have had less ammunition, I think, if Fine had not only omitted this passage but had been more explicit in admitting that NOA is, as Jarett Leplin has lately said, "not an alternative to realism and antirealism, but a preemption of philosophy altogether, at least at the metalevel."[17] Leplin is right to say that Fine's "idea that 'scientific theories speak for themselves,' that one can 'read off' of them the answers to all legitimate philosophical questions about science, cannot be squared with the rich tradition of philosophical debate among scientists over the proper interpretation of theories." So I think that Fine should neither take the Einstein-Bohr debate at face value, nor try to rehabilitate notions like "ontological commitment." He should grant to Leplin that "Philosophy of science in the role of interpreter and evaluator of the scientific enterprise, and realism in particular, as such a philosophy of science, are superfluous."[18] We felt the need for such an interpreter, evaluator, and public-relations man only so long as we thought of natural science as privileged by a special relation to nonhuman reality, and of the natural scientists as stepping into the shoes of the priests.

II

So much for my broad-brush account of the wonderful new philosophical prospects that I see Fine, Davidson, and Brandom opening up. In the time that remains, I want to explain why anyone who enjoys these prospects should be suspicious of the notion of "philosophical method" and of the idea that philosophy has always dealt, and will always deal, with the same recalcitrant problems. I shall offer sixteen metaphilosophical theses that sum up my own suspicions.

Thesis One: A recent "call for papers" for a big philosophical conference refers to "The analytic methodology which has been so widely embraced in twentieth century philosophy [and which] has sought to solve philosophical problems by drawing out the meaning of our statements." Such descriptions of twentieth-century philosophy are ubiquitous, but they seem to me seriously misleading. "Drawing out the meaning of our statements" is a pre-Quinean way of describing philosophers' practice of paraphrasing statements in ways that further their very diverse purposes. It would be pointless to think of the disagreements between Carnap and Austin, Davidson and Lewis, Kripke and Brandom, Fine and Leplin, or Nagel and Dennett as arising from the differing meanings that they believe themselves to have found in certain statements. These classic philosophical stand-offs are not susceptible of resolution by means of more careful and exacting ways of drawing out meanings.

Thesis Two: The philosophers I have just named belong to, or at least were raised in, a common disciplinary matrix—one in which most members of anglophone philosophy departments were also raised. Philosophers so raised do not practice a common method. What binds them together is rather a shared interest in the question, "What happens if we transform old philosophical questions about the relation of thought to reality into questions about the relation of language to reality?"

Thesis Three: Dummett is wrong in thinking that such transformations suggest that philosophy of language is first philosophy. His picture of the rest of philosophy as occupied with the analysis of "specific types of sentence or special forms of expression,"[19] analyses that can be guided or corrected by discoveries about the nature of meaning made by philosophers of language, has no relevance to the actual arguments that analytic philosophers invoke.

Thesis Four: The diverse answers to the question of the relation between language and reality given by analytic philosophers do indeed divide up along some of the same lines that once divided realists from idealists. But Dummett is wrong to think that this earlier division was marked by disagreement about which sentences are made true by the world and which by us. Rather, the division between Bain and Bradley, or between Moore and Royce, was one between representationalist atomists and nonrepresentationalist holists. The latter are the people whom Brandom refers to as his fellow inferentialists. They include all the people traditionally identified as "idealists," just as the representationalists include all those traditionally identified as "empiricists."

Thesis Five: Antirepresentationalists do not use a different method than representationalists, unless one uses the term "method" synonymously with "research program," or "leading idea," or "basic insight," or "fundamental motivation." Such uses are misleading. The term "method" should be restricted to agreed-upon procedures for settling disputes between competing claims. Such a procedure was what Ayer and Carnap on the one side, and Husserl on the other, thought had recently been discovered. They were wrong. Nagel and Dennett no more appeal to such a procedure than did Cassirer and Heidegger. Neither logical analysis nor phenomenology produced anything like the procedure for settling philosophical quarrels that the founders envisaged.

Thesis Six: When "method" is used in this restricted sense, as meaning "neutral decision procedure," there is no such thing as either philosophical or scientific method. There are only local and specific agreements on procedure within such specific expert cultures as stellar spectroscopy, modal logic, admiralty law, possible-world semantics, or Sanskrit philology. There is no method shared by geologists and particle physicists but not employed by lawyers and literary critics. Nor is there any method shared by Kripke and Davidson, or by Nagel and Dennett, that is more peculiarly philosophical than ordinary argumentative give-and-take—the kind of conversational exchange that is as frequent outside disciplinary matrices as within them.

Thesis Seven: The idea that philosophy should be put on the secure path of a science is as bad as the idea, mocked by Fine, of awarding prizes for scientificity as one awards blue ribbons to prize goats. It is one thing to say that philosophers should form a distinct expert culture, but quite another to suggest that they ought to be more like mathematicians than like lawyers, or more like microbiologists than like historians. You can have an expert culture without having an agreed-upon procedure for resolving disputes. Expertise is a matter of familiarity with the course of a previous conversation, not a matter of ability to bring that conversation to a conclusion by attaining general agreement.

Thesis Eight: If twentieth-century analytic philosophy gets favorable reviews in the writings of intellectual historians of the twenty-second century, this will not be because those historians are impressed by its exceptional clarity and rigor. It will be because they have seen that following up on Frege's suggestion that we talk about the statements rather than about thoughts made it possible to frame the old issue between representationalist atomists and nonrepresentationalist holists in a new way. Representation in the relevant sense is a matter of part-to-part correspondence between mental or linguistic and nonmental or nonlinguistic complexes. That is why it took what Bergman called the "linguistic turn" to get the issue into proper focus. For thoughts do not have discrete parts in the right way, but statements do. Frege's dictum that words only had meanings in the contexts of sentences will be seen by future intellectual historians as the beginning of the end for representationalist philosophy.

Thesis Nine. The issue between the nonrepresentationalists and the representationalists is not a matter of competing methods. Nor is the issue about whether a proper graduate education in philosophy should include reading Hegel and Heidegger or mastering symbolic logic. Both are matters of what one thinks it important and interesting to talk about. There is not now, and there never will be, a method for settling disputes about what is interesting and important. If one's heart leads one toward realism, then one will take representationalism and research programs for analyzing complexes into simples seriously. If it leads one elsewhere, one probably will not.

Thesis Ten: The idea of method is, etymology suggests, the idea of a road that takes you from the starting point of inquiry to its goal. The best translation of the Greek *meth' odo* is "on track." Representationalists, because they believe that there are objects that are what they are apart from the way they are described, can take seriously the picture of a track leading from subject to object. Antirepresentationalists cannot. They see inquiry not as crossing a gap but as a gradual reweaving of individual or communal beliefs and desires under the pressure of causal impacts made by the behavior of people and things. Such reweaving dissolves problems as often as it solves them. The idea that the problems of philosophy stay the same but the method of dealing with them changes begs the metaphilosophical question at issue between representationalists and nonrepresentationalists. It is much easier to formulate specific "philosophical problems" if, with Kant, you think that there are concepts that stay fixed regardless of historical change rather than, with Hegel, that concepts change as history moves along. Hegelian historicism and the idea that the philosopher's job is to draw out the meanings of our statements cannot easily be reconciled.

Thesis Eleven: Antirepresentationalists are sometimes accused, as Fine has been by Leplin and I have been by Nagel, of wanting to walk away from philosophy. But this charge confuses walking away from a certain historically-determined disciplinary matrix with walking away from philosophy itself. Philosophy is not something anybody can ever walk away from; it is an amorphous blob whose pseudopods englobe anyone attempting such an excursion. But unless people occasionally walk away from old disciplinary matrices as briskly as Descartes and Hobbes walked away from Aristotelianism, or Carnap and Heidegger from neo-Kantianism, decadent scholasticism is almost inevitable.

Thesis Twelve: Sometimes those who walk away from worn-out disciplinary matrices offer new philosophical research programs, as Descartes and Carnap did. Sometimes they do not, as in the cases of Montaigne and Heidegger. But research programs are not essential to philosophy. They are of course a great boon to the professionalization of philosophy as an academic specialty. But greater professionalization should not be confused with intellectual progress, any more than a nation's economic or military might should be confused with its contribution to civilization.

Thesis Thirteen: Professionalization gives an edge to atomists over holists and thus to representationalists over nonrepresentationalists. For philosophers who have theories about the elementary components of language or of thought and about how these elements get compounded look more systematic, and thus more professional, than philosophers who say that everything is relative to context. The latter see their opponents' so-called elementary components as simply nodes in webs of changing relationships.

Thesis Fourteen: The big split between "Continental" and "analytic" philosophy is largely due to the fact that historicism and antirepresentationalism are much more common among nonanglophone philosophers than among their anglophone colleagues. It is easy to bring Davidson together with Derrida and Gadamer, or Brandom together with Hegel and Heidegger. But it is less easy to find common ground between somebody distinctively "Continental" and Searle, Kripke, Lewis, or Nagel. It is this difference in substantive philosophical doctrine, rather than any difference between "methods," that makes it unlikely that the split will be healed.

Thesis Fifteen: Philosophical progress is not made by patiently carrying out research programs to the end. Such programs all eventually trickle into the sands. It is made by great imaginative feats. These are performed by people like Hegel or Wittgenstein who come out of left field and tell us that a picture has been holding us captive. Many people on both sides of the analytic-Continental split are spending much of their time waiting for Godot. They hope someone will do for us what *Philosophical Investigations* or *Being And Time* did for our predecessors—wake us from what we belatedly realize to have been dogmatic slumber.

Thesis Sixteen: Waiting for a guru is a perfectly respectable thing for us philosophers to do. One side of humanism, in the sense in which I am using the term, is the recognition that we have no duties to anything save one another. But another side is the recognition that, as Yeats put it, "Whatever flames upon the night/Man's own resinous heart has fed." Waiting for a guru is waiting for the human imagination to flare up once again, waiting for it to suggest a way of speaking that we had not thought of before. Just as intellectuals cannot live with pathos, they cannot live without gurus. But they can live without priests. They do not need the sort of guru who explains that his or her authority comes from a special relation to something nonhuman, a relation gained by having found the correct track across an abyss.

NOTES

1. Arthur Fine, "The Natural Ontological Attitude" in his *The Shaky Game: Einstein, Realism and the Quantum Theory* (Chicago: University of Chicago Press, 1986), 116n.

2. *Revue Internationale de Philosophie* 53.207 (1999): 7–20.

3. F. C. S. Schiller, *Humanism: Philosophical Essays*, second edition (London: Macmillan, 1912), xxv.

4. These papers include, in addition to "The Natural Ontological Attitude" and "And not Anti-realism Either" (both in Fine's *The Shaky Game*), the "Afterword" to *The Shaky Game* and "Unnatural Attitudes: Realist and Instrumentalist Attachments to Science", *Mind*, Vol. 95 (April, 1986), 149–179.

5. "NOA," 130.

6. "And Not," 63.

7. Ibid., 63.

8. "Afterword," 184.

9. Robert Brandom, *Making It Explicit* (Cambridge, Mass.: Harvard University Press, 1994), 444.

10. Donald Davidson, *Inquries Into Meaning And Truth* (Oxford: Oxford University Press, 1984), 219.

11. Ibid., 222.

12. Ibid., 222.

13. "NOA," 127.

14. "And not Anti-realism Either," 62.

15. "The Viewpoint of No One in Particular," *Proceedings And Addresses Of The American Philosophical Association*, vol. 72 (November 1998), 19. In this volume.

16. See Musgrave's "NOA's Ark—Fine for Realism", in *The Philosophy of Science*, ed. David Papineau (Oxford: Oxford University Press, 1996), 45–60.

17. Jarret Leplin, *A Novel Defense Of Scientific Realism* (New York and Oxford: Oxford University Press, 1997), 174.

18. Leplin, 139.

19. Michael Dummett, "Can Analytical Philosophy Be Systematic, and Ought It to Be?" in his *Truth and Other Enigmas* (Cambridge, Mass.: Harvard UP, 1978), 442.

8

❧

Barry Allen

What Knowledge? What Hope?
What New Pragmatism?

"I sowed in them blind hopes."

Aeschylus, *Prometheus Bound*

*P*hilosophy and Social Hope offers a restatement of Richard Rorty's themes
since *Philosophy and the Mirror of Nature* twenty years earlier. Longstanding
antiepistemological, antimetaphysical, polemically metaphilosophical themes
are freshly formulated and combined with a social philosophy, which, like the
very word "pragmatism," was all but unspoken in the earlier work.

1. Metaphilosophy

"I enjoy metaphilosophy."[1] Indeed, Rorty seems never to miss an opportunity
to make a polemical remark against the empty promises and fantastic dichotomies of classical and modern philosophy. This relentless attack on the
respectability of philosophy may be one reason for the hostility Rorty's work
sometimes encounters from his professional colleagues. He asks rude questions about the point of the expensive things they do. It is not easy to say,
especially not when you are an analytic philosopher trained in a specialization
whose point cannot be explained to anyone without an advanced degree. At

least scientists, equally specialized, can say they are contributing their bit to the progress of science and technology. But what should David Lewis or Crispin Wright or John McDowell say?

Looking for Rorty's latest on this long-standing interest, I find that his arguments implicitly distinguish four activities that can be called "philosophy."

1. Platonism, also known as Metaphysics. This is what Western philosophy has mostly been. It is the history of philosophy. John Searle proudly identifies it as the Western Rationalist Tradition. Rorty disparagingly calls it intellectual baggage inherited from Plato. It is a tradition of abstract absolutes (The Good, The True) and the inevitable dichotomies (appearance/reality, subject/object) they create. Metaphysical Truths, like wild orchids, are "numinous, hard to find, known only to a chosen few," and proudly indifferent to use.[2]

2. Epistemology. The history of philosophy has not really been a history of Platonism, unless "Platonism" includes the discontent that inspires Kant's critical philosophy. With Kant philosophy became conscious of itself as a special discipline standing in a special relation to natural knowledge as a whole. Philosophy as epistemology is philosophy as theory of representation, and as inspector of epistemic credentials, certifier of "objective validity."

3. Therapy. This is what the later Wittgenstein called "philosophy" and where Rorty is most comfortable with his own identity as "philosopher." In this point of view, the best philosophy undermines the feeling that there is something valuable for philosophy to do. The problem for philosophical work in this sense is simply the appearance of so-called philosophical problems. The best philosophy is one that overcomes the impulse to philosophy. As Wittgenstein said, "The real discovery is the one that makes me capable of stopping doing philosophy when I want to. The one that gives philosophy peace, so that it is no longer tormented by questions that bring *itself* in question."[3]

4. Poetry, or Imaginative Redescription. In a use of the term that cannot be related to those I have discussed, Rorty says that "philosopher" is "the most appropriate description for somebody who remaps culture—who suggests a new and promising way for us to think about the relation among various large areas of human activity." This is not Epistemology or Metaphysics, which strive for the eternal, for the deepest, for the most permanent truths. And it is not philosophical therapy, which is preoccupied not with the articulation of new alternatives but the debunking of exhausted, sclerotic, counterproductive ones. Philosophy as poetry is not what Plato did and not what Pragmatism is but, for instance, what Derrida does, and what links him in Rorty's mind to what Davidson does. "Philosophy" in this sense is an honorific term, a term of praise, and not the name of an academic specialization. As imaginative redescription, philosophy is "an aid to creating ourselves rather than knowing ourselves," and "not a field in which one achieves greatness by ratifying the community's previous intuitions."[4]

Platonism and Epistemology are distinguished for polemical refutation, and Poetry is what Rorty celebrates in the "philosophers" he most admires, while Therapy seems to be his preferred self-consciousness *qua* philosopher. "I agree with Dewey," he says, "that the function of philosophy is to mediate between old ways of speaking, developed to accomplish earlier tasks, with new ways of speaking, developed in response to new demands." He quotes more than once Dewey's words in *Reconstruction in Philosophy* (1920): "The task of future philosophy is to clarify men's ideas as to the social and moral strifes of their own day." Dewey thought that required philosophy to become more scientific and to develop a pragmatic theory of knowledge, or logic of inquiry. Rorty thinks it requires philosophy to champion fuzziness and work linguistic therapy on the urge to take Philosophy (that is, Metaphysics or Epistemology) seriously. "The particular charge of philosophy is to make sure that old *philosophical* ideas do not block the road of inquiry—that continued use of the normative language employed in the moral and social strifes of an earlier day does not make it harder to cope with contemporary problems."[5]

For Wittgenstein, therapy proved to be as interminable as it was for Freud. Each problem, each confusion, each worry that perhaps the language-game is not alright just as it is, meets the same patient therapeutic response as the next resistance or transference in psychoanalysis. Wittgenstein's text is endless, never finishes with anything. Rorty is the opposite—brash, impatient, refusing to allow the therapeutic intervention to become a new way of carrying on philosophy. For Rorty, so-called philosophical problems, whether Platonic problems about appearance and reality or Cartesian problems about subject and object, are no more than artifacts of entirely optional vocabularies—and that is—or should be—the end of it.

2. UTOPIA

The "hope" of *Philosophy and Social Hope* has two faces. Sometimes it appears as generalized hope, the hope for hope. There is no content to this hope; it is just the hope that people are in their infinitely different ways hoping "that the future will be unspeakably different from, and unspecifiably freer than, the past." For this mood, everything good is on the highway: "The vista, not the endpoint, matters." All questions of "validity" depend not on changeless epistemological norms but the future—*Is it good? Is it true?* I hope so; we'll see. Hence Rorty's "principled fuzziness." Don't let worries about "validity" or "methodology" get in the way of imaginative experiments. "To say that one should replace knowledge by hope is to say . . . that one should stop worrying about whether what one believes is well-grounded and start worrying about whether one has been imaginative enough to think up interesting alternatives to one's present beliefs."[6]

Elsewhere the hope is filled in with social content. It becomes the utopian hope "that the human race as a whole should gradually come together in a global community, a community which incorporates most of the thick morality of the European industrialized democracies." In his antithetical manner, Rorty argues that it is not knowing the truth but trust and cooperation that are the best things we do, "where our humanity begins and ends." The hope for more perfect trust and cooperation, or for social justice, is "the only basis for a worthwhile human life."[7]

Rorty seems to think this hope is peculiarly European or Western, perhaps even nineteenth century. He praises what he calls "European democratic ideals" and the "utopian social hope which sprang up in nineteenth-century Europe," "the liberal utopia sketched by Mill." He adds: "We pragmatists are not arguing that modern Europe has any superior insight into eternal, ahistorical realities. We do not claim any superior rationality. We claim only an experimental success: we have come up with a way of bringing people into some degree of comity, and of increasing human happiness, which looks more promising than any other way which has been proposed so far."

Europeans supposedly discovered the value of "mak[ing] the particular little things that divide us seem unimportant," as well as the idea of "moral progress" as "a matter of increasing *sensitivity*, increasing responsiveness to the needs of a larger and larger variety of people and things."[8] I don't think there is much that is deeply, originally European or Western about Rorty's utopia. What he presents as the relatively recent invention of one culture and its experience can also be seen as a tradition that cannot be identified with any one culture—the five thousand-year world history of urbanism, people living in cities.

Cities are far from self-contained, self-sustaining capsules. If you want practically infinite self-sustainability, you have to go back to the farming culture of the time before cities. Cities are big parasites, major ecological strains on their environment. They are also improbable social forms: improbably dense, with people everywhere; and improbably heterogeneous, with many different kinds of people. Under other conditions the combination might be lethal, but something about cities—about the ones that last, about the culture or ethos that grows there—counteracts these potential dangers (while creating new ones) and makes the urban social form not simply viable but the most dynamic, creative, prosperous social form in one hundred thousand years of modern human beings.

Partly that is because cities transform the older culture of kinship into an urban culture of social associations. Many different ethnic folk enter into new relationships as urbanists and neighbors. Only in a city can a stranger, an outsider, become a full member of a community without having to satisfy a requirement of real or mythical kinship. Everything about a city breaks down inherited social and economic structures based on family, caste, and status, and substitutes new urban orders, including vocational and residential contiguity. "In a small community," says a sociologist of the city, "it is the normal man, the man without eccentricity or genius, who seems most likely to succeed. The small community often tolerates eccentricity. The city, on the contrary, rewards it."[9] Individual success is linked to performance rather than status, and the urban economy amplifies the interdependence, specialization, and synergy of the different arts and sciences. Individuals become increasingly dependent upon the community, and the community (its prosperity) likewise comes to depend on individuals, their performance, and their cooperation.

Morality is not an invention of the city, nor is there one morality peculiar to urban conditions everywhere. Instead, the city becomes a crucible of different moralities—not just the tribal differences of immigrant peoples, but also the differences of morality, or moral practice, among individuals, free to make moral choices. In folk society the moral rules bend, but cannot be made afresh. In cities the dignity of the traditional moral order may suffer, but it is because the moral order is, to some significant degree, opened up to deliberation, compromise, and the tolerance of alternatives. Taking morals in charge is one way urban culture accomplishes an essential task—the peaceful assimilation of socially heterogeneous immigrants. "Everywhere that it made its appearance—in the Middle Ages, in Antiquity, in the Near and Far East—the city arose as a joint settlement by immigration from the outside. . . . The city, thus, has always contained elements from most varied social situations."[10]

To contain them takes more than walls. It takes particular cultural forms, infinitely various and always compromised, but recognizably practices of sensitivity to and tolerance of moral differences. And immigration is not the only source of challenges to tolerance. As Simmel observed, a city "conduces to the urge for the most individual personal existence."[11] The improbable concentration of highly specialized, and perhaps in other ways "special," individuals in the arts and knowledges means that urban tolerance must extend not merely to the construction of ethnic neighborhoods, but to the construction of individuals. Thus does everything about cities, from concentration and density to economic activity and immigration, promote differentiation, refinement, personal distinction, and enriched public needs, as well as the ethos of urban tolerance.

The Greeks did not invent citizenship. They talked about it, wrote about it, argued it in a way that earlier citizens of earlier cities did not. It may even be said that "the culture of Periklean Athens formed a sustained hymn to the ideal of poiesis, the city conceived as a work of art."[12] That made a big difference to historical consciousness, but it is not the origin of the idea, which is in an older urban practice the Greeks brilliantly adapted but did not invent. This original urbanity, of which every city on earth offers a variation, is defined, first, by a tolerance not only of other religions or races but of idiosyncracy and individuality too. Thus it is secondly an urbanity of experimental freedom, the freedom of individuals to try and do things differently. One result of such freedom, and a third quality of urbane culture, is the synergy of concentrated arts and sciences. Like the symbiosis of squash and beans or wheat and clover, the desirability of this urban ethos seems to be something human beings figure out for themselves wherever they have settled in cities that last. The great discovery was that such an ethos makes the urban concentration synergistic instead of lethal, and as the world becomes more consistently and densely urban, it will increasingly become the only ethical culture that works anywhere on earth.

A city is a hope as much as it is the effects of that hope on earlier generations, building the architecture of a city's urban culture. A contemporary describes an ecclesiastical household in Jerusalem at the beginning of the twentieth century: "The kawass [principal servant] and the stable boy were Muslims, the cook and the kitchenmaid Bethlehem women (Greek Orthodox Christians, that is), the housemaid an Armenian, the gate-keeper a Moor, and the gardener as great a rogue as ever came out of the Greek Levant. They all got on excellently together, and the breezes, chiefly on religious topics, though lively at the time, were short and infrequent."[13] Despite its history of conflict, or perhaps because of it and the memories it bequeathed, Jerusalem, continuously inhabited for over three thousand years, has contributed more to the desirability of Rorty's utopia than the collected works of J. S. Mill or the European nineteenth century. Before people were describing themselves in Mill's terms, they had been preferring and practicing what he gave formal description to. They were doing it in cities, because they found out early that it works.

I want to describe Rorty's utopia as not European or Western but originally and enduringly urban, an ethos of urbane tolerance as old and as global as life in cities, and provided I can redescribe it this way, I share his hope that a political culture inheriting the best of five thousand years of urban civilization should become the preferred one for a planet that is now practically a single global urban net. If you strip it down as Rorty does, "liberalism" reduces to urban tolerance and loses its Europeanness. The ideological liberalism or social democracy he identifies with this is a late recodification of ethics cultivated since the first cities.[14] And while I don't expect Rorty would feel much urge to take on my redescription of his utopia, which it seems important to him to pin on Europe or the West, I find the hope resonant under my description.

The politics of cities should matter more than they do when we think that the real politics are elsewhere, on a more spectacular stage. Many of the obstacles to Rorty's utopia are wrapped up with the forces driving an urbanism with orders of magnitude more parasitic than at any time since there were cities, and on a diminished and increasingly polluted nonurban base. The skein of cities that now envelops the planet, home to half the global human population, is the ultimate context within which we either address or evade the most pressing threat to our survival, which is simply ourselves, or more precisely, our cities.

3. KNOWLEDGE

Philosophy and Social Hope includes the text of three lectures, previously published as separate books in German and French, called "Hope in Place of Knowledge: A Version of Pragmatism." It is an admittedly idiosyncratic version and "makes no pretense to being faithful to the thoughts of either James or Dewey." Elsewhere Rorty describes it as "a version that delights in throwing out as much of the philosophical tradition as possible." All that is "new" about the so-called new pragmatism, of which Rorty's work is so large a part, should, he says, "be viewed merely as an effort to clear away some alder and sumac, which sprang up during a 30-year spell of wet philosophical weather—the period that we now look back on as 'positivistic analytic philosophy.'" The difference from classical pragmatism is, first, the linguistic turn, whereby pragmatism takes on the nominalism of Carnap and Quine; secondly, its openness to the critique of positivist philosophy of science, especially by T. S. Kuhn. This second legacy has made practically every version of the new pragmatism averse to the idea, common to Peirce, James, and Dewey, of pragmatism as a more perfect application of "scientific method." Another difference, peculiar to Rorty, is his "conviction that James's and Dewey's main accomplishments were negative."[15] This surely distinguishes Rorty's pragmatism from that of Hilary Putnam. Rorty works hard to make pragmatism say as little as possible, and one may be forgiven the suspicion that the result is something the founders of American pragmatism never dreamed of—a philosophy for those who have lost faith in the value of philosophy.

Rorty begins these lectures with the unexpected claim that "there is no reason why a fascist could not be a pragmatist, in the sense of agreeing with pretty much everything Dewey said about the nature of truth, knowledge, rationality and morality."[16] I can't picture it. Fascists believe in will, "unshakable determination," a *Führerprinzip;* and in all consistency reject democracy in politics, individuality in ethics, and experimentalism and fallibilism in the theory of knowledge. Where is the room for consensus with Dewey's pragmatism? A pragmatic Nazi would have to prefer democracy as the most consistently modern form of government. A pragmatic Nazi would have to be a fallibilist; he would have to have the capacity, notably lacking in the biography of every Nazi I've read, to say that he made a mistake, that he was wrong, that events proved him fallible, that unshakable will turns out not to be nearly so effective as Mussolini and Hitler led him to believe. The only Nazis who admit this are ex-Nazis.

Dewey viewed pragmatism as the most consistent working out of the implications of the revolutions of modern science and democracy. He was convinced that democracy was the right politics for a scientifically sophisticated and consistently pragmatic culture. In both its methods and results, modern experimental science smiles on democracy and withers under alternative regimes. Why was Greek science so limited, formal, and useless? Slavery. Why were the European Middle Ages so indifferent to discovery and innovation? Feudalism. Fascism, by contrast, wanted to be an alternative modernity, a different path to a different future. What has been called the "reactionary modernism" of German fascism "succeeded in incorporating technology into the symbolism and language of *Kultur*—community, blood, will, self, form, productivity, and finally race—by taking it out of the realm of *Zivilisation*—reason, intellect, internationalism, materialism, and finance"— in other words, relieving technology of everything that pragmatism celebrates and reinscribing privileged knowledge in an esoteric elite.[17] The only way I can imagine a Nazi "agreeing with pretty much everything Dewey said about the nature of truth, knowledge, rationality and morality" is if "pretty much everything" means only something negative, a claim about what truth, knowledge, rationality, and morality are *not*. Even then I think a reflective Nazi may have qualms, but I suppose it was on the assumption that Dewey's best thought on these subjects was entirely negative that Rorty could imagine this unlikely comparison.

Certainly one of Dewey's arguments has this negative quality, when he says that "knowing" is not the best thing we do, not the noblest activity of our highest faculty. Knowledge is not a contemplative, self-sufficient, intrinsically valuable end-in-itself. It is a good thing, to be sure, but it is not The Good. Knowledge is a tool kit with which individuals and groups can construct their many and different goods. Rorty is very close to this position, and may even claim it for his own, but there remains a characteristic difference. His argument is only partly Dewey's, that knowledge is *not* intrinsically good, *not* an end in itself; knowing the truth, knowing reality, is *not* the most distinctive, praiseworthy thing we do. He goes on, though, to develop this point in a way more his own when he says that we should trust and cultivate hope *in place of* knowledge. Knowledge is not merely demoted but replaced outright. It is our capacity to hope, trust, and cooperate, not to know, that is the source of all value or validity in ideas. What is important about an idea is the solidarity it inspires, the community it serves, the consensus it builds. The epistemological virtues— validity, objectivity, foundation, rationality, certainty—are unimportant, indifferent, distinctions that don't make a difference.

Rorty will say he has no theory of knowledge, only the suggestion that a theory of knowledge is not required. Yes, if "theory of knowledge" means a classical sort of theory about a classical sort of knowledge, in other words, a theory of representation. But give the expression a less procrustean reading, to mean something like "philosophical idea of knowledge," and this pragmatism is a theory of knowledge too, though one that tries to hew an entirely negative, debunking, deflationary line, and nearly succeeds. The reason it cannot do so entirely is simply because Rorty does have an idea about what knowledge positively amounts to. "There is no activity called 'knowing' which has a nature to be discovered, and at which natural scientists are particularly skilled. There is simply the process of justifying beliefs to audiences."[18] Setting aside the bit about scientists, why isn't "the process of justifying beliefs to audiences" an "activity called 'knowing' which has a nature to be discovered"? This activity, this justification, these audiences *are* where Rorty finds the good of knowledge, what makes it worth taking seriously, and that is a philosophical idea about knowledge, about what it *is*—namely, agreeable, justified discourse.

Another argument about knowledge concerns what Rorty calls the relativity of descriptions. Because "all the descriptions we give of things are descriptions suited to our purpose," any claim to know the true description of anything inherits this linguistic and social relativity.[19] Philosophically, epistemologically, practically, all that is at stake in the question whether a given claim is "knowledge" (not rather opinion, mere belief, error, and so on) is whether the description works, or perhaps merely whether one hopes that it may work.

Rorty thinks he is free of the reductive penchant because he thinks that reductive thinkers reduce everything to one vocabulary, like Quine's idea that only the language of fundamental particles tells unvarnished news, every other vocabulary merely repackaging its ultimate truth. Because Rorty believes nothing like this, he regards himself "as cleansed of reductivist sin."[20] But that is not the only or even the most objectionable way thinking may be reductive. What "reductive" really means is an aggressive indifference to differences. Reductive thinkers don't want a complicated picture, don't want distinctions, don't see differences, want things neat and simple. And this reductivism is no stranger to Rorty's pages.

We describe relative to a point of view, but is that point of view determined, conditioned, straightened by "needs and interests" or "utility"? *I can use it, I can do something with it*—that is not always a perception of need or interest or utility. Rorty's reference to "needs and interests" is either so bland as to say no more than that the descriptions that work in the way we call knowledge are called knowledge, or it is a reductive utilitarianism after J. S. Mill's heart, which may be how Rorty regards it. It is reductive because it flattens out differences and imposes a simplifying, rationalizing unity over the entire field of knowledge.

For another example, Rorty states: "the *only* thing that is specifically human is language. But the history of language is a seamless story of gradually increasing complexity."[21] It is poor evolutionism to say that "language" is the only human distinction, because you cannot separate language from the organism that speaks. You cannot separate language from the neurology that makes speech possible, and you cannot separate that neurology from the entire evolution that made *it* possible. What distinguishes us is the distinctness of our species, which is to say its genealogy, the whole evolution of the whole organism. To set all of that aside and hold up "language" as *the* difference is an aggressively simplifying indifference to differences that, in the case of human evolution, made all the difference in the world.

Reductive linguistification is practically ubiquitous in Rorty's work. It seems to be important to be able to say things like "'thinking' [is] simply the use of sentences," or "language provides our only cognitive access to objects," or "all our knowledge is under descriptions."[22] Of course we enjoy no direct, intuitive, spontaneous, unmediated cognitive contact with anything. Thoughts, awareness, choice, intention, and action are invariably mediated—by artifacts, symbols, preferences, neurology, culture, ecology, evolution. But why set all of that aside, single out "language," and attribute *all* mediation (or all that matters to knowledge) to that late and specialized formalism? The ubiquity of mediation obviously implies the ubiquity of media, but that does not mean (just) language. Cognitive, intelligent, effectively knowing mediation is neither invariably nor preeminently linguistic, nor are the values realized by the accomplishment of knowledge limited to the conversational or discursively articulated.

"Psychological nominalism" is Rorty's antidote to mystery, mystification, and the notorious obscurity of a philosophy of "consciousness" or "pure experience." He believes he has banished the ineffable from philosophy, meaning by ineffable "an appeal to a kind of knowledge that cannot be rendered dubious by a process of redescription."[23] However, that cannot be a useful way to use the word "ineffable." Consider any interestingly complex accomplishment of knowledge. There are many to choose from! It could be a challenging yet successful surgical operation, or one of the bridges designed by Robert Maillart, or Darwin's accomplishment in *The Origin of Species.* How should we imagine any of these being "rendered dubious by a process of redescription"?

I suppose Darwin could be "redescribed" in something like the way Einstein redescribed Newton, though it was the confirming experiments that rendered Newton dubious, and even then not so much dubious as simply not the last word. But what "redescription" would make Maillart's bridge less an accomplishment of knowledge? What redescription would render the surgical operation dubious? Even if its techniques or technology should seem crude by future standards, that doesn't mean it never was an accomplishment of knowledge. It seems to me that much perfectly respectable knowledge is "ineffable" according to Rorty's definition, while nothing that *could be* "rendered dubious" by a process of redescription was ever knowledge in the first place.

Hope can be more or less realistic, as hoping shades into dreaming, dreaming into fantasy, fantasy into obsession. To propose the formula "hope in place of knowledge" is to liberate hope from the constraints that make it realistic. According to the myth, Prometheus gave people both their best, most effective knowledge and the capacity for blind hope. Hope is good because knowledge, good as it is, cannot overcome tragedy. Prometheus stole as many tools as he could for us, but not even our best technology can overcome tragedy or make us immortal. Thus the great supplement of blind hope. For Rorty, though, hope is not a supplement but a substitute for knowledge. Hope is liberated from the reality principle and set free on the seas of poetic imagination. Which is fine for poets, but is it a good philosophy for a technological civilization on the brink of ecological catastrophe? Hope is all very well, but only as a supplement, and never in place of knowledge.

4. POLITICS

I suppose hope wouldn't be hope if it were dissuaded by improbability. Rorty hopes for "a utopia in which everybody has a chance at the things only the richer citizens of the rich North Atlantic democracies have been able to get— the freedom, wealth, and leisure to pursue private perfection in idiosyncratic ways." That can be read two ways. Read one way, freedom, wealth, and leisure are classic urban values, enjoyed (or withheld) in as many different ways as there are and have been cities. Read this way, Rorty hopes for a global urbanity as the fitting political culture of a global urban economy or system of civilizations. Like Rorty, I think that would be wonderful. But his utopia also has connotations of what John Dunn calls facile eudaemonism: "Advanced capitalist society cultivates in its citizens a mood which may very fairly be described as one of facile eudaemonism. To hope to extend such happiness as it makes available within itself to the vastly increased population of the world as a whole in the future without the most drastic political reorganization of this world and without considerable modification of the concept of happiness which it has fostered is not a coherent project."[24]

Perhaps when hope takes the place of knowledge it doesn't have to be realistic. Yet Rorty does sometimes confront the improbability of the global Western-style affluence he hopes for. In "Love and Money," for instance, he writes: "The fear that is beginning to gnaw at the heart of all us liberal gentlefolk in the North is that there are no initiatives which will save the southern hemisphere, that there will never be enough money in the world to redeem the South."[25] Undisguised pessimism is rare in Rorty, and he doesn't try to redescribe the problem away. What he does instead ("all I can offer") is to suggest "that we Northern gentlefolk at least keep ourselves honest . . . love is not enough." It's going to take power, not just eloquence and good intentions.

Insofar as they imagine they may change the things they denounce, the work of "intellectuals" (teaching, writing, research, critique, deconstruction, problematization) is impotent love, hysterical and self-deceived. "All the love in the world, all the attempts to abandon 'Eurocentrism,' or 'liberal individualism,' all the 'politics of diversity,' all the talk about cuddling up to the natural environment will not help."[26]

Rorty apparently wants to chastise those who engage in any sort of critical examination of the instruments or effects of Western domination—our technology, our ecology, our eurocentrism, or individualism. What should "intellectuals" do, if they can't do that? "The most socially useful thing we can do is to continually draw the attention of the educated publics of our respective countries to the need for a global polity."[27] "Know yourself" is emphatically not a motto of this pragmatism. Don't engage in demoralizing cultural introspection. Don't ponder what went wrong. Don't doubt yourself (or your culture). Look instead for ways to keep alive the hope that the people with power and money will do what the intellectuals of impotent love know that they should.

When hope takes the place of knowledge, failure loses its disconfirming value. Just because something failed doesn't mean it wasn't the Right Thing, the to-be-hoped-for thing. Failure is disappointing, but must not be demoralizing. If "intellectuals" want to be socially useful, they should work on hope rather than stoke the will to know what went wrong. Rorty singles out critics of "technology." The urge to question this dimension of our culture and ask whether serious alternatives can be realistically imagined is "a nervous, self-deceptive reaction to the realization that technology may not work." "Maybe technology and central planning will not work. But they are all we have got. We should not try to pull the blanket over our heads by saying that technology was a big mistake, and that planning, top-down initiatives, and 'Western ways of thinking' must be abandoned. That is just another, much less honest, way of saying what [E. M.] Forster said: that the very poor are unthinkable."[28]

I doubt that any serious person holds the view that "technology may not work." *Which technology? Whose work?* Rorty's devastation of a straw man evades the issue, which is not as easily dismissed. I don't understand why, at the very point where the difficulties are unprecedented, where one might think nothing *short* of a revaluation of tenacious presumptions stands a chance of working, Rorty forgets about imagination, diminishes the power of redescription, and dismisses the work of those who try to make serious alternatives seem urgent if not always hopeful. "Maybe technology and central planning will not work. But they are all we have got." When was that decided? Why is Rorty sure that here, where we most need it, hope for something different must be rebuked and dismissed? And why is he convinced that only "some as yet unimaginable bureaucratic-technological initiative, [and] not a revaluation in values," will give the teeming billions of the southern hemisphere a place at the table in utopia?[29]

Much of the best work Rorty dismisses as "anti-technology talk" tries to do the very thing he elsewhere (and more characteristically) praises. It tries to "understand how we tricked ourselves in the past . . . exhibiting the unexpected and painful consequences of our ancestors' attempts to do the right thing."[30] Writing elsewhere, with different concerns, he praises the poetry that "make[s] invidious comparisons between the actual present and a possible, if inchoate, future," and "appeal[s] to a still dimly imagined future practice." I don't understand what happens to this hopeful experimentalism when it comes to questions like world government, central planning, or the International Monetary Fund or World Bank. I don't understand why there is nothing to learn from the spectacular failures of central planning, whether Stalin's collectivism or Le Corbusier's city of Chandigarh; or from the devastation wrecked by the top-down bureaucratic initiatives that destroyed indigenous farming in so-called Third World countries, only to replace it with the expensive and unsustainable (but immensely profitable) methods of Western agribusiness.[31] I think these suggest something badly wrong with the sort of initiative, the sort of bureaucracy, the sort of planning, and the sort of government that was responsible for them. To Rorty that's defeatism. "The rich democracies of the present day already contain the sorts of institutions necessary for their own reform." They are not distorted "by anything more esoteric than greed, fear, ignorance, and resentment."[32] We don't need new directions, new alternatives, new values. All we need is for people not to be greedy and resentful, and let Western institutions finally do the right thing.

"Every top-down liberal initiative, from the abolition of slavery through the extension of the franchise to the establishment of the International Monetary Fund and the World Bank, has been driven by the hope that someday we shall no longer need to distinguish gentlefolk from those others, the people who live like animals." You can't buy publicity like that! To favorably compare the moral achievement of abolition and suffrage to predatory institutions indifferent (when not openly hostile) to democratic governance is another example of Rorty's aggressive (reductive) indifference to differences. In a text he cites elsewhere, the American social-gospel thinker Walter Rauschenbusch (Rorty's grandfather), condemns those "servant[s] of Mammon . . . who drain their fellow man for gain . . . who have made us ashamed of our dear country by their defilements . . . [and] who have cloaked their extortion in the gospel of Christ."[33] Change "gospel of Christ" to "gospel of Globalization" or "gospel of Free Trade" and you have a good description of what Rorty blandly compares to the struggle against slavery and disenfranchisement.

Far from having to "redeem" the South, we are presently witnessing what UN Undersecretary-General Maurice Strong calls "the first stages of a major shift of economic power from North to South." In 1955 Southern Hemisphere developing countries contributed 5 percent to world manufacturing; today it is 60 percent. The same countries now account for 33 percent of world energy use, a figure expected to rise to 55 percent within thirty years. The same South that already has 75 percent of the world's population will increasingly account for a larger share of economic growth.[34] Economically the South is taking off (however unevenly). It is poised for wealth, and if it pursues it the same way we did, it will destroy us, and them, and life as we know it. The problem is not how to redeem the South. It is how to prevent the coming economic take-off in the South from driving our kind to extinction. It is how to persuade not just southern or so-called developing countries, but all countries and transnational corporations everywhere, to conform to a system of international agreements designed to keep economic predation ("growth") within limits that respect the ecological and humanitarian conditions of human life on earth.

Rorty believes that "achieving a liberal utopia on a global scale would require the establishment of a world federation, exercising a global monopoly of force," and this too is very much to be hoped for.[35] Because we already have the right values, because it is merely a question of applying them with renewed determination, hoping for a lucky break, hoping people will be less greedy and resentful, it is logical that Rorty should envision the universalization of present-day institutions. It is one thing to hope, as both Rorty and I do, "that the human race as a whole should gradually come together in a global community," one which incorporates what Rorty calls "the thick morality of the European industrialized democracies," and what I would call the best of the global traditions of urbanism. It is something else to hope for a world-state or a global administrative-enforcement apparatus, such as what Rorty once called "half a million Blue [UN] Helmets."[36]

Not only does utopian global urbanity not require such an entity, it would probably be incompatible with it. There are unquestionably issues alive in the world today that transcend national frontiers and cannot be solved in the context of the old nation-states. But the answer is not a global state-like power. Instead, we need agreements on new contexts in which state power can form and exercise new alliances with other states, as well as with local powers, business, and civil society. We need serious internationalism recognized as a necessary ingredient of sound national policies. We need more effective local-global linkages. Perhaps the most hopeful (though unlikely) development would be for the city to eclipse the nation-state, in a global urban network that links the most local level of governance with similar localities all over the planet. Strong local cities together with effective global institutions and agreements, possibly under a reformed UN, may be the ideal implementation of the principle that government is most effective and should be carried out at the level closest to the people its decisions affect.[37]

I think Rorty paints himself into the corner of defending the indefensible in order not to seem to betray the poor. Yet it is not the armchair radicals of the academy, or not them alone, but also those who have been closest to it, who have directed its operations, who tell us that large-scale, top-down, bureaucratic (i.e., nondemocratic) initiatives don't work. It's just not a good way to get people to cooperate, or win their trust, or improve their lives. To acknowledge that does not consign them to the unthinkable. It challenges us to find new ways to think and act.

If there are to be real solutions to the dangerous problems of ecology and poverty in the Third World and globally, they lie in a democratic process, not a management process, especially not an imposed, top-down, bureaucratic one enforced by a global state-like power. Such management despises democracy almost as much as it does seriously new alternatives. Its instinctive reaction to anything from outside its own structures is to say *No;* to cast suspicion on innovation; to accuse new ideas of naivety or ignorance; to respond to error by refusing to admit it and denying responsibility. Thus, as the stakes get higher, it becomes increasingly improbable that a top-down bureaucratic initiative, however unimaginably bold, could do more than accelerate collapse.

The problem with world-state power, aside from the extraordinary violence that would go into its realization and the fact that nothing useful it might do could not be achieved by agreements among more human-scale polities given the political will to do so, is that it would be a death trap for the human species. The tendency of bureaucracies to proliferate has been called "perhaps the best example of a unidirectional trend furnished by any class of social phenomena. . . . There may be no increase in corruption, rigidity, incompetence, extravagance, or willful inefficiency, yet less gets accomplished."[38] Imagine that on a global scale: a global bureaucratic authority would drown in its own garbage. A world state would be the least efficient, most destructive polity in the history of civilization. It would be impossible to sustain, and as crisis set in it would become the hollow shell within which the final, and most violent, phase of the human species plays out under an increasingly hot and radioactive sun.

NOTES

1. Richard Rorty, *Truth and Progress, Philosophical Papers, vol. 3* (Cambridge: Cambridge University Press, 1998), 119.

2. Rorty, *Philosophy and Social Hope* (Harmondsworth, U.K.: Penguin, 1999), 8.

3. Rorty, *Social Hope*, xxi; Ludwig Wittgenstein, *Philosophical Investigations*, 3d ed., trans. G. E. M. Anscombe (Oxford: Blackwell, 1967), 133.

4. Rorty, *Social Hope*, 175, 187.

5. Ibid., 66; *Truth and Progress*, 306. I discuss Rorty's criticism of epistemology in "What Was Epistemology?," *Rorty and his Critics*, ed. Robert Brandom (Oxford: Blackwell, 2000).

6. *Social Hope*, 120, 28, 34.

7. Ibid., xxxii, xv, 204.

8. Ibid., 86, 81.

9. Robert Park, "The City," *American Journal of Sociology* 20 (1916); in *Classic Essays on the Culture of Cities*, ed. Richard Sennett (Englewood Cliffs, N.J.: Prentice-Hall, 1969), 126. See also Murray Bookchin, *From Urbanization to Cities* (London: Cassell, 1995).

10. Max Weber, *The City*, trans. and ed. Don Martindale and Gertrud Neuwirth (New York: Free Press, 1958), 92. See also Aidan Southall, *The City in Time and Space* (Cambridge: Cambridge University Press, 1998), 20.

11. Georg Simmel, "The Metropolis and Mental Life," in Sennett, *Classic Essays*, 58. Jonathan Raban observes that "the very plastic qualities which make the city the great liberator of human identity also cause it to be especially vulnerable to psychosis and totalitarian nightmare." *Soft City* (London: Harvill Press, 1974), 9.

12. Richard Sennett, *Flesh and Stone: The Body and City in Western Civilization* (New York: Norton, 1994), 85.

13. Cited in Martin Gilbert, *Jerusalem in the Twentieth Century* (New York: John Wiley, 1996), 18.

14. To regain its historical individuality liberalism has to become a good deal more ideological than Rorty likes. What is specific and different about "liberalism" in Western political thought is to elevate to a principle of rational politics the suspicion that we govern too much, a critique of the irrationality peculiar to excess government. See the summary of a course on liberalism by Michel Foucault, *Ethics, The Essential Works of Michel Foucault*, ed. Paul Rabinow (New York: New Press, 1997), 1:73–79; and my "Foucault and Modern Political Philosophy," *The Later Foucault: Philosophy and Politics*, ed. Jeremy Moss (London: Sage, 1998).

15. Rorty, *Social Hope*, xiii, 96; *Truth and Progress*, 130. I discuss Rorty's relation to classical pragmatism in "Is It Pragmatism? Rorty and the American Tradition," in *A Pragmatist's Progress: Richard Rorty and American Intellectual History*, ed. John Pettegrew (Lanham, Md.: Rowman and Littlefield, 2000). On similarities and differences with Putnam, see my "Putnam und Rorty über Objektivität und Wahrheit," *Deutsche Zeitschrift für Philosophie* 42 (1994): 989–1005; and "Critical Notice of Putnam," *Canadian Journal of Philosophy* 24 (1994): 665–688.

16. *Social Hope*, 13.

17. Jeffrey Herf, *Reactionary Modernism: Technology, Culture, and Politics in Weimar and the Third Reich* (Cambridge: Cambridge University Press, 1984), 16. Writing in *Deutsche Technik*, March 1939, Goebbels says, "National Socialism never rejected or struggled against technology. Rather, one if its main tasks was to consciously affirm it, to fill it inwardly with soul, to discipline it and to place it in the service of our people and their cultural level ... National Socialism understood how to take the soulless framework of technology and fill it with the rhythm and hot impulses of our

time." In *Mein Kampf* Hitler defined Aryan culture as a synthesis of Greek *Geist* and Germanic technology. *Mein Kampf*, trans. Ralph Manheim (Boston: Houghton Mifflin, 1943), 194.

18. *Social Hope*, 36.

19. Ibid., xxvi.

20. *Truth and Progress*, 94: "I define reductivism as the insistence that there is not only a single web [of causal relations] but a single privileged description of all entities caught in that web ... I regard myself as cleansed of reductivist sin."

21. *Social Hope*, 74–75.

22. Ibid., 55, 48; *Truth and Progress*, 298.

23. Ibid., 281.

24. Ibid., 324. John Dunn, *Political Theory in the Face of the Future*, 2nd ed. (Cambridge: Cambridge University Press, 1993), 118.

25. *Social Hope*, 226.

26. Ibid., 227.

27. Ibid., 233.

28. Ibid., 228.

29. Ibid., 217, 228.

30. *Truth and Progress*, 242. Examples of the work I have in mind are Vandana Shiva, *Monocultures of the Mind* (London: Zed Books, 1993); Wolfgang Sachs, ed., *The Development Dictionary: A Guide to Knowledge as Power* (London: Zed Books, 1992); John Ralston Saul, *Voltaire's Bastards* (Toronto: Penguin Books Canada, 1992); and James Scott, *Seeing Like a State* (New Haven, Conn.: Yale University Press, 1998).

31. See Madhu Sarin, "Chandigarh as a Place to Live In," in Russell Walden, ed., *The Open Hand: Essays on Le Corbusier* (Cambridge, Mass.: MIT Press, 1977); James Holston, *The Modernist City: An Anthropological Critique of Brasília* (Chicago: University of Chicago Press, 1989); and the work collected in Frédérique Apffel Marglin and Steven Marglin, eds., *Dominating Knowledge: Development, Culture, and Resistance* (Oxford: Oxford University Press, 1990), and *Decolonizing Knowledge* (Oxford: Oxford University Press, 1996).

32. *Truth and Progress*, 326.

33. *Social Hope*, 225; Rauschenbusch is cited in *Achieving Our Country* (Cambridge, Mass.: Harvard University Press, 1998), 59.

34. Maurice Strong, *Where on Earth Are We Going?* (Toronto: Knopf Canada, 2000), 37, 38, 368, 370.

35. *Social Hope*, 274. I don't know how to square these remarks with what Rorty says elsewhere: "The current leftist habit of taking the long view and looking beyond

nationhood to a global polity is as useless as was faith in Marx's philosophy of history, for which it has become a substitute." *Achieving Our Country,* 98.

36. Rorty, "Half a Million Blue Helmets?" *Common Knowledge* 4. No.3 (1995).

37. This is Strong's "principle of subsidiarity." *Where on Earth,* 313.

38. G. L. Cowgill, "Onward and Upward with Collapse," in *The Collapse of Ancient States and Civilizations,* eds. Norman Yoffee and George Cowgill (Tucson: University of Arizona Press, 1988), 263.

9

~

WOLFGANG WELSCH

Richard Rorty: Philosophy beyond Argument and Truth?

Translated by Andrew Inkpin and William Egginton

1. INTRODUCTION

Intent

Richard Rorty's position within American philosophy is paradoxical.* Once he bore all the hopes of analytic philosophy,[1] but ever since his *Philosophy and the Mirror of Nature* of 1979,[2] in which he criticized this school of thought, he has been practically ignored by most analytic philosophers. His shift to pragmatism has also brought him little recognition.[3] Analytic philosophers have reproached him for his excessive criticism, the pragmatists for his lack of orthodoxy. On the other hand, the general intellectual audience has taken notice of Rorty's emphasis on contingency and his ideas about liberalism—as well as, recently, his plea for a renewal of social-democratic thought.[4]

Rorty links the analytic and continental philosophical traditions as few other philosophers do (and I think that such a link will also prove increasingly decisive in this country). Nevertheless, in Europe as well Rorty's reputation is predominantly negative. Rorty the speaker attracts an audience, but the reaction of the philosophers' guild ranges from reserved to aggressive.

I consider this scepticism towards Rorty to be partially well-founded; philosophically, however, one should not only point out dangers and put up warning signs, as intellectuals are prone to do, but rather sound out argumentatively precisely wherein the tenable and untenable lies; and one should also ask whether some parts of the untenable could be corrected so as to become tenable. This is what I would like to attempt in the following.

I shall limit myself to the analysis of a single thesis—albeit a central and particularly objectionable thesis of Rorty's,[5] one found time and time again ever since the *Mirror of Nature*.[6] Rorty says that, strictly speaking, it is not possible for one philosophical position to argue against another. All that one can do is to play one's own vocabulary off against the other's and make one's own position appear attractive.[7] Sometimes Rorty even links this renunciation of interconceptional argumentation with the call to abandon the idea of truth.[8]

I hope to be able to show that this provocative thesis, which touches upon the very nerve of philosophy,[9] is not sound.[10] At the same time, however, my criticism has a constructive component. I believe that some of Rorty's points can be better defended than he himself has done.

A brief characterization of Philosophy and the Mirror of Nature *and* Contingency, Irony, and Solidarity

I shall refer primarily to the two books *Philosophy and the Mirror of Nature*, from 1979, and *Contingency, Irony, and Solidarity*, from 1989.[11] I would like, therefore, to outline briefly their theses beforehand.

In *Philosophy and the Mirror of Nature* Rorty criticizes what he sees as the guiding epistemological model since the seventeenth century, according to which the mind is a mirror of the world whose purpose is to reproduce reality as accurately as possible, making it necessary—by means, say, of a critique of reason or logical analysis of language—to polish this cognitive mirror and thus free it of blind spots. Rorty considers the modern representational model of cognition to be fundamentally flawed and pleads for an understanding of epistemological—or, as he also puts it, 'systematic'—philosophy based on this model as being just one type amongst several,[12] as well as advocating a stronger shift towards another type, for which he coins the collective name "edifying philosophy," adducing Dewey, Heidegger, and Wittgenstein as prime examples.[13] The aim of edifying philosophy is the invention of new, interesting, and fruitful self-descriptions[14] as well as keeping going (rather than systematically winding up) philosophical conversation.

In *Contingency, Irony and Solidarity*, Rorty makes the connection between edifying philosophy and awareness of contingency more precise, emphasizes the distinction between private and public, and outlines a utopian combination of private irony and liberal hope. He attempts to show that the concept of edifying philosophy is the one best suited to assist liberal democ-racy—and although he is unable to substantiate this claim, he also considers it in no need of philosophical substantiation.

2. RORTY'S ANTIARGUMENTATIVE THESIS

To begin with, I want to cite some formulations of Rorty's antiargumentative thesis. The actual reasoning will follow afterwards.

Philosophy and the Mirror of Nature

In *Philosophy and the Mirror of Nature* Rorty says that the edifying philosopher doesn't provide arguments, but merely suggests a new set of terms.[15] This alone, at any rate, is what he would prefer to do and does best. Rorty, however, is aware of the precariousness and apparent inadmissability of such a procedure. First of all, it runs counter to the basic notion of philosophy, according to which philosophy is an argumentative business.[16] Secondly, it violates a philosophical meta-rule that states that a deviation from the established standards is permit-ted only when one can give reasons as to why the new paradigm will be better able to fulfill the philosophical task than the established paradigm.[17]

It is exactly this, however, which edifying philosophy makes no claim to do. It intends not to better solve the classical problems of philosophy, but rather suggests a transition to different issues and problems, a change from a system-atic to an edifying orientation.[18] This is why, according to Rorty, there is no possibility of argument between epistemological and edifying philosophy.

Contingency, Irony, and Solidarity

In the altogether more mature book *Contingency, Irony, and Solidarity,* Rorty says that one should not demand arguments against preceding types of phi-losophy from philosophers of his kind.[19] The change from one type to an-other never takes place de facto on the basis of criteria or through conscious choice. Rather, a shift simply occurs. For example, Europe "did not *decide* to accept the idiom of Romantic poetry, or of socialist politics, or of Galilean mechanics. That sort of shift was no more an act of will than it was a result of argument. Rather, Europe gradually lost the habit of using certain words and gradually acquired the habit of using others."[20] All rhetoric commending things new misinterprets itself by presenting itself argumentatively; it ought to be probabilistic and pragmatic instead. For example, one should say: "try to ignore the apparently futile traditional questions by substituting the fol-lowing new and possibly interesting questions," and then see how we get on.[21] That is why Rorty—'true to his own principles'—offers no arguments against the vocabulary he wants to replace: "Instead, I am going to try to make the vocabulary I favor look attractive by showing how it may be used to describe a variety of topics."[22]

3. RORTY'S REASONS FOR ABSTINENCE FROM ARGUMENT, OR THE IMPOSSIBILITY OF INTERCONCEPTIONAL ARGUMENT

How does Rorty justify his abstinence from argument and the alleged impossibility of interconceptional argument in general?

So as to avoid one misunderstanding from the start: Rorty does not dismiss argument point-blank. First of all, argument *within* a philosophical conception remains possible and necessary—for example, in order to examine its consistency. Secondly, Rorty evidently considers *meta-argumentation* practicable with regard to the impossibility of interconceptional argument. Indeed, he himself presents just such an argument. It is just that the result of this is that interconceptional arguments as such are to be excluded. Why, and in which cases?

Differences between paradigms versus differences between types

Rorty distinguishes two kinds of relationship between conceptions. Conceptions either have a common basis, representing different versions (paradigms) of one and the same type; or they have no such common basis, belonging to different types. In the first case—with reference to the common basis—interconceptional argument is possible; in the latter—where such a basis is lacking—it is not.

Within the traditional type of epistemological philosophy, for example, arguments between normal and revolutionary positions are possible. Rorty, drawing support from Kuhn, understands normal philosophy to be the dominant conception at a particular time, which is then confronted by a revolutionary paradigm—which, if successful, subsequently becomes the normal philosophy. Because the normal paradigm and the revolutionary paradigm, with all their other dissimilarities, share the basic premise that the concern is to render the real as adequately as possible, an argumentative dispute between them is possible with reference to this premise: the new paradigm propounds reasons as to why the common aim is better attained by its means.[23] In this sense it is possible, for example, for Hegel to argue against Kant, or analytic philosophy against philosophy of consciousness.

In the conflict between epistemological and edifying philosophy, however, it is not paradigms of the *same* type, but of *differing* types that confront one another. Edifying philosophy, as opposed to epistemological philosophy, is not only not normal, but even more than revolutionary: it doesn't create a new paradigm within the same basic framework, but rather attempts to leave the old field of play and to engender a new type of philosophy. The elementary premise of epistemological philosophy—that representing what's real is at stake—is no longer found here. Edifying philosophers, Rorty says, do "something different" than "offering accurate representations of how things are."[24] They do not claim that their terms "are the new-found accurate representations of essences."[25] They don't seek "to find objective truth."[26] As a result of this difference in type, argument between such positions is no longer possible.

So much for Rorty's reasoning on the impossibility of argument between typologically-different conceptions. I consider these expositions to be sound in principle (later I shall come to speak of certain limitations). Moreover, the argumentative logic of this thesis is not altogether new: "contra principia negantem non est disputandum" was already a proven maxim of the philosophical tradition.

Strong demands

To conclude this introductory section by accentuating the positive component once again: Rorty by no means brushes aside argumentative obligations as being burdensome, as is sometimes suggested. He hasn't left his analytic schooling behind him in favor of a cynical relativism. Rather he intends to make clear, with analytic precision, the very standards of possible and impossible argument and to urge that they be taken into account.[27] And he demands strict performative consistency—from himself just as from others.[28] He points out time and time again that philosophers of his school would be performatively contradicting themselves if they were to claim suddenly that their view is the true view, the one corresponding to the essence of things and reality.[29] He criticizes, as examples, Nietzsche and Derrida for having fallen prey to this temptation.[30]

4. PROBLEMATIC CONSEQUENCES FOR EDIFYING PHILOSOPHY

Before I come back to Rorty's restriction of the possibility of argument, I want to discuss the consequences of Rorty's abstinence from argument for edifying philosophy, the type of philosophy he recommends.

Conversation in place of argument

Rorty's recommendation for the transition to this type falls under the aspect of fruitfulness. Edifying philosophy, he says, will lead to "new, better, more interesting, more fruitful ways of speaking." [31] However, abstinence from argument and fruitfulness fit together badly. More precisely: it is exactly the exclusion of argument that seems to me to render the remaining practice of edifying philosophy regrettably unfruitful. According to Rorty, it should be a matter of practicing "conversation" in place of argument.[32] But the way Rorty defines conversation reveals a dilemma. He says three things: that edifying philosophers are "conversational partners" for other edifying philosophers;[33] that, the continuation of conversation, not the discovery of objective truth, constitutes the aim;[34] that "keeping a conversation going" in this way represents a "sufficient aim of philosophy."[35] Rorty depicts philosophy as a *conversatio perennis*.

He does not, however, say what this conversation should actually be about, or what kind of exchange is still possible there.[36] I fear that he would be unable to state this either, for this conversation—in so far as it complies with Rorty's description—is no longer really about anything. Conversational partners provide one another, at best, with stimulation and a basic encouragement: they "have the courage to develop a new, deviant description, one which might even seem mad at first."[37] But all processes of refutation, falsification, of argumentative discussion and clarifying dispute are eliminated. Hence it is to be expected that this results not, as Rorty says, in "keeping a conversation going,"[38] but rather in the opposite: in the bogging down of these conversations, in which nothing is really at stake, in peaceable conversational murmurs, in discursive entropy.[39] Rorty's theory of conversations seems better suited to high-brow parlor talk amongst the educated and their inspiriters than to the business of philosophy.

Does philosophy mean "just saying something"?

Neither does Rorty shy from obviously minimizing definitions of philosophy. According to him, in some circumstances the edifying philosopher "might just be *saying something*."[40] This is what philosophy is supposed to be from now on. As prime examples Rorty even adduces Heidegger and Wittgenstein.[41] Yet, both of them would turn in their graves if they were to hear that they had only "*just said something*." Heidegger and Wittgenstein strove life-long with the utmost of exertion for cogent evidence, sound arguments, and reliable alternatives. One can certainly question their value, but one cannot ignore or suppress their clarifying efforts as such. Heidegger and Wittgenstein didn't just talk out of the blue; they weren't the antecedents of the contemporary "That's how I see it, full stop, that's all there is to it, finished; you're welcome to view it differently—so much the better, that way the wealth of human viewpoints grows."

Heidegger drew attention to the transition that took place with Plato from *aletheia* to *orthotes* and saw this as planting the seeds of the "calculative thinking" that has progressed ever since, culminating in the "atomic age," and whose abandonment in favor of "contemplative thinking" is imminent.[42] In all of this his claim was first to accomplish argumentatively a relativization of calculative thinking; second to develop the concept of a history of being that embraces both calculative and contemplative thinking; and third to present grounds for distancing from the metaphysical tradition. And when Wittgenstein said that traditional problems of philosophy result from a fundamental misunderstanding and misuse of language,[43] he was convinced that this could be proved by many points and that this would eventually be one of the reasons why subsequent generations would make the transition to another type of philosophizing. Heidegger and Wittgenstein did not simply play off a new vocabulary against an old one and most certainly did not "just say something"; they analyzed and argued insistently.

Rorty could counter that if Heidegger and Wittgenstein thought they had done more than simply play off a new vocabulary against an old one, then they misunderstood themselves. However, it is noteworthy that Rorty doesn't level this accusation, which he does make against Nietzsche and Derrida. For what reason? Heidegger and Wittgenstein did in fact do something other than Nietzsche and Derrida. The latter claim (according to Rorty) to state truthfully how things stand in reality. Since, on the other hand, they declare this to be impossible, they rightly acquire themselves "charges of self-referential inconsistency."[44] Heidegger and Wittgenstein, however, claim only to criticize argumentatively a preceding view. This should indeed be impermissible according to Rorty's demonstration of the impossibility of argument, but once again: Rorty doesn't make this accusation with regard to Heidegger and Wittgenstein. Is it possible after all in some cases, in Rorty's own estimation, to argue between heterogeneous conceptions and bring about refutations?

I will now return to the main focus of my considerations, the problem of argument. Using an example, I will show that Rorty himself de facto goes beyond his own restrictive thesis.

5. RORTY'S REFUTATION OF THE EPISTEMOLOGICAL MODEL

In *Contingency, Irony, and Solidarity* Rorty presents a refutation of traditional epistemological discourse, one which to me seems sound. What's wrong is not this refutation, but Rorty's playing down of its value and penetrative force.

Antirepresentationalism

Rorty's argument proves that the assumption that our cognition has a representationalist status is untenable. And not because we have suddenly gained some experience or insight that things in truth behave quite differently and just how things really are, but rather because the representational model contains a *conceptual* error. It sets out from the assumption that there is first of all a reality, which is then to be represented as accurately as possible in cognition. In this, reality is conceived of as being prior to, outside of, and independent of our reference to it. In the following I would like to call this kind of reality "alpha-reality" for short (in contrast, say, to understandings of reality in the life-world or in individual sciences). Reference to such an alpha-reality is fundamental to the representational model and all its variants, which reach from realism through to antirealism and from criticalism through to agnosticism, and which individually state, with respect to this alpha-reality, that we are able to cognize it authentically, or merely in translation, only approximately, or not at all.

How does Rorty argumentatively demonstrate that the talk of an alpha-reality makes no sense conceptually, that alpha-reality is a pseudoidea, in respect of which there is neither anything to be known nor to be missed? How does the argument run that at the same time lifts the representationalist cognitive model off its hinges?

The basic form of the analytic-philosophical argument: the dependence on language games of all reference to reality

The argument is of an analytic-philosophical kind. I would like, first of all, to state three of its elements and then develop it further.

First: truth is a characteristic of sentences, not of objects. Whenever we talk of the true state of objects, we actually mean the truth of corresponding sentences. "This board is black" means that the *sentence* making the claim is true. Second: sentences belong to vocabularies or language games and are dependent on these for their meaning—the identical-sounding sentence "Peter towered over all" has a different meaning in the anthropometric context than in the historical one.

Now—thirdly—one would like to be able to refer to reality independently of the conditions of such language games. Or one would like to make a decision between different descriptions of reality, suggested by different language games, by measuring their degree of adequacy to reality against reality itself. But this cannot be done. It would require language-free access to reality, and there is no such thing. And even if there were, it would be of no use for the purpose named, because—as a result of its nonlinguistic nature—one would be unable to derive from it sentences like "reality as such behaves in such and such a way." Yet it is precisely such sentences that one would need in order, as intended, to speak about reality as such, or to be able to decide between different descriptions thereof.

As such, the boundedness of all reference to reality to language games represents an ultimate limit that cannot be transcended. The idea of a reality-in-itself, an alpha-reality, is *in stricto sensu* impossible, because it can only occur within a language game—but then it is no longer the idea of an alpha-reality, of a reality completely independent of language games. Our talk of reality is always the talk of a "reality-under-a-certain-description."[45]

So much for the basic form of the argument.[46] In the next step, I would like to discuss an objection, and by doing so get to the core and pure form of the argument.

The realistic language game as counterevidence?

a) The basic thesis of the realistic language game

Among philosophical language games there are some that make use of reference to an alpha-reality: namely, the language games of the representationalist group. They operate with the idea of a reality that precedes our cognition and exists independently of it. Let us consider, for the sake of brevity, this group's leading paradigm alone, the realistic language game—the result will apply to the other versions too.

The realistic paradigm states that the task of cognition is to apprehend alpha-reality as exactly as possible, no matter how difficult this might be. Moreover, this paradigm insists on the exacting notion that a cognition-independent reality is indispensable for the concept of cognition, because without it cognition would degenerate into mere self-application.

b) The realistic language game as one amongst others—
  no chance of external refutation

What can Rorty make of this countermodel, one which—contrary to his analytic philosophical thesis of the impossibility of reference to an alpha-reality—nonetheless operates with such an idea? Now, "conforming to [his] own precepts,"[47] Rorty must—as surprising as this might seem at first—*recognize* this language game. For it is precisely when language games represent an impassable horizon of meaning and argument, as Rorty claims, that one is unable to criticize or refute this language game in the name of another language game or a general insight that overarches language games.[48] It may well be that other language games get by without the predicate "real," but "real" has an indispensable function for the realistic language game, and one must seek out and discuss the predicate "real"—just as with all other predicates—wherever it makes sense, and within the realistic language game it undoubtedly makes sense.

c) Immanent criticism of the realistic language game—
  "alpha-reality" as an interpretative concept

It is this finding—the requisite recognition of the opposing model precisely under Rorty's premises—that first makes it necessary to uncover the actual core and penetrating point of Rorty's argument.[49] Let us consider whether the realistic language game is consistent—whether, above all, it is consistent in its central point, with regard to the use of the expressions "real" and "reality." These expressions should, as I've said, refer to an alpha-reality, that is to a reality prior to, external to, and independent of all interpretation. Do they really do this? Obviously not. For these expressions already contain—contrary to their intention and pretension—a particular exposition of the X to which they refer, moreover an exposition that is *anything but self-evident*.

It is a *particular* exposition insofar as the truth is claimed of the proposition that this alpha-reality exists prior to, eternal to, and independent of our cognition. With this, however, some claims about this reality have already been made. That what is concerned here is in no way a *self-evident* exposition becomes clear as soon as one bears in mind that historically there have been quite different ways of understanding reality, say the ancient thesis of a basic commerciality between reality and cognition, or the apprehension in modernity of an interactionism between cognition and reality. These comparisons show that the talk of an alpha-reality is heavily laden with content—but with this it is elementarily self-contradictory. It claims to talk of a reality prior to, external to, and independent of each and every interpretation, but by so doing it already undertakes a highly consequential interpretation of this reality. This contradictory trait—the claim that reality, so interpreted, is a reality prior to all interpretation—even constitutes the core of the realistic paradigm. It is just because of this ascribed meaning of being independent of and prior to cognition that the whole emphasis is placed on this reality and that this becomes the measure of all descriptions and any cognition.

To put it another way: the realist does something other than he thinks and claims he is doing. He believes he is pointing to a reality free of interpretation, but in truth he has already unavoidably provided this reality with a certain interpretation. To this extent, the talk of alpha-reality is fundamentally inconsistent. And there is no way of escaping from the dual character of the asserted independence from interpretation and the factual interpretative status—unless one no longer wanted to say anything at all, in which case one could not then advocate the alpha-thesis and the whole paradigm simply wouldn't exist.[50]

The realistic position would only be remediable if it were to recognize the interpretative status of the alpha-reality it postulates. It would have to proceed from belief in its reference to an interpretation-free reality, to the understanding that it references a reality interpreted in a certain way (albeit perhaps a very meaningful way). It is only in this modified form that the paradigm would be consistent, whereas in its original form it abrogates itself.[51] Seen in this light, the result of these considerations is not a flat rejection of the realistic paradigm, but rather the call for a conceptually adequate grasp of that position, one familiar to us all and intuitively credible, called realism.

Allow me to add three more observations. First: my development of Rorty's argument goes beyond the standard analytic-philosophical objection, according to which we can refer to reality only through propositions, that is within language, so that it is impossible in principle to refer to things transcending language (say, to a reality transcending language)—in Rorty's words: "[. . .] *no* linguistic items represent *any* nonlinguistic items."[52] This might be right, but is not sufficient. The general condition of sentences—their immanence in language—is one thing. The specific contouring of a certain meaning, however—in this case the meaning of the alpha-reality—is something else. The decisive argumentative point is not that the realist can speak of a reality transcending language only within language,[53] but rather that the predicate 'reality' used by him inevitably attributes a *certain* meaning to its referent, whereas it is precisely this which is allegedly not to be the case.

Secondly, I would like to point out once again that this criticism of the realistic language game in no way makes use of a view of how things are in reality. One is not saying that reality is a construction, that it doesn't even exist, or that we are not capable of knowing it. This would indeed be self-contradictory, because the impossibility of such insight is the core of Rorty's argument. Rather, the refutation results simply and solely from an examination of the consistency of the representationalist paradigm. Such an utterance is not about reality as such, but about the conditions, misunderstandings and the correct understanding of all propositions in which we use predicates like "world," "real," "reality," etc.

Thirdly, the argument against the representational model, in spite of its penetrative force, is of course not to be understood as conclusive, one irrefutable for all times. It is quite conceivable that another argument will some day be found that overrides, modifies, or refutes Rorty's argument.[54] One thing can, however, be said safely: within the framework of those concepts available to us—those developed until now—nothing can be seen to detract from Rorty's argument. In this sense the argument is (for the time being) a valid one, a reliable proposition according with all standards known to us.

The cogency and penetrative force of Rorty's argument

What have we established? The consideration of what appears to be its greatest opponent, the realistic language game, results in a confirmation of Rorty's thesis, according to which the idea of a reality exempt from description is untenable. With this, however, Rorty's refutation of the representational model *as a whole* proves itself to be penetrative. Reality is always—in the realistic language game, too—reality-under-a-certain-description. Rorty's argument—which is already found in similar form in Wittgenstein, Sellars, Goodman, or Davidson (and which of course, in its content, was already Hegel's argument)—is sound in every respect.[55, 56]

Rorty has, at least according to all standards known today, achieved a valid refutation of the representational model.[57]

6. LIMITS OF ARGUMENT? ARE TYPOLOGICALLY DIFFERENT CONCEPTIONS HETEROGENOUS IN EVERY RESPECT?

With a glance at Rorty's conception, however, this result is itself double-edged. For it might confirm his refutation of the epistemological outset, but it evidently contradicts his thesis about the restricted possibilities of argumentation.

Recall Rorty's declaration that argument and refutation are not possible between typologically different conceptions. We have just met an example in which Rorty himself convincingly refutes a typologically contrasting position. There must be something wrong, therefore, with the restriction of argumentation. What is it?

On the design of typologically different conceptions:
complete heterogeneity or common features after all?

Rorty is misled by imprecisions and overgeneralizations in his definition of typologically different positions. He stylizes their difference into total difference. Whereas *paradigmatically* different conceptions, according to him, most certainly have something in common—namely their basis (Locke and Kant, for instance, in spite of all other differences, had the idea of representational cognition in common)—*typologically* different conceptions (say Kant's transcendental philosophy and Dewey's pragmatism) no longer exhibit a common basis—and hence, Rorty concludes, no longer have *anything at all in common*. As a result all reciprocal argument between them is excluded.

Now, in so far as conceptions are in fact fully heterogenous, the rejection of argumentative possibility would certainly hold. And of course—this constitutes in my eyes the healthy core of Rorty's restriction—any *direct basis argument* between such positions is impermissible. Wanting to refute the base assumptions of *one* concept with recourse to the axioms of a typologically *different one* would be logically incorrect and at best rhetorical. But it is precisely that explanation that is needed as to how Rorty himself can succeed in refuting a typologically contrasting concept—that of alpha-realism—by way of obviously interconceptual argument.

It was obviously specific linguistic-analytic reflection on the functioning of concepts (such as is originally alien to realist discourse) that provided the key to refutation here. It is revealing, however, that Rorty did not simply bring forward axioms of his model against the other approach, but succeeded through an *examination of immanent consistency* of the opposing concept. On the other hand, however, this means that the refutation follows in a manner contradicting both the total difference of typologically varying conceptions that Rorty insinuates and his thesis as to the impossibility of argument that he derives from this. Obviously even conceptions with basic differences are not so totally heterogenous that the impossibility of *all kinds* of interconceptual argument might, as Rorty claims, result from their dissimilarity.

Possibilities of interconceptual argument—
right through to fundamental criticism

To put it another way: one must make the concept of interconceptional argument more precise and differentiated. Interconceptual *basis*-arguments— the refutation of one basis in the name of the content of another—are indeed impossible. Rorty is thus far right. Interconceptual *detail*-arguments however—arguments relating to singular assumptions or constituents of a conception—are most certainly possible. This Rorty has overlooked. The fact that fundamentally different conceptions are heterogeneous in their basic assumptions in no way means that they must be heterogeneous *in all* of their elements. Herein lies Rorty's error. On account of their different bases he stylized typologically-different conceptions into structures heterogenous *everywhere* and hence (like Lyotard) obscured all intersections and all common features between them. Yet it is obvious that such conceptions also exhibit common features: they have at least logical structures and, equally, general conditions of theory such as coherence and consistency in common. In addition, intersections in content often exist.[58] All this opens up possibilities for argument and criticism even between a conception and one with a different basis, which on the one hand comes from outside, but on the other hand—and this is decisive—is at the same time internally legitimate and relevant insofar as it refers to imminent components of the criticized position and takes place in the name of standards that are also recognized by this position.[59]

Such criticism can, moreover, be very helpful in arriving at a more reliable version of the conception in question. It can, of course, even necessitate the reformulation of leading elements—right through to the reformulation of the base assumption. Rorty's refutation of alpha-realism provided an example of this.

To summarize: because typologically different conceptions, notwithstanding all basic differences, still have some common elements (logical, cross-theoretical, content elements), a whole range of interconceptual argument remains possible—beyond coarse basic arguments, which Rorty, wrongly, considers alone but, rightly, rejects. They can, moreover, extend as far as might be wished, namely, right through to the (merely nondirect, but, so to speak, indirectly effected) refutation of basic assumptions.

7. DEPARTURE FROM CLAIMS TO TRUTH OR DIFFERENTIATION BETWEEN TYPES OF UNDERSTANDING OF REALITY?

Rorty would presumably not agree with my reconstruction. He would not like to admit that his objections to the representational model amount to a refutation in the strict sense. He would rather have us believe that he had only played off one vocabulary against another.[60] Such restraint is personally honorable, but to me it seems more than problematic philosophically. With this I come, in conclusion, to the subject of truth—or to Rorty's underdetermination thereof.

Departure from the adequationist understanding of truth

Rorty rightly avoids the claim that the antirepresentationalism he advocates represents the truth, that his "sort of philosophy corresponds to the way things really are."[61] It is exactly such an idea of truth that has had the ground removed from beneath its feet. But does this also mean that truth is no longer to be spoken of at all in the new context? This would only follow if the concept of truth were bound exclusively to the adequational model. But there is no reason for this assumption. If a particular formulation of truth—here, the adequationalist one—proves itself to be untenable, then it is in general replaced by another. The adequationalist concept of truth is not the only one possible: pragmatic, coherence, or consensus based, etc., concepts of truth are possible in the same way. One can very well make the transition from representational to edifying philosophy—but one should then also clarify which altered contours truth assumes in this transition.

Explication of an altered understanding of truth—
Rorty's conservatism and its shortfalls

Rorty, however, neglects this task. He equates the departure from the representationalist idea of truth with the departure from truth altogether. He says we should cease to "see truth as a deep matter, as a topic of philosophical interest."[62] But this seems to me to be exaggerated. This consequence would result, as I've said, only if the objectivist apprehension of truth represented the only possible understanding of truth. It is almost paradoxical that Rorty, on the issue of truth, continues to follow the stipulation of the adequationalist position refuted by him. It is for this reason alone that he can equate the breakdown of this position with the abandonment of truth altogether—that is, throw out the baby with the bath water.

De facto of course, Rorty cannot help but raise claims to truth. The whole business of his critical explanations shows that even in the context of edifying philosophy one does not just say or accept arbitrary things. Besides which, Rorty himself once said the edifying philosopher "agree[s] with Lessing's choice of the infinite *striving* for truth over 'all of truth.'"[63] This is something quite different from straightforward abstinence from truth. On the other hand, Rorty thinks he can spare himself a clarification of his understanding of truth through the sweeping equation of the idea of truth with the adequation theorem. Recently, he has been fond of declaring straightforwardly that truth is not an interesting subject for the pragmatist—something that permits no philosophically fruitful work.[64]

Argument and truth as persisting constituents of philosophy

I must confine myself here to these few remarks on the subject of truth, which I cannot unfurl here to its full extent. But two things can be said with certainty. First, there is sufficient room for a whole series of intermediate positions between Rorty's downright abandonment of claims to truth on the one hand and the old concept of absolute objective truth on the other; second, true things can obviously still be said, at least in the sense of being *more true*—of being argumentatively more correct and superior. So there is cause not to abandon the issue of truth, but on the contrary to take it up again in more precise rational conditions.

In this essay my intention has been to show the extent to which some of Rorty's arguments are better than his declarations about them would indicate, and to deny his postphilosophical claims. Today still, philosophy does not have to become bogged down in a *conversatio perennis*, but can continue to be an exciting field of argument and endeavouring for truth.

AFTERWORD: MAY 2000

1. Argumentation: In footnote 11, I had said that I had not found any fundamental changes in Rorty's work concerning the question of argumentation after 1989. Nevertheless, one point is becoming increasingly clear. Although Rorty makes continuing use of argumentation, it has for him a clearly different status than in the genuine language game of argumentation. It is characteristic of this language game that argumentation should still be able to affect all *foundations*. For Rorty, on the contrary, it consciously affects only certain clarifications within an assumed position. For example, Rorty argues on the basis of evolved convictions like democracy and the diminution of suffering for their consequential and broadened application. However, he considers it senseless to want to argue for these convictions as such; properly speaking, this could simply not be done (cf. *Contingency*, 54). Thus Rorty in general turns away from the fundamental assumption of the language game of argumentation, on the basis of which one still is able to argue about the

foundations. Now, I showed before how some of Rorty's insights can themselves be just as well used in the language game of argumentation. (I am, in fact, different from Rorty, still interested in this language game.) Of course: to do this is not in Rorty's interest. And this is, in the sense of the limited role argumentation plays for him, completely consequential and legitimate. If there is to be a debate, then, it would have to revolve around the following question: Is the language game of argumentation for its part only a specific sociocultural language game (the traditionally occidental or philosophical one), which should now be abolished by another (the pragmatic or postphilosophical one)? Or does the first language game retain some right, even when philosophers like Rorty decide to go over to another language game? The status of argumentation as relevant to the foundations or merely relevant within—that is the alternative whose decision seems to be presupposed at any one time—in favor of the foundations-relevant type in my case, and in favor of the insider-relevant type in Rorty's case. What can Rorty now bring forth in favor of his option? He cannot, of course—in a consequential way—give a reason for this option, but only *recommmend* it. In any case he wants to proceed in this way. Does he really do so?

2. Monotypic of philosophy? What Rorty has had in mind ever since *Philosophy and the Mirror of Nature* is a paradigm shift in philosophical activity, from epistemological to edifying philosophy, which later has meant: to pragmatism or to postphilosophical culture. My question is now: whether Rorty's plea has, all in all, a consistent form. I think that on at least one point this is not the case: namely, where Rorty says that we would do best to realize the paradigm shift he suggests. The mistake seems to me to lie in the demands of exclusivity to which he ties it. First of all there is no satisfying reason to assume that we would *best* serve our social interests through the suggested paradigm shift—one cannot be certain of this, even if it may be plausible that Rorty's suggestion is a good way to serve such interests; but it could easily be that other philosophical strategies also—at least in the long run—serve quite well for this purpose. Secondly, all polemics against other orientations of philosophizing are out of place, because first of all it cannot (according to Rorty himself) be shown (but rather in all cases circularly clarified) that these other orientations have failed, and secondly, Rorty's polemic is for this reason no better than the reverse polemic of other orientations against Rorty. This is finally—in the third place—the truly irritating point: that Rorty (therein certainly no "post-modern" thinker) calls out a new unified kind of philosophy and likes to speak about other kinds only in shoulder-shrugging or discrediting ways. Against this, Rorty's observation at the end of *Philosophy and the Mirror of Nature* was too golden for words: that it cannot be excluded that "mirror-imagery and 'mainstream,' systematic philosophy will be revitalized once again by some revolutionary of genius"

(*Mirror*, 393). If we are to think in a democratic and liberal way, then plurality of philosophical options should not at the same time be reduced to one—pragmatic or postphilosophical—model.

NOTES

*The following contribution is the further elaboration of a talk given at the University of Jena, Germany on January 18, 1977.

1. Cf. *The Linguistic Turn: Essays in Philosophical Method*, edited by Rorty in 1967 (Chicago and London: The University of Chicago Press, 1967). Admittedly, Rorty had already formulated a detailed critique of analytic philosophy at the end of his introduction. As a result the volume became a point of departure for postanalytic schools of American philosophy.

2. Richard Rorty, *Philosophy and the Mirror of Nature* (Princeton, N.J.: Princeton University Press, 1979).

3. Cf. *Rorty & Pragmatism*, ed. Herman J. Saatkamp Jr. (Nashville, Tenn. & London: Vanderbilt University Press, 1995).

4. Richard Rorty, *Achieving Our Country: Leftist Thought in Twentieth-Century America* (Cambridge, Mass.: Harvard University Press, 1998).

5. I have discussed Rorty's position in more detail in my *Vernunft. Die zeitgenössische Vernunftkritik und das Konzept der transversalen Vernunft* (Frankfurt a. M.: Suhrkamp, 1995, stw 1996), 211–244.

6. Cf. especially Richard Rorty, *Contingency, Irony, and Solidarity* (Cambridge: Cambridge University Press, 1989).

7. Cf. Ibid., 73, 9.

8. Thus Rorty says: "[. . .] there is little to be said about truth." Richard Rorty, "Truth without Correspondence to Reality," in *Philosophy and Social Hope* (New York: Penguin Books, 1999), 23–46, 32 "[. . .] a pragmatist theory about truth [. . .] says that truth is not the sort of thing one should expect to have a philosophically interesting theory about. For pragmatists, 'truth' is just the name of a property which all true statements share. [. . .] Pragmatists doubt that there is much to be said about this common feature." "Pragmatists think [. . .] that there is no interesting work to be done in this area." Rorty, *Consequences of Pragmatism*, (Minneapolis: University of Minnesota Press, 1982), xiii–xiv. "Pragmatism" would be understood in one sense as "comprising nothing more than the dissolution of the traditional truth problematic."Richard Rorty, "Pragmatismus, Davidson und der Wahrheitsbegriff", in: *Die Wahrheit der Interpretation. Beiträge zur Philosophie Donald Davidsons*, eds. Eva Picardi und Joachim Schulte (Frankfurt a. M.: Suhrkamp, 1990), 57. Hence, one should no longer waste one's efforts on the issue of truth, but work instead towards the establishment of a postphilosophical culture. Cf. ibid., xiii ff. and xxxvi–xliv.

9. Hence his appeal for a "post-philosophical" culture.

10. In doing this I will, for reasons of space, try to piece together an account of Rorty's position from several sources in such a way that I give them a clearer or more tenable form from the start, without setting out in detail the steps leading from analysis of the text through to this distilled form. Rorty's utterances seem to me not always to be consistent. My account thus provides a reconstruction of Rorty's position rather than reproducing the wording of his utterances. The difference between this reconstruction (which, I believe, is completely in Rorty's spirit) and my criticism will, however, remain clear.

11. Rorty's later publications do not seem, at least on the theoretical level, to comprise any changes as regards the question here under consideration.

12. *Mirror*, 360.

13. Ibid., 368.

14. Ibid., 360.

15. Ibid., 370.

16. Ibid.

17. Ibid.

18. "This sort of philosophy [. . .] says things like 'try to ignore the apparently futile traditional questions by substituting the following new and possibly more interesting questions.' It does not pretend to have a better candidate for doing the same old things which we did when we spoke in the old way. Rather, it suggests that we might want to stop doing those things and do something else. But it does not argue for this suggestion on the basis of antecedent criteria common to the old and the new language games. For just insofar as the new language really is new, there will be no such criteria." *Contingency*, 9.

19. Cf. *Contingency*, 8.

20. Ibid., 6.

21. Ibid., 9, 8.

22. Ibid., 9. Wittgenstein had already said: "In a certain sense I canvass *for* one style of thought and *against* another." Ludwig Wittgenstein, *Vorlesungen und Gespräche über Ästhetik, Psychologie und Religion* (Göttingen: Vandenhoeck & Ruprecht, 1971), 55, no. 37.

23. For the sake of clarity I will go slightly beyond Rorty's statements here. Rorty tends to present paradigmatic differences as being just as incisive as differences in type—at least with regard to their results. Thus he speaks, for example, of incommensurability and irreducibility, without further differentiation, in relation to the difference between revolutionary and normal paradigms within a type as well as in relation to the difference between types (Cf. *Mirror*, 388). Another case of such inexactitude is that Rorty once describes (imprecisely) both edifying and paradigmatically revolutionary philosophers as revolutionary philosophers (Ibid., 369), whereas a little

later (precisely and correctly) he contrasts the type of the edifying philosopher and the type of the revolutionary philosopher. The decisive point is that more argument is always possible between paradigmatically differing positions than between typologically differing positions. Rhetoric may always be in play, but in the first case it is not everything, whereas in the latter case it seems that it must be everything.

24. *Mirror*, 370 ff.

25. Ibid.

26. Ibid., 377.

27. Rorty reminds not only systematic, but in particular edifying philosophers too, not to ignore the argumentative preconditions outlined and not to pass off their position as the true one.

28. The argument is naturally directed against systematic philosophers too, who only know their own type of philosophizing and hence, when faced by edifying philosophers, demand from them unjustified arguments—such as would only be possible within the systematic type.

29. Cf. *Mirror*, 377; *Contingency*, 8. See also the general criticism of the schema of "seeing" (*Mirror*, 371).

30. Nietzsche often seems to think that his criticism of belief in reality does in fact state the way reality in truth is: "NB. *Appearance*, as I understand it, is the real and sole reality of things." Friedrich Nietzsche, "Nachgelassene Fragmente. Juli 1882 bis Herbst 1885. 2. Teil: Frühjahr 1884 bis Herbst 1885," in Nietzsche, *Sämtliche Werke. Kritische Studienausgabe in 15 Bänden*, eds. Giorgio Colli and Mazzino Montinari (Munich: Deutscher Taschenbuch Verlag, 1980), 11: 654. With Derrida it is, in my opinion, different. He does not claim, as Rorty suggests, that there is no reality of the kind claimed by metaphysicians, but that metaphysicians' statements in this repect could only superficially lay claim to such being, even though precisely viewed they would be forced to attribute this being with a sense other than the one they believed. Derrida speaks—like Rorty—not about reality, but about modes of reference to reality (i.e., about the law of "difference" to which all such reference is subject).

31. Ibid., 360.

32. Within edifying philosophy argument is only possible still within a paradigm—for the purpose of increasing or establishing its consistency—but no longer between alternative paradigms. For just this reason Rorty consistently suggests another model of interaction: that of "conversation."

33. *Mirror*, 372.

34. Ibid., 377, 373.

35. Ibid., 378. In this Rorty even sees the "philosophers' moral concern" (*Mirror*, 394).

36. Rorty attempts to define edifying philosophy as the love of wisdom; yet in this the decisive role is not, of course, played by the love of argument, because here

wisdom refers to "the practical wisdom necessary to participate in conversation" (*Mirror*, 372). Rorty, however, provides not a positive, but only a negative, definition of this practical wisdom: it is acquired not "in finding the correct vocabulary for representing essence," and it seeks to prevent "conversation from degenerating into inquiry, into a research program" (ibid.).

37. The only precise form in this exchange consists in what Rorty calls "hermeneutics with polemic intent" (*Mirror*, 365). This is certainly an interesting example of the (legitimate) kind of reference to other conceptions that is still possible now. But it cannot lead to refutations, rather only to proposals and suggestions, and thus there is no more argument. Reciprocal hemeneutics goes further than "hermeneutics with polemic intent"—which seeks only to set out "how the other side looks from our own point of view" (*Mirror*, 364). Rorty undertakes such reciprocal hermeneutics in, for example, "Overcoming the Tradition: Heidegger and Dewey," in *Consequences of Pragmatism*, 37–59: "In what follows, I propose to offer sketches of Dewey as he would presumably look to Heidegger and of Heidegger as he would presumably look to Dewey" (42). I portrayed the possible reasonable achievements of a consequent and fully realized reciprocal interpretation in "Vernunft und Übergang: Zum Konzept der transversalen Vernunft", *Ethik und Sozialwissenschaften - Streitforum für Erwägungskultur* 11.1 (2000): 79–91.

38. Ibid., 378.

39. Toulmin sarcastically notes: "Reading Rorty's essays, we carry off the image of a party of ex-soldiers disabled in the intellectual wars, sharing, over a glass of wine, memories of 'old, forgotten, far-off things, and battles long ago.'" Stephen Toulmin, *Cosmopolis. The Hidden Agenda of Modernity* (New York: The Free Press, 1990), 10.

40. *Mirror*, 371.

41. Ibid.

42. Cf. Martin Heidegger, *The Principle of Reason* (Bloomington & Indianapolis: Indiana University Press, 1991).

43. "For philosophical problems arise when language *goes on holiday*." Ludwig Wittgenstein, *Philosophical Investigations* (New York: Macmillan, 1958), §19, 38. "The confusions [. . .] arise when language is like an engine idling, not when it is doing work." Ibid., §51, 132. "When we do philosophy we are like savages, primitive people, who hear the expressions of civilized men, put a false interpretation on them, and then draw the queerest conclusions from it." Ibid., §79, 194. "[. . .] the clarity that we are aiming at is indeed *complete* clarity." Ibid., §51, 133.

44. *Contingency*, 8.

45. *Mirror*, 378.

46. *Contingency*, 4 ff., 21.

47. Ibid., 9.

48. Cf. Ibid., 8 ff.

49. Which is why—unlike Rorty—I have included the realist objection in the run of the argument.

50. So as not to be misunderstood: I am not saying that this interpretation of independence is—so to speak, objectively—false. I am simply pointing out that—in contrast to its self-understanding—it already contains a certain interpretation, exegesis, and understanding of alpha-reality. Without some understanding or other it would be quite impossible even to speak of reality; one could have no idea thereof and would be unable to use the term "reality," which would then also have only some meaning or other—as vague as this may be.

51. Such a reflected form is found, for example, in Putnam's "internal realism" (however much in need of criticism one may hold this concept in other contexts).

52. This, according to Rorty, is a basic thesis of his "antirepresentationalism." See Richard Rorty, *Objectivity, Relativism, and Truth, Philosophical Papers, vol. 1* (New York: Cambridge University Press, 1991), 2.

53. This is formulated by Rorty, for example, as follows: "We have to drop the notion of correspondence for sentences as well as for thoughts, and see sentences as connected with other sentences rather than with the world." *Mirror,* 371 ff.

54. An example of this requisite awareness of provisionality can be found towards the end of the *Mirror of Nature*, when Rorty writes: "It may be that mirror-imagery and 'mainstream,' systematic philosophy will be revitalized once again by some revolutionary of genius" (*Mirror,* 393).

55. In the introduction to his *Phenomenology*, Hegel showed for the first time the contradictions in which the idea of cognition as a "tool" or "medium" entangles itself if it is to serve to grasp the absolute. He explained that the aspects of Being-in-self (*An-sich-sein*) and Being-for-another (*Für-ein-anderes-sein*) both fall *within* consciousness. This was, from the basis of the philosophy of consciousness, a form of expressing the view that—whenever we speak of an alpha-reality—we can do nothing other than conceive this by way of a construct of consciousness (an idea). Cf. Rorty's reference to this in "Representation, social practise, and truth," in Rorty, *Objectivity, Relativism, and Truth,* 151–161, 158, as well as his portrayal of the young Hegel as a thinker who founded "an ironist tradition within philosophy" whose "practice undermined the possibility of the sort of convergence to truth about which the older Hegel theorized." *Contingency,* 79. It is exactly the *Phenomenology* which Rorty understands as being "a paradigm of the ironist's ability to exploit the possibilities of massive redescription." Ibid., 78. Analytic philosophy has certainly developed this argument with more clarity and sharper conceptual means than Hegel—but the insight as such was already Hegel's. Furthermore, on the one hand it is nothing short of a piece of objective irony that analytic philosophy thus finally arrives at a realization that, two hundred years previously, had already been a basic insight of that very philosopher whom the analysts least of all believed capable of things meaningful. (I pursued some surprising factual convergences and congruences between Hegel and the new analytic philosophy in my Jena inaugural lecture, "Hegel und die analytische Philosophie: Über einige Kongruenzen in Grundfragen theoretischer Philosophie"; a shortened version appears in *Information*

Philosophie 1 (2000): 7–23). On the other hand, this insight has painful consequences for analytic philosophy itself, in that it necessitates the departure from the very project for the sake of which analytic philosophy had embarked upon its clarifications. It had set about the "logical analysis of language" precisely in order to make it the sharp instrument which—in place of the vaguenesses of the traditional philosophy of consciousness—ought finally to be suited to the clean and efficient execution of the project of a precise rendering of reality—the old project of representation. A sharpening of these means was indeed attained, but at the same time the untenability of the project was discerned. It is just this that Rorty makes clear in his *Mirror of Nature.* In this sense he states elsewhere that he intends to argue for the view "that the internal development of analytic philosophy had led that movement to conclusions which contradicted those of its founders, conclusions which sound more like James than Russell, and much more like Dewey than like Frege or Moore." Richard Rorty, "Comments on Sleeper and Edel," in *Symposium on Rorty's Consequences of Pragmatism. Transactions of the Charles S. Peirce Society* (1985): 21: 39–48, 39 ff.

56. One could indeed ask whether this insight (in constrast to Rorty's construction of relationships in the *Mirror of Nature*) had not already belonged to the whole endeavor of modern age thinking. Already Descartes's new science aimed not to copy a preexisting reality, but at a construction of reality. Kant apprehended our reality as a construction within the framework of transcendentally given prerequisites (forms of intuition and categories). Spectacularly, this led finally to Nietzsche's thesis that the human is above all an *animal fingens*—a being that creates and is confronted by fictions.

57. Two other ways in which Rorty formulates his rejection of an interpretation-free reference to reality are his rebuttal of assumed "essences" (e.g., *Mirror,* 367, 370) and of the assumption of an "intrinsic nature" (e.g., *Contingency,* 4, 8, 9). These are, so to speak, more traditional and thematic versions (relating to the world, humanity, or society) of the subject "reality" and, as such, other varieties of realism. These would also demand access to an entity lying beyond the diverse descriptions.

58. Cf. on this point my detailed observations on the interweaving character of paradigms and on the relation of conceptions (*Vernunft,* 593 ff., 853–908).

59. Rorty rightly says that the usual expectation is that central components of a vocabulary could be shown to be "'inconsistent in their own terms' or that they 'deconstruct themselves'. But that can *never* be shown." *Contingency,* 8. If an inconsistency of this kind existed then the vocabulary or paradigm concerned would be so nonfunctional that it would, in all probability, be unable to establish itself for any duration at all. But Rorty overlooks the other possibility that such untenability can in some cases be recognized from outside and then also more or less demonstrated internally. Hence there are often good reasons as to why an older position is dropped once a new one has been developed. This must be explained not in a straightforwardly behavioristic manner—as a transition from one habit to another—but in a falsificationist one at the same time.

60. Cf. *Contingency,* 73.

61. Ibid., 8.

62. Ibid. This passage, which is characteristic of Rorty's strategy, amounts to equating the abandonment of the idea of objective truth with a move away from the idea of truth altogether (that is, it neither presents this abandonment as ultimately argumentative, nor allows the ground thus arrived at to appear as a ground on which claims to truth are still possible): "To say that we should drop the idea of truth as out there waiting to be discovered is not to say that we have discovered that, out there, there is no truth. It is to say that our purposes would be served best by ceasing to see truth as a deep matter, as a topic of philosophical interest, or 'true' as a term which repays 'analysis'. [. . .] But this claim about relative profitability, in turn, is just the recommendation that we in fact *say* little about these topics, and see how we get on." Ibid.

63. *Mirror*, 377.

64. See footnote 8.

10

〜

WILLIAM EGGINTON

Keeping Pragmatism Pure: Rorty with Lacan

Given Richard Rorty's oft-confessed appreciation for the work of Freud, it is curious that he has had so little to say about Freud's most influential follower, Jacques Lacan. This would not be so surprising if Rorty were universally suspicious of the French intellectual style of which Lacan was so infamous an example. But if there is one European thinker for whom Rorty has confessed an even greater appreciation than for Freud, it is Jacques Derrida—a philosopher whose syntactical acrobatics and love of poetic wordplay were forged in the intellectual world built at least in part by Lacan. Nevertheless, with the exception of a disparaging reference to a contemporary enthrallment with phrases like "the unconscious is structured like a language" and a passing suggestion that his thought may simply be too bizarre to be worth bothering with,[1] Rorty has never written anything, positive or negative, about Lacan.

The purpose of this article is to commend certain aspects of Lacan's thought to Rorty as being compatible with his pragmatist project. The aspect that I wish to commend may seem at first glance the one most antithetical to Rorty's project: namely, Lacan's notion of the real. The concept of the real could be taken as opposed to Rorty's project for two reasons: first, in that it would seem to connote an ultimate reality, one that could be taken as a foundation for truth; second, in that Lacan himself describes the real as that which exceeds symbolization, hence something that is part of human experience and yet beyond the ken of language, in direct contradiction to Rorty's nominalism. The first ground for disagreement is easily dismissed, because the Lacanian notion of the real does not connote what *is* but rather what *is desired*. Lacan's notion of the real as an integral aspect of human being, as opposed to something outside it that grounds it, is entirely compatible with Rorty's refusal to consider truth-as-correspondence versus truth-as-coherence to be a serious philosophical problem.

The second reason for disagreement, on the other hand, is substantial. Rorty's nominalism, his conviction that "nothing is better than a something about which nothing can be said," leads him to an intransigent refusal of any notion of ineffability or of any concept that purports to *refer to* that which cannot be *talked about*. But it is precisely here that the Lacanian notion of the real becomes useful for pragmatism, because with it Lacan developed a vocabulary for discussing human experience and behavior that takes into account—that gives utmost importance to—the effects of ineffability on human behavior. And it is precisely insofar as pragmatism gives precedence to behavior, precisely insofar as it respects vocabularies that are better able to predict and explain behavior, that pragmatism should pay attention to Lacan.

The intellectual position I sketch out in the pages that follow is that of the "psychoanalytic pragmatist," the pragmatist who has a use for, as Rorty has said we should have a use for, the language of psychoanalysis.[2] But the psychoanalytic pragmatist is also a specifically Lacanian pragmatist because, as I will argue, Rorty's obvious preference for Freud notwithstanding, it was Lacan's focus on the linguistic dimension of being that ultimately pragmatized psychoanalysis, transforming it from a discourse involved in the positivistic search for truth to one that understands the subject as a process of poetic self-creation or, in Žižek's words, an effect that posits its own cause.[3]

Rorty, in very much the way Lacan would do, reads Freud "strongly," making of him one of the heroes of early pragmatism: "He [Freud] is not interested in invoking a reality-appearance distinction, in saying that anything is 'merely' or 'really' something quite different. He just wants to give us one more redescription of things to be filed alongside all the others, one more vocabulary, one more set of metaphors which he thinks have a chance of being used and thereby literalized."[4] But the problem with trying to make of Freud a pragmatist is that one often runs into passages like this: "[T]he ego must observe the external world, must lay down an accurate picture of it in the memory-traces of its perceptions, and by the exercise of the function of 'reality-testing' must put aside whatever in this picture of the external world is an addition derived from internal sources of excitation."[5] Nevertheless, my point is not to bicker with Rorty over whether Freud really believed in truth as correspondence, but rather to suggest that the Lacanian vocabulary of subjectivity is a strong ally for pragmatism, an ally that enables one to avoid some of the problems into which Rorty's "purer" pragmatism has led him.[6]

These problems are the following: Rorty's attraction to nominalism, to the motto that nothing is better than a something about which nothing can be said, has led him to a dogmatic refusal of the notion of first-person experience. Since what would remain irreducibly first-person about such experience is precisely everything about it that one could not communicate to another person, and because, according to (a certain interpretation of) the above dictum, there is *nothing* you could *not* communicate to another person, it follows that first person experience and everything that goes along with it—consciousness, "raw feels," sensory perception—simply do not exist. Coming to such a conclusion is what I call using Occam's razor to cut your own wrists. For not only is such a conclusion patently absurd in its own right, it also and ultimately cripples pragmatism's ability to confront what is for psychoanalysis the central component of human being: desire. Where Rorty rejects the notion that "the unconscious is structured like a language" on the grounds that it tempts people to think of language as something that might have a structure and that therefore might make for a philosophically interesting problem, psychoanalysis insists that it is just that, a structure, and furthermore one whose principal ramification, desire, is and ought to be *the* fundamental philosophical problem. This problem, which has manifested itself in the history of philosophy as the desire for an ultimate or *metaphysical* ground, cannot, the pragmatist's own desire notwithstanding, merely be disposed of as a category mistake, for ultimately it is an analysis of this problem that allows us to make sense of so much of human behavior. The behavior such an analysis illuminates includes not only the pragmatist's own central desire, the desire for progress, but also the extraordinary passion with which humans cling to their ethical worlds—the worlds, in other words, composed of their final vocabularies.

A discussion of the Rortian and Lacanian understanding of the role of metaphor in language and in the construction of these final vocabularies brings me to a critique of Rorty's public/private distinction, namely, that the activities relegated by Rorty to the private realm determine in part the individual's final vocabulary, which itself determines in part how the individual relates to those outside of his or her community, and hence to the degree of cruelty he or she is capable of engaging in or of tolerating. Therefore, whereas Rorty believes the problem of cruelty can be solved by more and better descriptions of the other's suffering, psychoanalytic pragmatism insists that description is irrelevant without identification, and that the capacity for identification with an outsider is a function of what for Rorty constitutes an intrinsically private matter, that is, the ultimate contingency of one's final vocabulary. Both Rorty and psychoanalysis hold this contingency to be a fact; the difference is that for Rorty this fact will ultimately not be a problem for an individual who simply stops playing certain language games, whereas for psychoanalysis metaphysical desire, the desire for our vocabulary not to be contingent, is not just a language game but is essential to being-in-language as such. Recognition of this fact implies that in some cases it is only a process of private humiliation, the implosion of certain fantasy structures, that will pave the way for the ultimate diminution of public cruelty.

Finally, I will only add that the purpose of this essay is not to offer a "reading" of Lacan; indeed, many of the "Lacanian" points I make might make some Lacanians indignant. My intention, rather, is to cull from Lacan— and in some cases from Slavoj Žižek, Lacan's most influential contemporary interpreter—another vocabulary, one palatable for pragmatists like me, without keeping any of the obscurantism that is the residue of Lacan's *Zeitgeist*. I will be doing (to quote Rorty on Heidegger) to Lacan "what he did to everybody else, and what no reader of anybody can avoid doing,"[7] i.e., reading Lacan by my own, pragmatist, lights.

NOMINALISM AND EXPERIENCE

If I were forced to sum up the core of Rorty's philosophy—his most passionate commitment, in one short phrase—I would say that his philosophy is one that endeavors always and everywhere to dismantle epistemology, to debunk the notion, entrenched in our culture since Descartes, of the human subject making judgments about the accuracy of its mental representations of the world-out-there.[8] An immediate objection to reading Rorty with Lacan is that while Rorty is explicitly anti-Cartesian, Lacan's model of subjectivity is explicitly Cartesian.[9] But Lacan's Cartesianism is itself the product of a "strong" reading of Descartes, one that removes the epistemological divide between the world and the subject's perception of the world and replaces it with a divide between the subject's world and its language.

For Lacan, Descartes founds the modern subject not only in that "the philosophical *cogito* is at the portal of that mirage that renders modern man so sure of being himself in the midst of his uncertainties about himself,"[10] but also and more importantly in that the language of his self-certainty becomes the model for the modern desire for self-identity. Rather than taking as the subject of psychoanalysis the strong and certain center of apperception that watches impressions go by in the theater of its mind, Lacan reads Descartes' *cogito ergo sum* as the description of a speaking thing chasing endlessly after its unconditioned being: "It's not a question of knowing whether I am speaking of myself in a way that conforms to what I am, but if, when I speak about myself, I am the same as he of whom I speak."

Phenomenologically (and here the term must be voided of any contrastive value with the real world) the subject inhabits what Lacan calls the imaginary, which we should take to mean the sum total of sensory experience. We need not distinguish here between what is fantasy and what is accurate

representation, because, in a sense very much in tune with Rorty's Darwin-
ism, the imaginary is an adaptive mechanism, a way of dealing with an
organism's environment.[11] Truth is simply not an issue for the imaginary;
there need be no question of separating the subject's phenomenal world from
the real world of objects. The subject is only what Lacan calls a subject,
however, insofar as it is a speaking being—a being who, as Rorty would put
it, exchanges marks and noises with other beings as a means of better adapt-
ing to its environment. These marks and noises have value (meaning) as tools
to be used and as a function of their relation to other marks and noises.
Because the environment (imaginary) is not made of marks and noises ("there
are no sentence-shaped objects"[12]), truth is not a matter of corresponding to
reality. The truth of a mark is a function of another mark.

The above Lacanian model, however, contains one element that might be
questionable to Rorty's pragmatism, namely, the distinction between language
and experience. In the following pages I hope to make explicit exactly what is
entailed in that distinction, to point out that Rorty is more ambiguous about
such a distinction than one might at first glance suppose, and finally to explain
why, if he in fact does not accept such a distinction, he should.

If Rorty disapproves of Cartesian dualism—the belief that there is a
philosophically interesting distinction to be made between the corrigible
impressions the "world-out-there" makes on our senses and the incorrigible
certitude that we are indeed receiving some such impressions—he is equally
disapproving of any attempt to distinguish between those things we can talk
about and those things that might be out there but for which we have no
adequate vocabulary. This second disapproval, called nominalism after Wilfrid
Sellars, is based on the later Wittgenstein's injunction not to try to "get
between language and its object." As both the later Wittgenstein and the
younger Heidegger knew, our language, like our historical and cultural world,
is coterminous with our ability to think. To try to transcend this condition
would necessarily lead to self-deception or inauthenticity.[13]

According to Rorty, whereas the younger Wittgenstein had hoped to be
able to find the "nonempirical conditions for the possibility of linguistic
description," he later "dropped the whole idea of 'language' as a bounded
whole which had conditions at its outer edges, as well as the project of
transcendental semantics": "He became reconciled to the idea that whether a
sentence had sense did indeed depend upon whether another sentence was
true—a sentence about the social practices of the people who used the marks
and noises which were the components of the sentence. He thereby became
reconciled to the notion that there was nothing ineffable."[14] Rorty's agreement with this form of nominalism leads him down a logical path from the
pragmatic and interesting claim of Sellars that "all cognition is a linguistic
affair" to a highly unpragmatic alliance with what I will call a priori physicalism (even if, as he claims, of a nonreductive sort) and its collapsing of

distinctions between machines, nonhuman animals, and humans. My suspicion is that this is an instance of Rorty's (in my view) healthy dedication to philosophical pragmatism being tainted by the temptation to keep his philosophy pure, of following a train of thought to its logical extreme. My own feeling is that there is no need to stay on the train that long, and that by maintaining one distinction—between experience and language use, a distinction that Rorty himself at times does seem to hold on to—one avoids making a number of rather absurd claims for the sake of philosophical purity and manages to explain significantly more human behavior in the process.

Where I would suggest getting off the train is in the middle of the quotation above, right before "He thereby became reconciled to the notion that there was nothing ineffable." Whereas Wittgenstein might have become reconciled to this notion, I will argue below that he should not have. And while I accept his dictum that "nothing is better than a something that does nothing," I will be arguing for a notion of ineffability, or at least of present "ineffedness," that in fact does quite a lot. But before pursuing that line of reasoning I will make clear why I think that the acceptance of the nonutility of the concept of the ineffable gets one into a great deal of trouble.

One of the first consequences that Rorty draws from his agreement with the tenets of nominalism is that once you have described a being's behavior to the best of your linguistic abilities, there is nothing left for you to say about it. There is no, as Nagel would call it, "something it is like" to be that being that your descriptions cannot get a hold on. There is, in other words, no irreducible first person perspective, no consciousness, no awareness of phenomena. "In contrast, followers of Wilfrid Sellars (such as George Pitcher, David Armstrong, Daniel Dennett, and myself) lump the neurological arrangements that make possible such differential responses to stimuli together with the internal states of (for example) thermostats. We treat perceptions as dispositions to acquire beliefs and desires rather than as 'experiences' or 'raw feels,' and hence we disagree with Thomas Nagel that there is 'something it is like' to have a perception."[15] Rorty here follows Dennett in believing that accepting the basic tenets of phenomenology, that there is something it is like to be you, leads to positing a distinction between "thinking . . . something seems pink to you and something *really seeming* pink to you."[16] Once you have posited such a distinction (as does Dennett's unfortunate straight man Otto, when he says in frustration, "I don't just *think* there seems to be a pinkish glowing ring, there *really seems* to be a pinkish glowing ring!"), the physicalist Dennett can gleefully point out that such a distinction is in fact illusory, and that the consequence of its being illusory is that "[t]here is no such phenomenon as really seeming—over and above the phenomenon of judging one way or the other that something is the case."

But let's look more closely at poor Otto's situation. Let's say you were given a pill that was supposed to grant you one wish.[17] Immediately upon swallowing the pill, however, you were overcome with unbearable stomach pains, such that you had to cry out "I wish I had never taken this pill!" The pain immediately stops, and the pill is back in your hand. When you express to your companion-in-adventure at this point how awful the experience of taking the pill was, he dutifully informs you that you never in fact took the pill, and that, therefore, you never really felt any pain. You insist; he goads; and before you know it, you come out with a sentence like Otto's: "Look! I mean it. I don't just *think* I felt terrible pain, I really *did* feel it!" The point is that by uttering this sentence you are not in fact positing a distinction between thinking you felt pain and actually feeling it. You are, like Otto, replying to your interlocutor's clever goading by denying what you take to be his suggestion: that a) there is such a distinction; and b) given that distinction, you merely *think* you felt the pain. The proper response then is not that there is "no such phenomenon as really seeming—over and above the phenomenon of judging in one way or another that something is the case," but rather that "thinking one is in pain" as distinct from "being in pain" makes no sense. It is the language game of "thinking," not that of "feeling," that is out of place.

Dennett, with Rorty's support, wants to do away with language concerning the experience of phenomena and with words referring to things like consciousness or raw feels, by explaining why there seems to be a difference between judging and feeling, when in fact there is not. But this strategy fails, if one refuses to be goaded into the distinction in the first place. For this distinction is not in fact what a phenomenology need be about. Let's take another example. I am sleeping but awake suddenly, certain that someone just called my name. I look around the house, but no one is there. I go back to sleep confident that I was mistaken, that I just "thought I heard someone call my name." But "thought" in this sentence functions merely to relativize a certainty that I at first felt. At first I heard someone calling my name. When later I say "I thought I heard someone," this is the language game I use to indicate that I was mistaken, that I heard something that turned out to be nothing. I am not terribly surprised, of course, because it is part of my daily experience to occasionally "think I heard" something. The Cartesian and the pragmatist need not be in disagreement about the phenomenological fact of this perception; the Cartesian simply goes on to make a philosophical point that the pragmatist finds useless: namely, that while I was mistaken about a voice being what I heard, I was not mistaken about the fact of the illusion that I heard it, and that therefore *truth* is a function of ascertaining how clearly and distinctly my perceptions accord with reality. For the pragmatist, however, there is no philosophically interesting difference between mistakenly hearing a voice and mistaking one friend in the distance for another: in each case the mistake is a function of a language game that seeks to classify perceptual reports as cohering or not cohering. In the case of the pain pill or a trip to the dentist, there is no difference between thinking something hurts and it really hurting, whereas there can be a difference between the doctor's needle entering your gum and the pain it causes. But to argue this is not to say that there is no such phenomenon as pain, or no such experience as seeing pink.

Nevertheless, Rorty will reply, we agree that there is no difference between thinking that something seems and something seeming. Now, we have a handle on "thinking something seems," because it involves the same propositional attitude we can take to any belief or desire: you say you see pink, I think you're a trustworthy person, so I take you at your word for it. What possible need is there for positing yet another distinction, or using yet another formulation to say the same thing: "not only do you judge/think/formulate a sentence about seeing pink, you actually have the phenomenological experience of seeing pink"? According to Rorty, this adds absolutely nothing to the picture we already have. But Rorty's opponents, philosophers like Nagel and John Searle, need to make this distinction in order to be able to claim that there is something—unique and ineffable—*it is like* to be a particular individual endowed with a sensory perceptive mechanism.

Rorty's response to this is that "the intuition that there is something ineffable which it is like to be us—something which one cannot learn about by believing true propositions but only by being like that—is not something on which anything could throw further light. The claim is either deep or empty. The pragmatist sees it as empty."[18] For Rorty, this claim is part and parcel with the claim he makes a little later in his famous essay "The World Well Lost," that "'the world' is either the purely vacuous notion of the ineffable cause of sense and goal of intellect, or else a name for the objects that inquiry at the moment is leaving alone."[19] But whereas I agree with this formulation, I do not see how accepting it ties me to his claim that there is nothing ineffable that it is like to be me. To deny that there is a "world" out there, separate from our perceptions and from the statements we make about it but nevertheless governing the truth of those statements, is not the same as believing that there is nothing "ineffable" it is like to be me. I prefer to fall back on a rule of thumb that is also one of Rorty's favorites: if a vocabulary makes a difference, then it is meaningful; if it does not, then it is not. Getting between the words and their objects in "the world out there" does not make a difference, but phenomenal experience and the category of the ineffable, as I will show below, do.

To take Rorty's position, one can certainly argue that because a) there is no describable difference (and hence no difference) between the world and its description, then b) the same standard should apply to the use of the word "consciousness," if we wish to claim it as a part of the world. Therefore, c) there is no need to accept the existence of something like awareness apart from the description of beings who act in ways that suggest to us beliefs and desires. Perhaps, however, the real disagreement lies with the term "ineffable,"

which Rorty, in the quote above, is using to describe Nagel's caveat for subjective experience: "we do not have the vocabulary to describe it adequately."[20]
What could "adequate" in this case mean? Perhaps it should be taken to mean
"in such a way that it is no longer exclusively first-person." In this case, we
could claim that our first-person perceptual reports are not adequate to our
experience because even if there is no difference *for me* between the world and
my perception of it (and I accept that deceptions and errors are part of my
world) it does not follow that there is no difference between that world and
my description of it *to a third party*. If no such difference existed, and if my
descriptions were "adequate," the third party would have no desire to experience what I am experiencing. But this desire is an observable behavior in
most speaking beings. Let's take an example: I live in California, but I have
a friend who lives in Vienna. I do not feel there is any use in positing a
difference between her experience of Vienna and Vienna as it is in itself. The
concept if Vienna as it is in itself has no apparent meaning to me. I also have
an uncle who lives in Vienna, a sixty-year-old ex-pat who has lived there half
his life. When he describes Vienna to me, I get an entirely different impression than when my friend describes it to me. But still, I have no need at this
point to posit experiences on their part different from their individual linguistic judgments of Vienna, and certainly no need to posit Vienna as it is in
itself, apart from these various impressions. So far so good. But now I experience a strange feeling. I miss my friend. I realize that I would like to be with
her, would like to experience being in Vienna with her. I call her and ask her
to tell me more, tell me as much as she possibly can about life in Vienna,
about herself, about what we would do together were I there with her. But
much to my surprise (being the good nominalist that I am), after all her
descriptions, I remain unsatisfied. I still want to experience it for myself.

This example is absurdly simplistic, but if we are to take nominalism
seriously—take seriously, that is, the claim that "nothing is better than a something about which nothing can be said"—then my need to actually be in
Vienna is irrational: once my friend has told me everything there is to be said
about it, there should be nothing left. But there is, and that something is called
desire. For, as should now be obvious, no one can ever say all there is to be said.
The inability to say everything is built into language, and is, in fact, one of the
conditions of our desire to speak. This is ineffability, or ineffedness. Lacan
begins his seminar *Télévision* with the lines "I always tell the truth. Not the
whole truth, since no one can manage that. To tell the whole truth is impossible, materially speaking: words fail. But it is just on this impossibility that
truth hangs onto the real."[21] As I discuss below, "truth hangs on to the real" is
Lacan's way of saying that, rather than truth being a function of an ultimate
correspondence between language and reality, it is supported in the final instance only by a series of metaphors, what he calls "signs of the lack in the
Other," words that stand in for the fact that we can't say everything.[22]

Now, it is quite clear that Rorty does not really think that there is an absolute correlation of language to experience in the sense described above. He is perfectly willing to grant that when I am using words like "conscious- ness," or "subjective," or "mental," I am using them to explain what he calls my "epistemological authority," an authority that organisms have to report back on internal states to which external observers have no access. Neverthe- less, he argues, we should not use words like "subjective" or "mental," because these words have the effect of convincing us that we are talking about some- thing special, unique, and mysterious, when in fact all they do is refer tau- tologically to that "epistemological authority."[23] But beyond the simply aesthetic and practical problems of using bulky phrases like "my judgment about which I have epistemological authority is that this butter tastes rancid," there is a philosophical issue involved: with this "epistemological authority," Rorty is in fact referring to the same problem of "adequacy" that, for someone like Nagel, is missing in any attempt to convey the entirety of first-person experience. For Nagel, this inadequacy indicates the existence of an intrinsically myste- rious entity: consciousness. For Rorty, it indicates merely the presence of a category mistake, an instance of the tendency in philosophy to treat a con- fusion in language as a serious philosophical problem. For the psychoanalytic pragmatist, however, it is this very inadequacy, this gap between experience and linguistic expression, that constitutes human being as such. Conscious- ness is not, in other words, a mysterious something beyond the ken of lan- guage; it is rather the name we give to the fact that our experience, and that of others, exceeds our ability to talk about it. It is the very fact that the other's words present themselves to me as a world that exists and that nevertheless is beyond my experience that produces my awareness of my own experience as being something unique—as being, in other words, first-person.

Let me stress that to make these arguments one need not distance oneself from nominalism. Rorty is right to follow Wittgenstein and Sellars in claiming that to become "aware of qualia is the same thing as learning to make judgments about qualia—a process that involves relating qualia to non- qualia."[24] All I want to stress is that awareness, judgment, and relation all take place against a greater backdrop of experience that, while not separable, de- scribable, or distinct, is nevertheless in excess of the former. I could not agree more when Sellars writes, ". . . all awareness of sorts, resemblances, facts, etc., in short all awareness of abstract entities—indeed, all awareness even of par- ticulars—is a linguistic affair. . . . [Not] even the awareness of such sorts, resemblances and facts as pertain to so-called immediate experience is pre- supposed by the process of acquiring the use of language."[25] But when Wittgenstein takes "a nothing would be as good as a something about which nothing can be said" to mean that we ought not speak about private sensa- tions, to my mind he has gone too far. There is a lot we can say about another person's private sensations, starting with the fact that we can't feel them ourselves. The need to have recourse to a vocabulary of private sensations is even required by nominalism, if we derive from Sellars's slogan "a difference that cannot be expressed in behavior is not a difference that makes a difference"[26] the positive statement "a difference that is expressed in behavior makes a difference and needs a vocabulary." For behaviors like my paying a large amount of money to fly to Vienna when I could just as well read about it are not explainable by vocabularies that collapse the difference between first person experience and third person description.

PRAGMATIC INEFFABILITY

It is my view that, as I stated above, many of these disadvantages of Rorty's thought may be avoided by not following him when he derives his doctrine of the nonutility of ineffability from Sellars's doctrine that all awareness is a linguistic affair. Rorty agrees "wholeheartedly," as do I, with this statement from Hilary Putnam: "elements of what we call 'language' or 'mind' *penetrate so deeply into what we call 'reality' that the very project of representing ourselves as being 'mappers' of something 'language-independent' is fatally compromised from the start.*"[27] But, unlike Rorty, I do not feel that holding this belief commits one to a further belief that there is nothing special or distinctive about language, that because language and reality are not distinguishable entities, it therefore follows that we cannot say anything interesting about language.

Rorty's interest in saying just that comes in part from his commitment to a Darwinian understanding of human development. Such an understanding views language as just one more complex tool for dealing with an environment: "According to this story [the Darwinian one that speaks of the brain, throat, and hands as organs that 'let humans coordinate their actions by batting marks and noises back and forth'], these organs and abilities have a lot to do with who we are and what we want, but have no more of a representational relation to an intrinsic nature of things than does the anteater's snout or the bowerbird's skill at weaving."[28] But the fact that language does not have a "representational relation to the intrinsic nature of things" does not mean that there is nothing specific or philosophically interesting that we can say about it. One of the difficulties Rorty apparently has with Lacan is that his thought leads people to treat language as if it were unique and philosophically interesting: "One begins to be enthralled by phrases like 'the unconscious is structured like a language,'[29] because one begins to think that languages must have a distinctive structure, utterly different from that of brains or computers or galaxies (instead of just agreeing that some of the terms we use to describe language might, indeed, usefully describe other things, such as the unconscious)."[30] At the same time he insists that "[l]anguage [should not] become the latest substitute for 'God' or 'Mind'—something mysterious, incapable of being described in the same terms in which we describe tables, trees, and atoms."[31] But if he allows that languages can be studied like trees, and that we can use words to describe them, then it seems pragmatic to allow that they might have a specific structure, that it might make more sense to use one vocabulary to describe languages and another to describe galaxies. In fact, much as he would like to deny it, Rorty is in a minority in claiming that there is nothing mysterious, or at least philosophically interesting, about language. Consider just a few examples from the litany of mysteries that language presents for a linguist like Noam Chomsky, who, incidentally, is no more a fan of structuralist approaches to language than he is of the "metaphysical naturalism" that the contemporary cognitive science Rorty finds so attractive presents for him. For Chomsky, no approach to the study of language has come even close to eliminating the problems brought up by twentieth-century thought's favorite whipping boy, Descartes: "the fact that it is un-bounded in scope, not determined by external stimuli or internal state, not random but coherent and appropriate to situations but not caused by them, evoking thoughts that the hearer might have expressed the same way—a collection of properties that we may call the 'creative aspect of language use.'"[32] Even Rorty at times finds qualities of language interesting enough to talk about: with Heidegger, that we are thrown into it, that it is the House of Being; or, with Wittgenstein, "[t]hat the search for nonempirical truth about the conditions of possibility of describability raises the self-referential problem of its own possibility."[33] This last point is close to one of the central notions of Lacan's understanding of linguistic structure, namely, that it represents everything for us, in that we cannot get outside of it, and yet it is "not all," in that there always remains something to be said. In other words, what is specific about language is that words fail. Lacan's innovation in saying that the unconscious is structured like a language was to point out that this interesting fact about language had some even more interesting and useful ramifications for psychoanalysis, and for understanding how people behave.

Let us return, then, to what a Lacanian version of linguistic ubiquitism looks like. For Lacan, as for Sellars, Wittgenstein, and Rorty, there is no separate "real world" to which our thoughts correspond; we are thinking things insofar as we inhabit what he calls the symbolic order. This symbolic order has much in common with "Quine's notion of 'the web of belief,' like Putnam's notion of 'cluster concepts' and Wittgenstein's image of overlapping strands,"[34] and like them helps to break the notion of semantic rules nested in our heads for answering questions. Furthermore, as with these other vocabularies, the symbolic order is not anchored to reality; there is, as Lacan puts it, no other of the Other;[35] it is not founded or guaranteed by anything. Truth cannot be a matter of correspondence because *we* speak, but things do not. Therefore, *our* world has a special character, one imposed by signification.

One aspect of this character we could call the symbolic order's incompleteness—not in the sense that we can stand outside of it and see where it stops short, but rather in the sense of coming to places in our language where words no longer refer back to other words for their meaning. Because our symbolic order ultimately is not founded on anything external to it, because it has no final, referential anchors—things, in Wittgenstein's terminology, that can be shown but not said—our words acquire meaning by virtue of their use in concrete situations (context) and by referring back to other constellations of words. This, then, is the meaning of Lacan's reworking of Sartre's *en-soi/pour-soi* distinction (the subject's alienation in meaning produces an aphanesis, a fading, of being): the speaking being's situation is such that it has no ultimate anchor in Being (because there is none), but also and for that very reason it desires such an anchor, such a certainty, much as the early Wittgenstein desired to stand outside the limits of language in order to calculate its a priori rules. Living in language then entails a loss of being, *but only insofar as the specter of that loss exists only in and for the speaking being's world.*

This Being that the speaking being perceives as lost is what Lacan called the real. The real, then, is not a *Ding-an-sich* supporting our phenomenal world, but rather is the name Lacan gave to the apparently irrepressible desire to seek out such a thing. To sum up, the real equals the finitude of signifiers over the infinitude of experience. But for thought or language to be finite does not mean that there are "limits of language" that we can go out to and explore. Like the closed universe of Dante or that of Riemannian space, the universe of language is finite but boundless; there is no getting outside of it.

Now, if experience—as opposed to reality—exceeds the symbolic, then it follows that there is something that is ineffable or, more specifically, some aspect of all experience that remains "ineffed"—something that Rorty heartily denies. But at times Rorty lets a belief in the ineffable slip out. People, he says, often feel grateful that they were not born disabled or mentally retarded. "This is in part because of a calculation of the obvious socioeconomic disadvantages of being so born, but not entirely. It is also the sort of instinctive and ineffable horror that noble children used to feel at the thought of having been born to non-noble parents, even very rich non-noble parents." Then he adds in a footnote: "This is the sort of ineffable horror that creates a sense of moral abomination (at, e.g., intercaste marriage), and thus furnishes the intuitions one tries to bring into reflective equilibrium with one's principles."[36] This use of ineffability is completely commensurate with one of the modalities of the real analyzed by psychoanalysts of an *Ideologiekritik* stripe like Žižek. The utility of such analysis is not that it explains the ineffable any better than Rorty does in the above-quoted section (for to explain it would be to eff it and hence to show that it was not ineffable), but rather that it fills in the above picture with some of the vocabulary provided by analytic experience, the experience of generations of humans dealing with the troubles other humans have with ineffable horrors and desires.

The vocabulary used for this purposes is that of what Lacan called *jouissance*, which Žižek translates as enjoyment, although, paradoxically, it is an enjoyment that can as easily be horrible as pleasurable.[37] One of the functions of "jouissance" is to name the bodily sensations that accompany our commitments to the various key words in what Rorty calls our final vocabulary: the flush that accompanies what we call righteousness when a liberal answers the unanswerable question of why homosexual love is just as good as heterosexual love with the words "Because it is, that's why!", or, conversely, the feelings of disgust and moral superiority of the bigot interrogating her when he responds that the liberal is as sick as the fag is. This is, perhaps, another way of describing what Rorty calls the "intuitions one tries to bring into reflective equilibrium with one's principles."

One model that helps to imagine the relation between language and experience is that of a sponge saturated with water. Like the sponge's relation to the water, our languages, again in Putnam's words, "penetrate so deeply into what we call 'reality' that the very project of representing ourselves as being 'mappers' of something 'language-independent' is fatally compromised from the start." Our thought, our ability to be conscious of things, extends only so far as the material of the sponge is in contact with the water. Nevertheless, there are pockets of water that the sponge does not touch, just as there are aspects of experience that we are not conscious of, that we do not eff, but which we nevertheless must posit in order to better describe our behavior, in particular the behavior that has to do with desire. Even if one could posit that the combination of all possible languages would be the equivalent of a sponge with no holes, one must realize that it is also in the nature of languages that, as Rorty says, "you cannot let all possible languages be spoken at once."[38] The ineffable, then, would be precisely the word that indicates this relation to what cannot be said at any given time.

METAPHYSICAL DESIRE

For the younger Wittgenstein, the sentence that summed up his *Tractatus*, and that hence, for Rorty, gets everything wrong, is "what can be said at all can be said clearly, and what we cannot talk about we must pass over in silence."[39] The problem with this sentence for the pragmatist is that it posits a clear distinction between the whole of language, which can be described in its full complexity, and the realm of the ineffable, of those things that can be shown but not said and hence must be left in silence. The psychoanalytic pragmatist also disagrees strenuously with this sentence, but for different reasons than does Rorty. The psychoanalytic pragmatist's reversal of this sentence would be: "What we do say is almost never clear, and every sentence we utter piques us with the possibility of something that has not yet been said." What the second half of this formulation suggests is that there can be a notion of the ineffable, or at least the persistently "ineffed," that does not thereby suppose the ability to "get between language and its object" and study or map out language as distinct from the world, and vice versa. The suggestion of the first half, which I will spell out in greater detail below, is that clarity in the sense of objective certainty as to the meaning of the other's speech, or total transparency of the other's intentions, is a phantom, the desire for which—whether exhibited by logical positivism or a priori physicalism—is in fact explicable in terms of the effects the ineffability of experience has in our unconscious.

Another way to put the distinction central to the *Tractatus* is as one between "the available and effable world and the unavailable and ineffable 'substance of the world.'"[40] This is a felicitous formulation in light of Žižek's Lacanian/Hegelian treatment of the notion of substance. *Jouissance*, according to Žižek, is the only substance acknowledged by psychoanalysis. But what we need to keep in mind when we read such a statement is precisely the fact that by means of it Žižek undermines any possible Tractarian effort to find an invariable substance upon which to found an analytic of knowledge. For substance, like the Lacanian real, is the word Žižek uses to refer to the "that which must stay the same in all circumstances," the God's eye view, the *Ding-an-sich*, and every and all such manifestation of what we can also call, quite simply, metaphysical desire[41] or the desire for something metaphysical. When he says, as he often does, that *jouissance* is not historical,[42] what he means is that what Rorty calls the "ambition of transcendence" has always haunted us, and part of facing up to one's finitude, or even facing up to one's contingency, involves the realization that if you can't found certainty on *jouissance*, you can't get away from it either.[43]

One of the few arguments against pragmatism that Dewey ever countenanced was made by G. K. Chesterton, when he said "[p]ragmatism is a matter of human needs and one of the first human needs is to be something more than a pragmatist." Although Dewey accepted the point, he believed that this human need was *merely* a need, one that, like a child's need for constant maternal attention, could be outgrown: "Dewey was quite aware of what he called 'a supposed necessity of the "human mind" to believe in certain absolute truths.' . . . But he thought that the long-run good done by getting rid of outdated needs would outweigh the temporary disturbance caused by attempts to change our philosophical intuitions."[44] Psychoanalytic pragmatism differs from Dewey's and Rorty's pragmatism by placing the yearning for transcendence, along with contingency and finitude, not as a human need that it makes sense to grow out of, but as a useful way of describing human being with which it makes sense to come to terms.[45] One way to describe the practice of psychoanalysis is as a method for helping humans beings deal with the disturbances metaphysical desire provokes in their physical, quotidian, mundane existence.

Rorty's term for this desire is the ambition of transcendence, which, "in the form it took in modern philosophy, gave us the distinction between the world and our conception of the world, between the content and the scheme we applied to that content, between the truly objective and the merely intersubjective."[46] But the ambition of transcendence is for Rorty a philosophical illness, something for which philosophy should serve as a therapy in that it should always do its best to extirpate it from any philosophical discourse. The late Wittgenstein and the early Heidegger wrote exemplary books in this sense, in that, "[f]rom the point of view of both *Philosophical Investigations* and *Being and Time*, the typical error of traditional philosophy is to imagine that there could be, indeed that there somehow must be, entities which are atomic in the sense of being what they are independent of their relation to any other entities (e.g., God, the transcendental subject, sense-data, simple names)."[47] Psychoanalytic pragmatism is of a kind with these books in refusing to posit such objects, but differs (at least from Wittgenstein and his nominalist followers) in that it sees as one of its purposes, and as an interesting philosophical project, the explanation of *why* people suffer from metaphysical desire,[48] the discussion of whether in some forms it might be socially and individually beneficial, and the consideration of how best to avoid its possible ill effects, both social and individual.

Ultimately, the fact of ineffability and its resultant metaphysical desire explains much of what Rorty wants to erase from traditional philosophy, but it also explains an aspect of Rorty's own belief system that would remain mysterious without it. This is the aspect of "progress" that is so important to Rorty as a liberal. For if we take seriously the notion that there is no "world out there" to which the ever-increasing correspondence of our linguistic practices is the motor of all knowledge, then what takes the place of that motor? What drives us "forward"? What constitutes progress?

Rorty defines progress in terms of the belief that the situation one sees in one's community is better now than what it was in the past, and the hope that it will be better in the future than it is now. For the pragmatist, "better" means merely having more of the things that her community—in its present historical condition—desires and less of what it abhors. What a liberal community most abhors is cruelty, so it follows that the liberal pragmatist sees progress in terms of a march from a greater to a lesser prevalence of cruelty in her community and in the world.

This is straightforward enough, and yet it seems reasonable to inquire not "on what does the pragmatist base her desire for progress," for that is the kind of senseless metaphysical question that pragmatists rightly dismiss out of hand, but rather "whence the various future options that constitute possible paths along which to progress?" For certainly one could imagine a world, perfectly in keeping with the pragmatist's nonessentialist view of language, in which a given community simply continues to play one and the same language game for all eternity, never desiring to change, because its members are not aware of the existence of other options and certainly are not being caused to change by environmental stimuli, given that their languages and tools do a pretty good job of managing and predicting their environment as it is. In other words, one could imagine a situation in which the idea of change simply never occurs. Why, then, if Rorty is right, does change occur? Why does it make sense to talk about progress the way he does?

Rorty himself acknowledges that for Dewey the notion of progress was a kind of transcendence. Dewey, he says, "wanted us to keep something vaguely like a sense of transcendence by seeing ourselves as just one more product of evolutionary contingencies, as having only (though to a much greater degree) the same sort of abilities as the squids and amoebas. Such a sense makes us receptive to the possibility that our descendants may transcend us, just as we have transcended the squids and the apes."[49] This interpretation of the transcendence of progress in Darwinian terms is, predictably, attractive for Rorty, because it allows him to explain human progress as simply a much more complicated manifestation of the same kind of change present in biological evolution: "The history of human social practices is continuous with the history of biological evolution, the only difference being that what Richard Dawkins and Daniel Dennett call 'memes' gradually take over the role of Mendel's genes."[50] This statement is useful for a metaphilosophical perspective that wishes to emphasize the random aspect of human events over their planned aspect. But random mutation seems an inadequate model for the notion of human progress as Rorty wants to describe it. For human beings use the human tool called language to *imagine* the future, to *sich vorstellen* (set before themselves) various scenarios, to choose from them, and then to try to realize these projects. In order to better do this, they invent new languages for the description of new possibilities. No vocabulary I have come across to discuss the random mutation of genes responsible for evolution would employ such terms.

Although in general Rorty would agree with the statement above—that progress depends on a process of inventing new vocabularies for new purposes—at times he seems to negate it in order to defend the discourse of liberalism against the possible intrusions that as yet unseen vocabularies might constitute. His principal disagreement with Foucault, for instance, is "about whether in fact it is necessary to form a new 'we.'"[51] In *Contingency, Irony, and Solidarity*, Rorty even suggests that there is something about being an ironic intellectual that inhibits one from being a radical, or even a "'progressive' and 'dynamic' liberal,"[52] because the ironist cannot offer the same kind of hope that the metaphysician can. But given that our selves and communities are nothing but webs of beliefs, "descriptive centers of gravity," it seems that the development of a new vocabulary is tantamount, in many cases, to the formation of a new "we."

Apparently—and fortunately, in my view—Rorty has changed his mind on this issue. In an essay on Catherine MacKinnon and the utility of pragmatism for feminism, he argues that it is precisely pragmatism's willingness to dispense with present vocabularies—and not to believe that these vocabularies are adequate to expressing all viable political goals—that makes it an ideal partner for political movements like feminism, political movements whose success depends on what Foucault would call inventing a new "we." "Universalist philosophers assume, with Kant, that all the logical space necessary for moral deliberation is now available—that all important truths about right and wrong can not only be stated but be made plausible, in language already to hand. I take MacKinnon to be siding with historicists like Hegel and Dewey and to be saying that moral progress depends upon expanding this space."[53] If the webs of beliefs and desires that constitute our identities perceive progress as doing things better than they used to be done, using more effective vocabularies than did our forbears, we must conceive of progress toward the future as continuing to allow poets and revolutionaries to develop new vocabularies for as yet unimaginable worlds. But this ability to invent new vocabularies, to imagine a "contrast between a painful present and a possibly less painful, dimly seen future,"[54] requires another factor, one that pure pragmatism does not account for: desire. It is not enough to answer the question of motivation with the same dismissive shrug that we answer the question of the ultimate foundations for our beliefs, claiming that people just desire change and that to ask why is an uninteresting question. The fact is that not everyone desires change. Progressives are the kind of people who do desire it. And, in contrast to Rorty's earlier claim above, that there is something incompatible between ironism and progressive liberalism, I would even say that the more ironic, the more nonmetaphysical one's belief system is, the more one will be devoted to progress (whether or not we like the direction that progress might take). Metaphysical desire, the desire that derives from our specifically symbolic being-in-the-world, requires transcendence, and if not expressed in one form, it will appear in another.

Of course it's doubtful that Rorty would accept such a formulation, given his tendency to think of desires as a subgenre of beliefs. There is little in common between the notion of a fundamental and unconscious desire, responsible for both the fact of human progress and the ambition for transcendence, and the sort of desire that one can treat as follows: "By a familiar trick, you can treat desires as if they were beliefs. You do this by treating the imperative attitude toward the sentence *S* 'Would that it were the case that *S*!' as the indicative attitude 'It would be better that *S* should be the case than that not-S should be."[55] I can only respond by pointing out that, by a less familiar trick, one can collapse the difference in another way and read indicative statements like "the things in the world are but shadows of forms," "the phenomena are our impressions of the things-in-themselves," or "all reality is ultimately explicable by corpuscular science," as instantiations of metaphysical desire—the desire to undergird the instability, uncertainty, and thrownness of our various worlds with some bedrock of apodictic truth.

METAPHORS AND QUILTING POINTS

Whatever we might believe about the utility of a metaexplanation for progress, I agree with Rorty about what it consists of: changes in the way people think, and hence in the way they use language. We are also in agreement about *how* languages change, and hence about how knowledge of any kind progresses. The basic idea is that vocabularies change when people accustomed to speaking in that vocabulary begin to "creatively misuse" it in one or another way. These creative misuses, however, are not *reasons* for changing one's beliefs (the reasons come afterward, justifications spoken in the new language for its superiority over the old); rather, they are *causes*.[56] In general, "there are three ways in which a new belief can be added to our previous beliefs, thereby forcing us to reweave the fabric of our beliefs and desires—viz., perception, inference, and metaphor."[57] Perception refers to the noninferential and nonrational causal influence our environments have on our bodies. Inference refers to how our languages are altered internally as a result of applying the consequences of one proposition to another. Such change is rational, because inferences *are* reasons for changing or adding a belief. The third way, metaphor, is different in that it belongs to the realm of use rather than of meaning: "Davidson's view is that there is a strict distinction between meaning (the property which one attributes to words by noting standard inferential connections between the sentences in which they are used and other sentences) and use, and that 'metaphor belongs exclusively to the domain of use.'"[58]

For Davidson and Rorty, the notion "meaning" refers to the way our words work in a limited, though constantly shifting, realm of usage, that is predictable and literal.[59] Words or phrases that have meaning in this sense can always be paraphrased with other words or phrases. They are usages that anyone with a working knowledge of the language should be able to engage with unproblematically and with limited possibility for confusion. Metaphors, while they are still "alive," are precisely those usages of language that cannot be paraphrased. When such a paraphrase becomes widely available, the metaphor dies, becomes literalized, becomes a piece of quotidian language.[60]

Words that mean, then, are words that refer back to other words. Metaphors do not mean, because they are not immediately assimilable into the constellation of words and sentences that constitute us at any moment. They are foreign intruders into our world of meaning, coming across at first glance as either nonsensical or downright false. Their appearance in our linguistic world then causes one of two possible reactions: we can ignore them offhand, or we can be intrigued by them and try to integrate them into our world. If the latter is successful, they will eventually die as metaphors, but in the meantime our knowledge, and our identity, will have incrementally (or radically, in some cases) changed.[61] Some now-famous former metaphors might be, "the earth revolves around the sun"; "the universe is finite but boundless", "class-struggle is the motor of history"; "the soul is the prison of the body"; and "the unconscious is structured like a language." The possibility that such metaphors will change our current beliefs is what Davidson and Rorty mean by their belonging to the realm of use. Without metaphor, we would still be able to form new beliefs by way of perception and inference, but our knowledge could not in any sense progress, because the fundamental structure of our belief system, what Rorty calls our final vocabulary, would forever remain unchanged.[62] When a new perception is so new—as when the telescope allowed men to see craters on the face of the moon—its integration can indeed cause a revolutionary change in belief, but the actual change will still be produced by metaphors, such as "the moon is made of corruptible substance."

The parallel with Lacanian semiotic theory would be as follows. There are basically two ways in which words relate to one another—and hence in which our symbolic order and unconscious function. The names for these, which he takes (in altered form) from Jakobson, are metonymy and metaphor.[63] Although he does not use the same terminology as Davidson, it is not too much of a stretch to say that, for Lacan as well, metaphor belongs to the domain of use, in that metaphor is the name Lacan gives to the words we use to stop the "metonymic" sliding of signifiers. At a microsyntactical level, the metaphoric function can be fulfilled by any element, word, gesture, indication, pause, or silence that serves to stop a sentence and inform the listener: "My most recent string of noises has ended, you should make sense of them now."[64] At a macrosyntactic level, metaphor is the active ingredient in any acquisition of knowledge, as it involves the insertion of a new word (or of an old word used in an initially unrecognizable way) into the normal, metonymic chain of words. Any constellation of words comprising one's knowledge (either about specific subjects or, theoretically, "the entirety of one's knowledge") consists of a great number of words related "metonymically"[65] to one another (in that one refers to another for its meaning and so on), and a very small number of words that hold the place of the constellation, that respond dumbly to the question "But why, finally, is that the case?", that do not refer back to the next word in the chain for their meaning but rather, tautologically, to the constellation as a whole.[66] These special words, which are also the principal elements of each individual's or group's final vocabulary, are called by Lacan quilting points (*points de capiton*), in that they hold together the webs of beliefs that constitute the "descriptive centers of gravity" that are ourselves and our communities.[67] Like "democracy" or "freedom" to an American, these are words that are conceived of as requiring no justification, as being desirable per se. There can be no communities without quilting points, and there can be no selves without them either.

If indeed it can be argued, as I am arguing, that Lacan's and Davidson's theories of metaphor are similar in a fundamental way, this is of some consequence for Rorty, because Lacan's theory implies a notion of ineffedness of the sort I have been advancing. Metaphors or quilting points, for Lacan, are produced and have their function precisely insofar as the symbolic order is limited in relation to the imaginary, precisely insofar, that is, as not everything can be said. Metaphors are "signs for the lack in the Other [symbolic order]," they stand in for the symbolic order's incompleteness, and as such are the principal symbolic element in the production of unconscious desire. Subjects acquire new metaphors only insofar as old ones die, insofar as they render up their promise of infinite *jouissance* and show themselves to be merely exchangeable concepts as opposed to containers of divinity—which is why, as I argued above, the critique of metaphysical certainties (otherwise described as a way of killing essentialist metaphors) can be such a powerful engine for progress.

The psychoanalytic pragmatism I am advancing is compatible in many ways with Rorty's thought, but in some ways it can be seen as being *more* pragmatic. Principally, the space this model creates for a notion of ineffedness allows for a viable and useful notion of desire, in contradistinction to Rorty's tendency to conflate desire and belief and his refusal to analyze desire on its own terms. The notion is pragmatic in that it is a difference that makes a difference, a distinction that helps to interpret successfully the ways people actually behave, instead of theorizing, due to a misguided desire for physicalist purity, their ultimate identity to machines. Finally, it also is a model that explains the imaginative, utopian thinking that is central to Rorty's theory of progress, recognizing in it the same impulse that manifests itself in traditional philosophy as the ambition to transcendence, but that, when turned away from the promise of metaphysical fulfillment, is instrumental in achieving the kind of society the pragmatist desires.

CONTINGENCY, INEFFABILITY, AND PSYCHOANALYSIS

Toward the end of *The Consequences of Pragmatism*, Rorty admits that his admiration for what he calls "textualism," the practice of strong misreadings in the intellectual's quest for self-creation, falls prey to one criticism in particular, namely, that "the stimulus to the intellectual's private moral imagination provided by his

strong misreadings, by his search for sacred wisdom, is purchased at the price
of his separation from his fellow humans. I think that this moral objection
states the really important issue about textualism and about pragmatism.
But I have no ready way to dispose of it."[68] Seven years later Rorty answered that objection, in *Contingency, Irony, and Solidarity*, by arguing for a
strict division between two realms of behavior: a private one in which all are
free to pursue idiosyncratic projects of self-creation and perfection, and a
public one in which the primary goal is the diminution of cruelty. In private
we can work to our heart's content to achieve autonomy *vis à vis* the rest
of the world and the particular intellectual, poetic, artistic, and familial
traditions and communities from which we hail. But in public it is our duty
to build solidarity, to make connections with as many people and as many
communities as possible, and ceaselessly to understand how what we in our
community are doing may be causing pain to others in theirs.

The person who can successfully balance these two poles of existence
is the liberal ironist. The liberal ironist is liberal in that he or she thinks
that "cruelty is the worst thing we do"; he or she is an ironist in that he or
she is "the sort of person who faces up to the contingency of his or her own
most central beliefs and desires—someone historicist and nominalist enough
to have abandoned the idea that those central beliefs and desires refer back
to something beyond the reach of time and chance."[69] Private irony is a
useful correlate to public solidarity because progress—which the liberal desires
in order to ensure that present levels of cruelty continue to diminish, rather
than simply stay the same—requires poets and revolutionaries to invent new
languages, not languages they keep to themselves but ones they circulate
among their communities, searching for new adherents.[70] But while this
freedom can contribute to liberal progress, it must nevertheless be kept
strictly separate, because, as Rorty has famously said, "I cannot imagine a
culture which socialized its youth in such a way as to make them continually dubious about their own process of socialization. Irony seems an inherently private matter."[71] Irony should be kept private because of its tendency
to put into question final vocabularies. Given that final vocabularies are
what define individuals and communities, while it should be everyone's
right to ironize about their own and other final vocabularies to themselves,
to allow it to be done in public is to risk subjecting others to humiliating
critique, precisely the kind of cruelty and pain that it is the liberal's vocation
to diminish at any cost.

The public realm, then, for Rorty, includes any and all actions (including uses of language) by which one risks causing others pain; the private
realm consists of those behaviors and uses of language that do not run that
risk. While at first glance this may seem a commonsensical and classically
liberal distinction, his interpretation of the kinds of language-use that might
constitute causing pain to others leads to curious passages in which he rec-

ommends relegating to the private realm the writings of certain philosophers who might see themselves as engaging in a public battle against cruelty, and hence as participating in the sort of debate for which the public realm exists.

> It is precisely this sort of yearning [for total revolution] which I think should, among citizens of a liberal democracy, be reserved for private life. The sort of autonomy which self-creating ironists like Nietzsche, Derrida, or Foucault seek is not the sort of thing that could ever be embodied in social institutions. . . . Most ironists confine this longing to the private sphere, as . . . Proust did and as Nietzsche and Heidegger should have done. Foucault was not content with this sphere. . . . *Privatize* the Nietzschean-Sartrean-Foucauldian attempt at authenticity and purity, in order to prevent yourself from slipping into a political attitude which will lead you to think that there is some goal more important than avoiding cruelty.[72]

This injunction to privatize forces us to consider two important questions: first, what exactly does it *mean* to privatize a writer; and second, who has the authority to decide when a writer is due for privatization? When Rorty claims that Proust confined his desire for autonomy to the private sphere, while Nietzsche and Heidegger should have, what exactly does this mean? Does it mean that they should have written in a different way, or that we should place warning stickers on the covers of their books saying "Caution! This book is for private perfection-seeking only. Any use in the public realm may lead to serious social problems like fascism or a generalized yearning for total revolution"?[73] Does it mean, rather, that fiction is inherently private and philosophy public, and that therefore Nietzsche and Heidegger should have written novels like Proust? Or does it merely mean that we should endeavor to *read* them only as private writers, while continuing to read Habermas and Rawls as public writers, as writers whose ideas and proposals have currency in the public realm?[74] As to the second question, it seems quite arbitrary to decide that a philosopher like Habermas should be considered a public thinker, while Foucault—whose life's work could certainly be interpreted as a battle against cruelty—should be privatized.

Further problems crop up when we turn to the question of progress. If the liberal's desire for progress is aided by the freedom granted to ironists to distance themselves from their own final vocabularies and hence to develop new vocabularies, the question arises of whether the work these ironists accomplish is in fact public or private. Given that "poetic, artistic, philosophical, scientific, or political progress results from the accidental coincidence of a private obsession with a public need,"[75] the modes of expression of these private thinkers must be publicly available, or else the accidental coincidence he describes will never have a chance to occur. It seems, then, that much of Rorty's position as outlined in *Contingency, Irony, and Solidarity* eventually runs afoul of the objection to his criticism of Foucault that I discussed above: namely, that to guarantee progress, to bring about dimly-sensed future possibilities for diminishing pain, he must allow for the possibility that new "we's" will be formed, and it is only the work of the thinkers he defines as private thinkers that will eventually bring that about. A strict divide, then, between the public and the private is not desirable if one cherishes, as Rorty does, the constant mutation of final vocabularies that constitutes progress.

Among the various practices that Rorty categorizes as private—in that they have to do with the individual's effort to define herself as autonomous over and against the "blind impresses" that have formed her and the final vocabularies into which she has been thrown—psychoanalysis holds a special place. Psychoanalysis is important to Rorty because it showed how every individual life, not just the poet's or the revolutionary's, can be seen as a poem, as a process of self-creation. "By seeing every human being as consciously or unconsciously acting out an idiosyncratic fantasy, we can see the distinctively human, as opposed to animal, portion of each human life as the use for symbolic purposes of every particular person, object, situation, event, and word encountered in later life. This process amounts to redescribing them, thereby saying of them all, 'Thus I willed it.' "[76] By recasting human being in terms of poetic self-creation, Freud helped distance us from the traditional Platonic model of morality in terms of which what one ought to do was conceived of as a function of a universal truth concerning human nature. Rather than working toward the Good, whose truth resided in each individual human being, Freud helped us see "moral consciousness as historically conditioned, a product as much of time and chance as of political or aesthetic consciousness."[77] If Plato's project had been to bring together the public and the private, by claiming that individual perfection was inherently commensurate with social justice, Freud's demonstration of the contingency of moral identity helped make it clear that the quest for self-perfection would not automatically lead to social justice, that in fact the opposite was just as likely true.[78]

Because the quest for self-perfection does not lead to social justice, Freud's own method for seeking autonomy—a method that constituted a valuable contribution because it conceived of this quest as available to everybody, not just poets—ought as well to be confined to the private realm. Rorty is, consequently, quite dismissive of attempts to make psychoanalysis a tool for social change, claiming that "Freudo-Marxist analyses of 'authoritarianism' have offered no better suggestions about how to keep the thugs from taking over."[79] But what Rorty fails to mention in his discussion of Freud is that while Freud may well have helped destroy any notion of the individual's conscience partaking of an essential, extraindividual morality, much of his writing nevertheless argues that it is precisely the interaction and overlap between the individual's private drives and the demands that society makes of him that is responsible for so much of the pain (and pleasure) that occurs both at the individual and the social level. Psychoanalysis, then, cannot be relegated purely to the private sphere, for the problems it treats are reflections of public norms and the individuals it helps create in turn change and affect those norms. If the purpose of public discourse is to find ways of ensuring that the thugs don't take over, it may turn out that some of the Freudian veins of *Ideologiekritik* that Rorty dismisses do have some proposals to make.

The problem of how to keep the thugs from taking over can also be stated as that of how to ensure a liberal society continues to be liberal in the sense of the word that Rorty emphasizes, i.e., that it continues to strive for the diminution of cruelty. The problem stems from the fact that, for Rorty, there is no such thing as a universal ethical sense, a built-in mechanism for recognizing the humanity in another human and automatically respecting it, treating it as an end in itself. Rather, individuals recognize others because they have something in common with them that is not something abstract and universal, like humanity, but is rather something concrete, specific—a series of shared beliefs and desires, ideals, experiences, and memories. When one identifies another as being "one of us," this term "is, typically, contrastive, in the sense that it contrasts with a 'they' which is also made up of human beings—the wrong sort of human beings."[80] How one distinguishes one of "us" from one of "them" has to do with one's final vocabulary, that constellation of words, beliefs, and desires that is the *non plus ultra* of one's identity, the destruction or changing of which would be tantamount to becoming a different person altogether. The vocabularies are final in the "sense that if doubt is cast on the worth of these words, their user has no noncircular argumentative recourse. Those words are as far as he can go with language; beyond them there is only helpless passivity or resort to force."[81] Since Rorty does not believe that we can do without final vocabularies, and as he doesn't much like the idea of a completely universalistic community, a community whose final vocabulary is shared by everyone on earth, the most he feels a liberal community can hope to achieve is to be as open and sensitive as possible to the final vocabularies of other communities without giving up on its own. If the intellectuals of that community are ironists too, their responsibility is to put into doubt the validity of their own final vocabulary, but to do so in private, so as not to disturb the socialization of the community at large. As contact with other communities increases, the hope is that the liberal community will propagate those elements of its final vocabulary that have to do with the diminution of cruelty, with the end of diminishing cruelty around the entire world, as well as among its own members.

As I pointed out in the discussion of metaphor above, Rorty's final vocabularies consist of words expressing values that need or stand no further *justification* because they form the subject's ultimate moral horizon: "I do the right thing because it's right." "Democracy is simply the best political system, even when it doesn't work." "Of course freedom is preferable to confinement, what planet do you come from?" "Men are supposed to sleep with women, not with other men." These are metaphors insofar as their function is defined paradigmatically in relation to an entire structure as opposed to in relation to their local position in a syntagm, as "red" and "tree" usually are. Each refers to a global semantic field, an ideology concerning what is right, what it means to be a man, etc., that goes far beyond being able to use a word correctly in a sentence. Of course these examples can also be defined by their position in a sentence, but when they function in a final vocabulary their *unjustifiable* nature is analogous to the metaphoric function of standing-in-for-something. Insofar as they function as metaphors, these words can also be seen in a Lacanian vein as being constellations of quilting points. The added benefit of thinking of them in these terms is that one realizes that insofar as the identity of an individual is constituted by a web of quilting points—words that stand in for the ultimate lack of foundation in some metaphysical reality, that stand in for the symbolic order's incompleteness *vis à vis* lived experience—it is also held together by the desire for the real that supports any system of meaning. In community politics, this desire manifests itself as that ineffable pleasure or horror that, as we discussed above, accompanies any invocation of the final vocabulary. Communities, then, are not only held together by agreement concerning fundamental beliefs and desire; they are also and more fundamentally held together by libidinal investments.[82] These libidinal investments are as responsible for all the good that is done in the name of a community—everything that a liberal like Rorty says we should be proud of when we think about our country[83]— as they are for all the evil that is done in ts name, racism and nationalistic violence being the prime examples.[84]

For Rorty, as long as one includes in one's final vocabulary the importance of not causing pain, then all one needs to guard one's society from becoming comfortable with the pain of others are good descriptions. "What would guard such a society from feeling comfortable with the institutionalized infliction of pain and humiliation on the powerless? From taking such pain for granted? Only detailed descriptions of that pain and humiliation— descriptions that brought home to the powerless the contrast between their lives and the lives of others (thus inciting revolution) and brought the same contrast home to the privileged (thus inciting reform)."[85] But such a prescription still demands that the participant *identify* with those who feel pain. Just as certain people feel pain or guilt at the killing of an animal, and as a consequence don't become hunters (even if they may not feel their pain deeply enough to become vegetarians), so people who do *not* identify with other people may quite easily cease to feel their pain, and cease to feel moral approbation at the thought of being the cause of their pain. What is needed is not *description*—torturers who are in direct contact with their victims do not need a description to know what they are feeling—but rather *identification*. Rorty's final prescription is for a society that knows how to distinguish the question of whether the other shares my final vocabulary from the question of whether she is in pain.[86] The psychoanalytic pragmatist thinks that one's relationship to one's final vocabulary—as well as the kind of final vocabulary one has—determines the extent to which one can identify with others and therefore recognize the pain one causes them, for it is precisely to the extent that a subject's fundamental fantasy presents his or her final vocabulary as a necessary order of things, as "grounded in the real," that the subject's psyche will need to produce "symptoms" to account for the failure of the fantasy, for the rifts in his or her world, for the difference in the way others describe the world. Psychoanalytic pragmatism sees many social ills as precisely such symptoms.

For Rorty, one of the main reasons why the intellectual ironist should keep her activities private is that ironizing threatens final vocabularies, and threatening final vocabularies is a form of causing pain, a very specific kind of pain: humiliation. "The redescribing ironist, by threatening one's final vocabulary, and thus one's ability to make sense of oneself in one's own terms rather than hers, suggests that one's self and one's world are futile, obsolete, *powerless*. Redescription often humiliates."[87] But the psychoanalytic pragmatist sees intellectual ironizing as being useful both in public and in private. You learn to redescribe and to distance yourself from your final vocabulary in private so that in public others don't have this power over you. In the private practice of psychoanalysis, the analysand suffers, in effect, a kind of humiliation, a realization that his fundamental fantasy is empty, not grounded in the real, that—in the less violent language of pragmatism—his final vocabulary is contingent. This process of humiliation is also essential to the racist becoming a nonracist: the realization that one hated the other's enjoyment (the other's presumed attainment of what one lacks oneself) out of a desperate attempt to avoid the humiliating fact that one's own enjoyment was lacking. The goal of Žižekian critique is thus to bring individuals to a point of identification with the ethnic, racial, or sexual other that they have constructed as their symptom—i.e., to a recognition that this other is a stand-in, a dupe for their own constitutive inability to ground their final vocabulary on something real or to make their fantasy of a seamless social body a reality. The analysis, then, should bring about a confrontation and ultimate acceptance of contingency and finitude, and a consequent dissipation of the particular *jouissance* that the destruction of the other seems to promise.

When Rorty confronts a hypothetical Nazi, he does not believe that philosophical argumentation will demonstrate to him the horrid nature of his beliefs. But he does "have some idea of how to set to work" converting the

Nazi, even if he has no guarantee that his method will work.[88] The method consists, of course, in describing to the Nazi "how horrible things are in the Nazi camps, how his Führer can plausibly be described as an ignorant paranoid rather than as an inspired prophet," etc. But is this not, in effect, a form of humiliation? All the psychoanalytic pragmatist adds is a way of understanding people's attachments to their final vocabularies and some techniques for dealing with that attachment that might make this necessary (from our perspective) process of humiliation more effective, less likely to (as it will in most cases) backfire and provoke a full-scale reaction. Again, we need not have too many scruples about resorting to this kind of humiliation. *From our perspective*, some final vocabularies are simply better than others; *because from our perspective* some are more likely to promote social ills than others; these are the ones we would like most to dismantle.

What we call social ills always have to do with vocabularies. One needs a vocabulary to make distinctions. This does not mean that, for instance, love is more natural than hate, but rather that the differentiation that supports both requires a vocabulary. There is no more likelihood of a "natural" aggression to the other prior to it meaning something (i.e., having a place in a vocabulary) than there is of a "natural" hatred of grass or small furry animals. The "natural" man might kill the furry animal, or might leave it in peace, but he is unlikely to feel that its eradication is necessary to his way of life. Psychoanalytic *Ideologiekritik* of the kind that Žižek promotes believes that such a desire to hurt or to eradicate the other is an indication that the other has been constructed as a symptom, that which is perceived as keeping the subjects of a community from truly being what their final vocabulary promises they really are. When this is the case, the only thing that will prevent violence is what Žižek calls "traversing the fantasy," coming to the realization that one's fantasy, the final vocabulary upon which one's community is founded, is contingent. This is humiliating. But sometimes what a society needs is a little humiliation just to keep it honest.[89]

Ultimately, whether in public or in private, in philosophy, *Ideologiekritik*, or clinical practice, pragmatism and psychoanalysis have the same goal: to make people more comfortable with contingency.[90] The psychoanalytic pragmatist sees that this goal has positive public consequences as well, because it sees racism, sexism, homophobia, and ethnic hatred as ways that people who are not comfortable with the contingency of their selves and their societies react to that contingency via a direct expression of their *jouissance*. In other words, it feels good to hate when one sees the object of one's hatred as responsible for what is wrong in one's world. But if one learns to recognize that what is wrong in one's world is wrong because worlds are human creations and human creations can never tap into the perfection of pure correspondence to an ideal (the metaphysical fantasy *par excellence*), then one can learn to direct one's *jouissance* in other directions. One can learn, for example, to sublimate one's ambition for transcendence into a desire for progress.

One last objection to these conclusions might be that, as nice as it sounds, one can't really "sublimate" one's ambitions for transcendence into a desire for progress, because there really isn't any difference between the two to begin with. All this talk about traversing the fantasy and thereby making people less racist is ultimately just that, talk—the kind of talk that participates in those endless leftist-intellectual fantasies (what Stanley Fish calls "leftist theory hope") about provoking social change without actually *doing* anything. In part, I'm sympathetic to this critique. I do not think that by becoming psychoanalytic pragmatists we intellectuals are going to become empowered to go about the world traversing racist fantasies. Nevertheless, I will not join in the facile and trendy belittling of intellectual activity implicit in such complaints. Intellectuals *do* do something: they create vocabularies. And it is ultimately the creation of vocabularies—assuming these vocabularies are adopted and disseminated—that is responsible for changing beliefs.

As I said at the outset, this essay is not intended as a pragmatist reading of Lacan, nor is it my hope to establish a new theory called "psychoanalytic pragmatism." My wish, rather, is to engage Rorty's pragmatism as a pragmatist and to present him and those who agree with him with the possibility of appropriating a vocabulary that pragmatism has as of yet failed to acknowledge. The intellectual position that might result from such an appropriation, what I have been calling psychoanalytic pragmatism, is in fundamental agreement with Rorty that the question of whether truth is a function of the correspondence between one's words and one's reality or merely of the coherence between one's words is a false question. It is a false question because it leads one to suppose that human beings inhabit worlds-out-there, worlds made of very different stuff (real stuff) from the stuff we are made of (ideas). Psychoanalytic pragmatism differs from Rorty's version in that it recognizes that, at least in modern cultures, this false question is on everybody's mind—in the form that I've called metaphysical desire—and is not merely a philosophical problem. Psychoanalytic pragmatism sees the prevalence of this question, along with its social and individual concomitants—metaphysical desire and its various offshoots, the desire for progress included—as having much to do with the notion of ineffability. But since metaphysical desire is a social and not just a philosophical phenomenon, it behooves us not to try, as Rorty does, to eradicate it from a minor discourse, but rather to analyze it, to think about the ways in which its manifestations act to increase pain, as well to imagine how it might be redirected toward better ends. All of this requires a vocabulary that refuses the temptation to keep pragmatism pure, that knows, in other words, how to talk about the ineffable.

NOTES

1. The first reference is to be found in *Essays on Heidegger and Others: Philosophical Papers, Volume 2* (Cambridge: Cambridge University Press, 1991), 4; the second reference is to "Wittgenstein Reads Freud: the Myth of the Unconscious," *New York Times Book Review* (Sun., Sept. 22, 1996): 42, col. 2.

2. Richard Rorty, "Freud, Morality, and Hermeneutics," *New Literary History* (1980): 177–185; 177.

3. See Žižek, *The Metastases of Enjoyment: Six Essays on Woman and Causality* (London: Verso, 1994), 30–33.

4. *Contingency, Irony, and Solidarity* (Cambridge: Cambridge University Press, 1989), 39.

5. Quoted in Charles Hanly, *The Problem of Truth in Applied Psychoanalysis* (London: The Guilford Press, 1992), 18. Hanly's agenda is to secure a correspondence theory of truth for psychoanalysis. I agree with Rorty against Hanly in thinking that psychoanalysis helps transcend the philosophical pseudoproblems of realism vs. antirealism and coherence vs. correspondence. The only difference is that I think Lacan is a better ally in this matter than Freud is.

6. The use of "pure" here and in the title is a reference to Rorty's criticism of philosophers' tendency always to seek purer methodologies and thereby arrive ever closer to the truth. See *Consequences of Pragmatism* (Minneapolis: University of Minnesota Press, 1982), 19. Although I do not wish to imply that Rorty believes one form of pragmatism comes closer to the truth than any other, I am suggesting throughout this paper that he has fallen prey to the temptation of another kind of purity, a purity produced by erasing as many distinctions as possible, sometimes before their usefulness has been exhausted. Thomas McCarthy also notices this tendency, calling it "Rorty's all-or-nothing approach to philosophy." See "An Exchange on Truth, Freedom, and Politics II: Ironist Theory as a Vocation: A Response to Rorty's Reply," *Critical Inquiry* 16 (Spring 1990): 644–55; 644.

7. *Essays on Hedeigger*, 49.

8. See Rorty, *Philosophy and the Mirror of Nature* (Princeton, N.J.: Princeton University Press, 1979), his polemic against dualism and representationalism.

9. See, for example, *Écrits* (Paris: Seuil, 1966), 856, where he identifies what he calls the subject of science with the historical period inaugurated by Descartes's *cogito*. See also Jonathan Scott Lee, *Jacques Lacan* (Cambridge, Mass.: MIT Press, 1990), 146.

10. *Écrits*, 517. Unless otherwise indicated, all translations are mine.

11. This is a simplification, as the subject at all times inhabits all three dimensions: real, imaginary, and symbolic. The point of this stipulation is to stress that the imaginary/real distinction is not one between what we perceive and what is really out there, but rather between the world of our conscious perception and that of our desire.

This distinction is developed in great detail in *Le séminaire. VII. L'Éthique de la psychanalyse* (Paris: Seuil, 1986).

12. The reference is to Strawson's "sentence shaped objects," of which Rorty says, "[i]insofar as they are nonconceptualized, they are not isolable as input. But insofar as they are conceptualized, they have been tailored to the needs of a *particular* input-output function, a *particular* convention of representation." *Truth and Progress: Philosophical Papers, Volume 3* (Cambridge: Cambridge University Press, 1998), 36. Another way of putting this is to say that in "a wider sense of 'social construction,' everything, including giraffes and molecules, is socially constructed, for no vocabulary (e.g., that of zoology or physics) cuts reality at the joints. Reality has no joints. It just has descriptions—some more socially useful than others." Ibid., 83.

13. *Essays on Heidegger*, 51.

14. Ibid., 57.

15. *Truth and Progress*, 20.

16. Dennett, *Consciousness Explained* (Boston: Little, Brown, 1991), 364; *Truth and Progress*, 98.

17. The example comes from an episode in Frank Baum's series of books about the land of Oz.

18. *Consequences*, xxxvi.

19. Ibid., 15.

20. Ibid., xxxvi.

21. *Télévision* (Paris: Seuil, 1974).

22. Jonathan Scott Lee also emphasizes the agreement between Lacan and pragmatism on issues of truth and representation, noting that Lacan explicitly rejects representational theories of knowledge in his seminar XI. See Lee, 154–55; Lacan, *Le séminaire XI. Les quatre concepts fondamentaux de la psychanalyse* (Paris: Éditions du Seuil, 1973), 201.

23. *Truth and Progress*, 111.

24. Ibid., 104.

25. Wilfrid Sellars, "Empiricism and the Philosophy of Mind," *Science, Perception and Reality* (London: Routledge, 1963), sec. 29; quoted in *Truth and Progress*, 124.

26. Ibid.

27. Hilary Putnam, *Realism with a Human Face* (Cambridge, Mass.: Harvard University Press, 1990), 20; quoted in *Truth and Progress*, 43.

28. Ibid., 48.

29. This metaphor (simile, in this case), which inaugurated Lacan's combination of structural linguistics and psychoanalysis, is actually of the kind that Rorty would

usually admire, because it initiated new possibilities of thought on the basis of an utterance that at first glance seemed absurd. See my discussion of metaphor below.

30. *Essays on Heidegger*, 4.

31. Ibid.

32. Noam Chomsky, *Language and Thought* (Wakefield, Rhode Island & London: Moyer Bell, 1993), 36.

33. *Essays on Heidegger*, 54. Rorty makes this point himself about that aspect of language he calls our final vocabularies: ". . . we do not *construct* final vocabularies. They are always already there. We find ourselves thrown into them. Final vocabularies are not tools, for we cannot specify the *purpose* of a final vocabulary without futilely twisting around inside the circle of that final vocabulary." Ibid., 38. Which is to say that at least some aspect of language, our final vocabularies, *is* unique, because we can describe pretty much everything else without twisting around in it. Rorty might add that the same thing can be said of "thought" or "brains" or "neurons." I agree, but I don't see how this is an objection to the statement that there might be something philosophically interesting to say about language.

34. *Truth and Progress*, 107.

35. Jacques Lacan, "Desire and the Interpretation of Desire in Hamlet," in *Yale French Studies* 55/56 (1977): 11–52, 25; an excerpt from the unpublished Seminar VI on *Le désir et son interprétation*.

36. *Truth and Progress*, 224.

37. See, for example, Slavoj Žižek, *Looking Awry: An Introduction to Jacques Lacan through Popular Culture* (Cambridge, Mass.: The MIT Press, 1991), 147–154, and *For They Know Not What They Do: Enjoyment as a Political Factor* (London: Verso, 1991) passim.

38. *Essays on Heidegger*, 46.

39. *Tractatus Logico-Philosophicus*, trans. D. F. Pears and B. F. McGuiness (London: Routledge and Kegan Paul, 1961), forward; quoted in *Essays on Heidegger*, 57.

40. Ibid., 58.

41. This phrase comes from Emmanuel Levinas, *Totality and Infinity: An Essay on Exteriority*, trans. Alphonso Lingis (Pittsburgh, Pa.: Duquesne University Press, 1969).

42. See *The Plague of Fantasies* (London: Verso, 1997), 50, for only the most recent example.

43. The ahistoricism of this account can made perfectly compatible with the pragmatist historicism that I share with Rorty by saying, on the one hand, that the statement "all human beings partake of metaphysical desire" implies merely that metaphysical desire is central to my (historically situated) definition of a human being and, on the other, that one can make any pronouncement one wants without thereby

assuming that the vocabulary one is using would be valid or comprehensible for all times.

44. *Truth and Progress*, 77.

45. Rorty denies that there "is something called 'philosophy' or 'metaphysics' which is central to our culture and which has been radiating evil influences outward," (*Essays on Heidegger*, 104), a view he attributes to Derrida. But my point is that metaphysical thought does exist (evidence: Rorty's own polemic against it), and that it can be understood as a symptom or manifestation of a more generalized "way people think about the world." Rorty later admits "that this claim has some plausibility" and comes up with some evidence of his own for it. See "An Exchange on Truth, Freedom, and Politics I: Truth and Freedom: A Reply to Thomas McCarthy," *Critical Inquiry* 16 (Spring 1990): 633–643; 636. Thomas McCarthy makes a similar claim to mine in "Private Irony and Public Decency: Richard Rorty's New Pragmatism," *Critical Inquiry* 16 (Winter 1990): 355–70; 360: ". . . whatever the sources, our ordinary, nonphilosophical truth-talk and reality-talk is shot through with just the sorts of idealizations that Rorty wants to purge."

46. *Truth and Progress*, 109.

47. *Essays on Heidegger*, 59.

48. Rorty has asked me whether psychoanalysis explains metaphysical desire, or whether it just renames it. My feeling is that if renaming a phenomenon allows one to think of it in a different way, and to make connections between it and other phenomena with which it wasn't connected before, this is explanation.

49. *Truth and Progress*, 196.

50. Ibid., 206.

51. *Contingency*, 64.

52. Ibid., 91.

53. *Truth and Progress*, 203.

54. Ibid., 214.

55. Rorty, *Objectivity, Relativism, and Truth: Philosophical Papers, Volume 1* (Cambridge: Cambridge University Press, 1991), 93.

56. *Truth and Progress*, 213.

57. *Essays on Heidegger*, 12.

58. Ibid., 13.

59. *Objectivity*, 164.

60. Ibid., 168.

61. "On Davidson's view . . . 'live' metaphors can justify belief only in the same metaphorical sense in which one may 'justify' a belief not by citing another belief but

by using a non-sentence to stimulate one's interlocutor's sense organs—hoping thereby to cause assent to a sentence." *Objectivity*, 169.

62. "[N]either knowledge nor morality will flourish unless somebody uses language for purposes other than making predictable moves in currently popular language-games" (Ibid., 169); and, ". . . metaphor is an essential instrument in the process of reweaving our beliefs and desires, without it, there would be no such thing as a scientific revolution or cultural breakthrough, but merely the process of altering the truth values of statements formulated in a forever unchanging vocabulary" (Ibid., 124).

63. Lacan develops his theory of the function of metaphor and metonymy in the unconscious in his "L'instance de la lettre dans l'inconscient ou la raison depuis Freud," in *Écrits*, 493–530. See, in particular 508: "one sees that metaphor is placed at the precise point where sense is produced in non-sense" and 515, for the relation between metonymy and metaphor in more detail. My interpretation, while tailored for greater commensurability with Davidson's theory, nevertheless also owes a great deal to J. D. Nasio's *Enseignement de Sept Concepts Cruciaux de la Psychanalyse* (Paris: Éditions Rivages, 1988). See 240 for his explanation of the association of metaphor with S1, the meaningless master signifier whose authority supports all knowledge.

64. This function is explained in "Subversion du sujet et dialectique du désir dans l'inconscient freudien," in *Écrits*, 798–828. Žižek's commentary throughout chapter 3 of *Sublime Object of Ideology* (London: Verso, 1989) is extremely useful.

65. It is certainly reasonable to dispute Lacan's use of this term, which ultimately seems to have little to do with the poetic device of the same name. The point to infer from his metaphorical appropriation of "metonymy" is that when words are used normally they may be understood to lie adjacent to one another in a chain, what structural linguistics refers to as the syntagm. This "metonymy" of words linked together in a signifying chain becomes itself Lacan's principal metaphor for desire because of the movement or sliding along the chain that occurs as we produce or listen to language, a sliding in which the meaning of the present word always hangs on the next, and so on.

66. The former Lacan refers to as S2, or knowledge, the latter as S1, or the master signifier (see note 63).

67. For the diachronic and synchronic effects of *les points de capiton*, and their identity with metaphor, see *Écrits*, 805.

68. *Consequences*, 158.

69. *Contingency*, xv.

70. This is actually my extrapolation. Rorty explicitly denies the usefulness of the ironist intellectual at times, saying that ironist theory is "at best useless and at worst dangerous" (*Contingency*, 68) to the quest for social justice. But his ambivalence on this issue is demonstrated by his belief, expressed at other times, that the ironist is needed to construct new vocabularies, as I indicated in the section on progress above.

71. Ibid., 87.

72. Ibid., 65.

73. Rorty's response to this rhetorical question is an emphatic "Yes!"

74. McCarthy also touches on this criticism in "Private Irony and Public Decency," 365. Later, in his reply to Rorty's reply, he asks a similar series of questions to mine, a series intended, like mine, as a *reductio* of Rorty's position. See "An Exchange on Truth, Freedom, and Politics II," 650.

75. *Contingency*, 37.

76. Ibid.

77. Ibid., 30.

78. Ibid., 34.

79. *Essays on Heidegger*, 162.

80. *Contingency*, 190.

81. Ibid., 73.

82. When Orthodox Jews in Israel band together and throw feces at conservatives and women trying to pray at the Wall, they are not driven to do so by an "agreement concerning fundamental beliefs and desires," but rather by the feelings of "enjoyment" that accompany striking a blow in God's name.

83. See his essay, *Achieving Our Country* (Cambridge, Mass.: Harvard University Press, 1998).

84. The source of this analysis is, of course, Žižek's *Sublime Object*, chapter 3, "Identification"; *passim*; although the theme is touched on in all of his books.

85. *Truth and Progress*, 322.

86. *Contingency*, 198.

87. Ibid., 90.

88. "On Truth, Freedom and Politics I," 637.

89. Žižek himself discusses Rorty's public/private split, in *Looking Awry*, 157–60. There he argues that the "very social law that, as a kind of neutral set of rules, should limit our aesthetic self-creation and deprive us a part of our enjoyment on behalf of solidarity, is always already penetrated by an obscene, 'pathological,' surplus enjoyment." Žižek's critique of Rorty is that he seems to be positing the possibility of a "universal social law not smudged by a 'pathological' stain of enjoyment" (160). But I don't see how this can be the case, given that Rorty (unlike Žižek) doesn't believe in anything "universal," much less a social law. In fact, while his language differs greatly from Žižek's flamboyantly "continental" psychoanalese, Rorty would probably agree completely with the notion that the fantasies or vocabularies that hold communities together are run through with particular libidinal investments. He just would refuse to derive from this the belief that therefore it makes no sense to strive

for solidarity. Where the two viewpoints should naturally meet would be an acknowledgment of the importance of an analysis of such libidinal investments for the establishment of local solidarities. For a discussion of Žižek's particular brand of universalism, see my "On Relativism, Rights, and Differends, or, Ethics and the American Holocaust," *Qui Parle* 9, no.1 (1995): 33–70.

90. "If one starts off from the view that freedom is the recognition of contingency rather than of the existence of a specifically human realm exempt from natural necessity, one will be more dubious about the social utility of philosophy than Habermas is." *Truth and Progress*, 326.

11

~

JOSEPH MARGOLIS

Cartesian Realism and the Revival of Pragmatism

I

Richard Rorty is widely credited with having revived pragmatism's sagging fortunes. And so he has. But it is hardly clear, whether what Rorty revived, beginning with *Consequences of Pragmatism* (1982), *is* indeed the recovery of pragmatism proper. Certainly, he has earned the pragmatist badge through sheer exuberance and drive and the inventive continuity he's forged between his views and the classic pragmatists'; but the connection seems to owe as much to a kind of squatter's rights and the skillful use of the *obiter dictum* as to any compelling, fresh version of a pragmatist argument or canon. Think, for instance, of Rorty's mistaken disjunction between the public and the private, offered as genuinely Deweyan[1]; or Rorty's deliberate deformation of Dewey in Heidegger's direction and Heidegger in Dewey's[2]; or, possibly even more puzzling, the flat-out reversal of the intent of William James's original theory of truth.

Rorty says straight out, in the Introduction to *Consequences of Pragmatism*: "The essays in this book are attempts to draw consequences from a pragmatist theory about truth. This theory says that truth is not the sort of thing one should expect to have a philosophically interesting theory about."[3] Informed readers will protest: "Whatever you make of the misunderstanding

223

between James and Peirce, James surely believed his theory of truth *was* the
most important conceptual plank in the whole of pragmatism." One may also
react to that reaction: "Well, Rorty never meant to dismiss James's theory, he
hardly thought it was pointless or misguided; he meant rather to salvage its
essential lesson!" But if you say that, you must ask yourself whether Rorty's
theory about theories of truth, especially James's, *is* sufficiently like James's
theory to count as an extension of it—hence, as an extension of pragmatism—or rather a clever subversion of James's doctrine. And then we'd be off
to the races.

My own sense is that, without Rorty's wide-ranging discussion of the
classic pragmatists, Dewey chiefly, there would never have been a revival at
all. After all, pragmatism was moribund by the end of the '40s. Even so, the
sense in which pragmatism has gained a second life may depend more on the
free-wheeling dispute that arose between Rorty and Hilary Putnam, which
began in the '70s before the publication of *Consequences*, than to any particular
thesis of Rorty's. The energy of those running debates effectively defined the
significance of the American revival—or, better, defined pragmatism's rein-
vention, which is now neither Rorty's nor Putnam's creation. Questions about
what pragmatism now means cannot possibly be answered in textual terms,
but neither are those questions pointless. Both Rorty and Putnam do exhibit
pragmatist loyalties, I concede, although neither can be said to have recovered
the force of any particular tenet favored by the original pragmatists.

Rorty and Putnam rather nicely feature (between them) a number of the
essential quarrels of our own time, which they designate (not altogether plausibly) as a debate about the nerve of pragmatism itself. They also define an
opportunistic space in which additional options opposing their own contest and
their own opposed doctrines suggest themselves and invite comparisons with
pragmatism's past. In any case, the pragmatist revival is the invention of a
substantially new confrontation drawn from the saliencies of our own time that
claim a measure of congruity with pragmatism's original "spirit"—not, however,
by adhering closely to any explicit pragmatist doctrine or program.

To see this is to see how little we may care to invest in terminological
quarrels. But it would be a blunder to ignore altogether the question of what
now to count as the essential pragmatist issue. There's a great deal of power
compressed in controlling the name—and, as a consequence, influence in
affecting the perceived validity of opposing arguments. The trick is to find a
strategy that can command a measure of attention collected at an unlikely
point of entry that might force an honest reckoning. I suggest beginning with
Rorty's account of his own attempt to present Donald Davidson's theory of
truth in a fair light, his candid report about Davidson's opposing his own
summary view, and his interpretation of what Davidson's rebuff signifies. I
doubt you will find a more perspicuous way of entering the heart of late
American philosophy or late pragmatism.

Here is what Rorty says about Davidson:

> In an article on Donald Davidson published in 1986 [Rorty's "Pragmatism, Davidson and Truth"[4]], I suggested that we interpret Davidson both as a sort of pragmatist and as a sort of minimalist—as someone who, like James, thought that there was less to say about truth than philosophers had believed. More specifically, I interpreted Davidson as saying that the word "true" has no explanatory use, but merely a disquotational use, a commending use, and what I called a "cautionary" use . . . . In an article of 1990,[5] Davidson partially repudiated my interpretation. He said that he should be considered neither a deflationist nor a disquotationalist. He defined "deflationism" as the view that "Tarski's work embraces all of truth's essential features" and said that I was mistaken in attributing this view to him on the basis of his eschewal of attempts to define "true" for variable L [designating one or another language] as opposed to defining "true-in-L" for particular values of L. [He] concluded that "[t]he concept of truth has essential connections with the concepts of belief and meaning, but these connections are untouched by Tarski's work."[6]

Davidson does indeed insist, contrary to what Rorty says, that truth has a distinct but dependent role in explanation. It's also true, as Rorty correctly reports, that Davidson's theory of the explanation of true belief remains thoroughly causal. The details need not concern us here.[7] But *that* hardly justifies Rorty's conclusion that "what Davidson adds to Tarski, when he displays the connections between the concept of truth and those of meaning and belief, has nothing whatever to do with the question of whether, or how, we can tell when a belief is true."[8] (This was meant to vindicate Rorty's saying that Davidson has only "partially repudiated" his interpretation.)

All Davidson actually says is this: that, regarding "certain familiar attempts to characterize truth," "[w]e should not say that truth is correspondence, coherence, warranted assertibility, ideally justified assertibility, what is accepted in the conversation of the right people, what science will end up maintaining, what explains the convergence on single theories in science, or the sources of our ordinary beliefs. To the extent that realism or anti-realism depend[s] on one or another of these views of truth we should [Davidson concludes] refuse to endorse either."[9] Very few would disagree with Davidson's judgment here, but it hardly entails truth not having any explanatory power (if that is what Davidson means) or not having any conceptual bearing on explanation (which is what Rorty means).

Certainly, it does not bear on James's distinctive claim (unless to reject it) or on what might be made of Davidson's claim read in James's way (which, of course, would violate Davidson's purely causal reading). It is not clear that Davidson could convincingly reconcile the different parts of his own theory. Even Tarski's account, which Davidson claims to espouse, has more than merely "semantic" force: it's plainly committed to a strong extensionalism *wherever it applies*—hence, it applies in epistemic rather than merely causal terms. Or, wherever Davidson actually invokes Tarski's model without relying on Tarski's own extensional analysis preparatory to truth-value assignment, Davidson's appropriation comes to little more than a vacuous version of the correspondence doctrine he himself opposes. (Tarski, of course, made a point of acknowledging the recalcitrance of natural-language sentences vis-à-vis the fruitful application of his conditions of analysis: that cannot be confined to an exercise in formal semantics alone; it is already implicitly epistemological in import.)[10]

As far as I can see—as far as Davidson succeeds in defending his own view—we ought not support any of the doctrines mentioned *if* they are thought to function criterially or in some cognitive or evidentiary way apt for justifying (and therefore explaining) why this or that belief about the ("independent") world is true. Davidson says nothing against the legitimacy of explaining why we *take* this or that belief to be true (on, say, a causal theory of belief and meaning and the conditions for assigning "true" and "false" in cognitive contexts): he "merely" opposes building an indubitably realist or antirealist force into the ordinary use of "true." I should say he was opposing what, in accord with his own view, may be called Cartesianism or skepticism.

On the substantive issue, that is what he intends: presumably, we can, by way of the causal theory of belief, explain why we treat particular beliefs as true. I am not convinced that a causal theory of truth could ever work; it would always require epistemic standing that it could never secure (or reduce in causal terms). Certainly, it goes beyond what Rorty reports Davidson as holding. Hence, when Rorty suggests that *we* should treat Davidson as a "pragmatist"—in the same way in which he (Rorty) treats James as a pragmatist—he gets both wildly wrong. I draw your attention to the improbable fact that, in recent writings, Rorty simply announces the following: "As I shall be using the term 'pragmatism', the paradigmatic pragmatists are John Dewey and Donald Davidson."[11] Dewey, of course, shared (in fact, improved) the main theme of James's theory of truth. There is no other explicit thread in Davidson's account of realism that could support Rorty's attribution, except his opposition to any criterial recovery of Cartesianism. But that would hardly distinguish Davidson from an army of philosophers who would not qualify as pragmatists.

If, intending to avoid any cognitivist reading of correspondentism and representationalism, James had offered his own pragmatist theory of truth to replace such views, he would still have intended to advance his theory in an explanatory way; but, if so, then anyone—Rorty, say—who offered an account of "true" in which truth had no explanatory function at all would have drastically distorted what we should rightly understand to be a revivified pragmatism. For, surely, if Rorty ever lost Davidson's support, he would have no grounds at all for insisting that "true" had no explanatory role to play—or for claiming that he himself was improving pragmatism's lot! At the very least, Rorty would have to explain the conceptual link between belief and meaning and truth (which, of course, Davidson undertakes to do); whereas Rorty, speaking as a postmodernist, simply holds that there is nothing there to know.

In fact, nothing would remain of James's pragmatism if it were denied that James had advanced a theory of truth that was meant to identify the key considerations in virtue of which beliefs are judged to be true. The fact that James was an innocent in his attempt (in *Pragmatism*) to give suitable form to his intuitions about truth is neither here nor there. What *is* extraordinary is that James should have hit on a fundamental element in pragmatism's theory of inquiry that was plainly within Peirce's grasp, but which simply eluded Peirce because of the latter's more ambitious vision. But Rorty cannot dismantle James's theory without dismissing James's standing as a pragmatist or without explaining how his doing so affects his analysis of Dewey. He fails to address these concerns.

What Rorty says in summarizing Davidson is also murky: he equates pragmatism with "naturalism" and construes both in a very thin postmodernist (or "postphilosophical") way. But Davidson is unwilling to tag along, and it's a fair question to ask whether pragmatism can, or should, be viewed as hospitable to the naturalist's claim. I think it should not. At times, the benefits of redefining pragmatism are stretched beyond all plausibility.

II

This piece of gossip, then, *is* philosophically worthwhile. It defines the most strategic question confronting American philosophy at the end of the twentieth century, hence also the best prospects for a redefinition of pragmatism if it is to proceed by way of its recent habit of conceptual piracy: the question, namely, what we should understand by the compatibility or irreconcilable contest between pragmatism and naturalizing—and, further afield, between pragmatism or naturalism and Rorty's brand of postmodernism. As it turns out, the larger question is more than a local matter; rightly interpreted, it is the American version of the most pointed question that now confronts the whole of Western philosophy. The quarrel between Rorty and Putnam is, then, another tribute to the cunning of Reason.

There is a single reference to Rorty in Putnam's influential little book *Reason, Truth and History*, which appeared a year before Rorty's *Consequences of Pragmtism* and which defined Putnam's "internal realism" (now abandoned or put at risk in a way that is not yet entirely legible[12])—which was, in effect, Putnam's candidate for adjusting pragmatism so that it might meet the most up-to-date puzzles of analytic philosophy. Putnam fastened quite explicitly on what he took to be risked in the way of pragmatism, realism, analytic philosophy, and philosophy in general as a result of Rorty's postmodernism (which Putnam read as a form of relativism, hence as incoherent).

In the last two paragraphs of *Reason*, Putnam emphasizes that answers to questions about "a more rational *conception* of rationality or a better *conception* of morality" (or even a better *conception* of truth) cannot proceed solipsistically, that such questions invite us instead "to engage in a truly human dialogue; one which combines collectivity with individual responsibility."[13] This may strike you as rather vague. I read it as indicating the sense in which both Putnam and Rorty favor very thin forms of the Hegelian theme that appears in Dewey and James and the later Wittgenstein; also, as anticipating Putnam's acknowledged sympathy for Jürgen Habermas's "dialogic" theme.[14] What the remark is meant to capture—the theme of the book's last chapter—is the "entanglement" of questions of objective fact and objective value that lie at the heart of Putnam's pragmatism, in particular his opposition to absolutism and Cartesianism, and his attack on relativism.[15]

The deeper significance of the vagueness noted comes out in the final paragraph of the book, which Rorty picked up very promptly and which, as I say, defines the contest between their two interpretations of pragmatism and realism—defines the very revival of pragmatism. Here is what Putnam says:

> Does this dialogue [referring to what has been just reported] have an ideal terminus? Is there a *true* conception of rationality, a *true* morality, even if all *we* ever have are our *conceptions* of these? Here philosophers divide, like everyone else. Richard Rorty, in his Presidential Address to the American Philosophical Association [1979], opted strongly for the view that there is only the dialogue; no ideal end can be posited or should be needed. But how does the assertion that "there is only the dialogue" differ from a self-refuting relativism . . . ? The very fact that we speak of our different conceptions as different conceptions of *rationality* posits a *Grenzbegriff*, a limit-concept of the ideal truth.[16]

This cannot be right and cannot even be defended on the grounds Putnam provides. It was entirely reasonable for Rorty to challenge Putnam's remark about his own remark ("only the dialogue") and Putnam's preoccupation with his would-be *Grenzbegriff*. "I would suggest," Rorty says, "that Putnam here, at the end of the day, slides back into the scientism he rightly condemns in others." "[W]hat is such a posit supposed to do, except to say that from God's point of view the human race is heading in the right direction?"[17]

You see, of course, how these questions implicate Davidson's rebuff of Rorty's postmodernism, also the warning's application to Putnam. For Davidson's resistance on the matter of truth entails the verdict that anything like a "limit-concept" would instantly generate Cartesian skepticism (a remark Putnam found puzzling).[18] Putnam and Rorty's running quarrel has become the very paradigm of the evolving effort to redefine pragmatism as well as the evidence that both Putnam and Rorty must fail; it has become a sign of the need for a more plausible reading of pragmatism's recovery.

The story runs as follows. Putnam believes that the loss of the *Grenzbegriff* of truth (or rationality), which would have followed from Rorty's postmodernism ("only the dialogue"), leads directly to an incoherent relativism. Rorty believes that insisting on the *Grenzbegriff* constitutes a form of scientism (or Cartesianism), which Putnam himself had rightly inveighed against. Putnam's objection does, indeed, betray his conflicting views and is ultimately self-defeating (as Rorty realized): "That rationality is defined by an ideal computer program [Putnam muses] is a scientistic theory inspired by the exact sciences; that it is simply defined by the local cultural norms is a scientific theory inspired by anthropology."[19] The first option answers to the extremes of positivism; the second, to the extremes of relativism. Yet, though he means to escape between these two horns, Putnam provides no third option accessible from his vantage. In fact, the only possible option would *require giving up all* Grenzbegriffe *and adopting a constructive realism instead* (which, I remind you, need not, as Davidson supposed, entail an unacceptable idealism). In any case, we cannot make sense of a regulative *Grenzbegriff* that has epistemic force that is not also constitutive of knowledge.

I cannot be certain of Putnam's train of thought. But I would be willing to bet that—after judging Habermas's "pragmatized" version of Karl-Otto Apel's *Grenzbegriff* to be congenial (in rational ethics) and reasonably in accord with the fact/value "entanglement"—Putnam was strengthened in his belief that there *should* be a pragmatized *Grenzbegriff* for truth as well. That is hardly an argument,[20] but it does explain Putnam's strong attraction to James. In fact, pragmatism could not possibly claim to have found a *Grenzbegriff* in practical or theoretical reasoning. He opposes *Grenzbegriffe* in either context: Apel and Habermas failed to notice that. Davidson seems to have believed that both Rorty's thesis about truth *and* Putnam's thesis about his *Grenzbegriff* would lead inexorably to skepticism: Rorty's, because it gives up important parts of fundamental philosophy; Putnam's, because it falls back to Cartesianism itself. Davidson has a point, though, for his part, Putnam is aware that Davidson slights the need to answer the epistemological question that realism poses.

I am not familiar with any sustained analysis of Davidson's version of realism from Putnam's point of view, except for brief remarks like those that appear in Putnam's *Pragmatism* (or what may be inferred from what McDowell offers[21]). But what Davidson says of his own position seems congruent with what Putnam says or might have said of it: "My form of realism [Davidson says] seems to be neither Hilary Putnam's internal realism nor his metaphysical realism. It is not internal realism because internal realism makes truth relative to a scheme, and this is an idea I do not think is intelligible . . . . But my realism is certainly not Putnam's metaphysical realism, for *it* is characterized by being 'radically non-epistemic', which implies that all our best researched and established thoughts and theories may be false."[22]

If I understand this correctly, then Putnam's objection to Davidson— which I must reconstruct from scattered remarks—would go this way: (1) although Davidson's realism has "epistemic" import, it lacks an "epistemological" rationale by which to legitimate true beliefs; and (2) Davidson's adherence here to causal explanation entails his failure to admit anything like a *Grenzbegriff* and, as a result, his failure to obviate relativism or (for that matter) arbitrariness. I think thesis (1) is justified but not (2), because Davidson and Rorty are right in thinking that Putnam's maneuver commits him to "Cartesianism" (hence, to skepticism). But if that is so, then the *only* way to secure a realism without paradox must be by means of a frank constructivism (a constructive realism), which of course neither Davidson nor Rorty would countenance.

There are also a number of difficulties Putnam raises against Davidson's realism. For one, the causal theory of belief, which favors, holistically, coherentist criteria of reliable belief, cannot help us with the determinate causes of particular true beliefs. (Think, for instance, of analogues of paranoid coherence.) Second, if the holism is to be parsed as if by "an omniscient interpreter," then the legitimative problem will return with a vengeance and will require a Cartesian resolution. (Think of Putnam's *Grenzbegriff*!) Finally, Putnam adds: "But the real worry is that *sentences cannot be true or false of an external reality if there are no justificatory connections between things we say in language and any aspects of that reality whatsoever*."[23] All three objections are compelling—and the third is surely a *reductio*.

The upshot of the entire exchange confirms that none of our three discussants—two who are self-styled pragmatists and one who is not a pragmatist at all—could possibly secure his own best doctrines against the objections of one or the other of the other two. Davidson clearly signals that Rorty probably misrepresents both James and Dewey (who is close to James on the matter of truth) and that neither James nor Dewey gets the matter right.[24] Putnam retreats to internal realism to overcome the threat of Cartesian realism but is forced back to Cartesianism by way of his *Grenzbegriff*. Rorty abandons "objectivity" for "ethnocentric solidarity," believing he can secure as much of commonsense realism (and of Davidsonian naturalism) as he wants; but he ends up with an arbitrary and vacant postmodernism. And Davidson finds that, to avoid the untenable options of Cartesianism that keep surfacing at every turn, he must abandon the pretense of having secured a defensible realism.[25]

III

Theorists like Davidson are too wedded to the notion of an objective science that knows the "mind-independent" world more or less directly. They therefore repudiate in advance all alleged interpretive *tertia*, the supposed intervention of conceptual schemes between ourselves and the world, relative to which (they fear) realism might be legitimated at too high a price. They themselves pay a price for relying on the supposedly higher rigors of "naturalism," which Rorty promptly equates with pragmatism.[26]

Davidson's formula seems straightforward: "Since we can't swear intermediaries to truthfulness, we should [he says] allow no intermediaries between our beliefs and their objects in the world. Of course there are causal intermediaries. What we must guard against are epistemic intermediaries."[27] Regarding the connection between realism and truth, *a fortiori* the question of knowledge, this simply means that "naturalism" is best served by causal explanation. Davidson does not actually affirm that naturalism avoids noncausal theories of any kind. Recall Tarski's theory of truth, in accounting for the realist standing of our sciences. Apart from advising us to avoid interpretive "intermediaries" (*tertia*, in Rorty's idiom), Davidson explicitly says that naturalism is constrained by the search for "a *reason* for supposing most of our beliefs are true that is not a form of *evidence*."[28]

The avoidance of "intermediaries" is supposed to preclude any taint of idealism, but the argument is muddy. If, on the one hand, we are talking about a world we can actually know—an "intelligible" rather than a "noumenal" world—then merely coming to know the world cannot meaningfully entail the offending doctrine (idealism)—for, of course, every realism would instantly become an idealism. In that case, "intermediaries" would make no difference. On the other hand, if we are talking about knowing an "independent" world—a world that, though known, remained unaltered by the effects of its merely being known—then, unless we were entitled to claim privileged access to that world, we could never argue convincingly that "interpretive intermediaries" (or *tertia*) did not affect the realism that we actually espouse. In that case, "intermediaries" of some kind would be unavoidable. But, of course, it remains entirely possible to abandon epistemic intermediaries that either force us to conclude that the "real" world is somehow "constituted" by the mind or is somehow known only through private mental states whose

evidentiary standing entails their being externally related to whatever part of
the independent world we claim to know. Davidson seems to be caught in a
trap of his own devising. In short, even a causal explanation of realist beliefs
would (if it worked) *be* an explanation of James's sort!

For his part, Rorty offers the following summary of what he means by
"pragmatism," what he takes Davidson to mean by "naturalism," and why, as
a consequence, he concludes that "Davidson and James are both pragmatists":

(1) "True" has no explanatory uses.
(2) We understand all there is to know about the relation of
     beliefs to the world when we understand their causal rela-
     tions with the world; our knowledge of how to apply terms
     such as "about" and "true of" is fallout from a "naturalistic"
     account of linguistic behavior.
(3) There are no relations of "being made true" which hold be-
     tween beliefs and the world.
(4) There is no point to debates between realism and anti-real-
     ism, for such debates presuppose the empty and misleading
     idea of beliefs "being made true."[29]

The most distinctive feature of Rorty's account is its uncompromising
commitment to doctrines more extreme than anything Davidson offers.
Davidson himself corrects doctrine (1), you remember. Because of its unyield-
ing assurance, doctrine (2) can hardly be read as anything but a Cartesian
formulation. And doctrines (3) and (4) oppose *tertia* because they violate the
naturalizing rigors of (1) and (2). It is odd that, as a know-nothing champion
of postmodernism, Rorty champions an unusually extreme form of naturalism. But, in doing that, he simply dismisses all the telling questions—as
Putnam has shown.

For his part, Putnam is flatly inconsistent; there's no gainsaying that. In
advancing his internal realism, he is aware that there cannot be "'a point at
which' subjectivity ceases and Objectivity-with-a-capital-O begins."[30] Nevertheless, fearful of the self-refuting relativism he believes he finds in Rorty's
"ethnocentric solidarity," he finds himself obliged to invoke his *Grenzbegriff*
without explicit Cartesian assurances—which presents an even weaker case
than the Cartesian claim. For in cognitive matters there cannot be a regulative norm that is not also constitutively grounded in our evidentiary powers.
It is impossible, therefore, to validate Putnam's realism any more effectively
than Davidson's or Rorty's naturalizing. Alternatively put, Putnam's theory is
hopelessly inconsistent with his own "internal realism."

Putnam is searching for an assurance of objective knowledge about an
"independent" world on grounds that are blind to the difference between the
subjective and the objective, whereas Davidson is searching for an assurance

of the objective truth of our beliefs about an "independent" world without regard to any evidentiary considerations applied to those beliefs. I take all three of our discussants to be Cartesian pawns despite their efforts to escape.

I remind you that these quarrels were aired at the end of the twentieth century! They belong by rights to the seventeenth and eighteenth centuries—with very slight adjustments. There is nothing in them that the pre-Kantians could not have envisaged. We have evidently not yet cast off the paralyzing assumptions of the Cartesian vision. In the Anglo-American world, it is of course the classic pragmatists who were the most promising opponents of Cartesianism running from the mid-nineteenth century to the middle of the twentieth. Now, in their "revival," what we find is a considerable muddle: effectively, a very large part of English-language philosophy, whether pragmatist or naturalist (or an amalgam of the two), turns out to be bent on pursuing various ways of converting pragmatism into the sparest form of Cartesianism.

Ever since Fichte and Hegel, continental European philosophy has never entirely lost the master thread of its anti-Cartesian metaphysics and epistemology, although it is apparent that the new American naturalism is making substantial inroads into Germany and France against that discipline. So it is reasonable to suppose the pragmatists' original resolve might be strengthened by daring to experiment selectively with themes drawn from the Hegelian and post-Hegelian tradition: from Marx, say, from Nietzsche, from Dilthey, Heidegger, Horkheimer and Adorno, Gadamer, Wittgenstein, Foucault at least. There is a risk, of course: we must bear in mind that no recent self-styled American pragmatist is more adventurous than Rorty in claiming to join the analytic and the continental; and yet, none is more likely to convert such an effort into a stiffening of Cartesianism itself—or, into a complete postmodernist ("postphilosophical") abdication of the essential philosophical motivation of both pragmatism and naturalism.

One reason theorists working in the pragmatist or naturalist orbit regularly fail to fashion a viable realism that is not a form of Cartesianism is this: nearly all who put their hand to the puzzle construe realism in Cartesian terms. Yet if the original pragmatists succeeded at anything, they succeeded in shaping realist and near-realist options that eluded any Cartesian weakness of the gauge we find in Putnam, Rorty, and Davidson.

So American philosophy has lost ground twice in its slim history: once, in failing to come to terms, in our end-of-century, with the full achievement of the post-Kantians, who first succeeded in exposing and overcoming all the Cartesian traps (meaning, by that, to span the work of Descartes and Kant himself, though Kant of course is the decisive, if equivocal, figure in the formation of modern philosophy's anti-Cartesian programs); and, again, in failing to hold fast, within pragmatism's "revival," to the original pragmatists' inventive simplification (almost invisible after Peirce) of the work of the post-Kantian themselves. It is, of course, true that Cartesian foundationalism and representationalism, as in Locke and Kant, have been largely retired—not entirely and none too soon if, in the European tradition, we bear in mind such figures as Husserl and Apel and closet Kantians like Heidegger; or, in the American tradition, figures like Roderick Chisholm and Wilfrid Sellars and, more surprisingly, Putnam,[31] or even James and Peirce at times. The history is quite confused, you see: small wonder pragmatism has slipped in the Cartesian direction.

What is still more interesting is that recent American philosophy has produced new Cartesian puzzles of its own: witness our exemplars. There will surely be others to be tracked in the same way: predictably, perhaps more fashionably, those drawn to computationalism, superventionism, reductionism, eliminativism, extensionalism, and the subtler varieties of the new naturalism. But it is surely a great gain to have discerned the intention of recent analytic philosophy to continue the Cartesian project as if it were the successor or continuator of pragmatism, particularly in the effort to reunite the strongest currents of Anglo-American and European philosophy closest to the post-Kantian.

I see no prospect of usefully recovering Cartesianism in any of its protean forms. It counts as a complete disaster in its effort to sustain a viable realism, the fatal first stroke at the beginning of the modern age that has deflected us for centuries from coherent alternatives to which we must still return. With hindsight, one may imagine that the alternative to Cartesianism was already incipient in Descartes's day—in, say, Montaigne's skepticism (which was no skepticism at all); for Montaigne did indeed anticipate Descartes's hyperbolic doubt—noted it and rejected it—which must have stiffened Descartes's resolve to affirm his *cogito*).[32] Montaigne is too weak a figure to rely on, of course, but his ruminations run in the right direction and cleave to the humanism of his century at least fifty years before Descartes's windfall.

Descartes's great contribution rests with having oriented the Western world to the primacy of epistemological questions in an effort to confirm an adequate scientific realism. But his own solutions, both the realism and the dualism (which are inseparable), have misled the entire genius of the era that culminates in Kant. The end result is that the double failing of late American philosophy takes on a grander meaning in its own thoroughly confused age.

IV

There is only one conclusion to draw—the single most promising finding to be gained from four centuries of speculation! And that is this: (1) every viable realism must be a constructivism (a constructive realism), in the sense that there can be no principled disjunction between epistemological and metaphysical questions, no neutral analysis of the disjunctive contributions to our science drawn from cognizing subjects and cognized objects; (2) the admission of (1) precludes all necessities *de re* and *de cogitatione*; (3) the admission of (1) and (2) disallows any principled disjunction between realism and idealism, as these are defined in the Cartesian tradition—in effect, confirms the unavoidability of interpretive intermediaries.

I explicitly spell out these consequences redundantly in order to avoid misunderstanding. But you must see that doctrine (1) already entails (2) and (3): for instance, it defeats Kantian constructivism hands down (the constructivism of the *First Critique*) and provides a space for the social constructivism and historicism of the post-Kantian movement, without falling back to idealism. For the *assignment* of what is subjective and objective in realism is itself an artifact internal to reflection in accord with (1)–(3). The entailment does not supply any particular form of realism especially suited to our own temperament: witness Putnam's uneasiness with his own internalism. But that is why the classic pragmatists attract us, if they attract us at all, and that is where the latent Cartesianism of Davidson and company goes entirely astray.

We are, therefore, empowered at the turn of the century to bring philosophy back to lines of speculation that are not self-defeating in the Cartesian way. That is reason enough to redefine pragmatism for our time. In American thought, pragmatism is nearly the only current that has resources enough to validate the philosophical "re-turn." The European tradition houses other currents closer to the original post-Kantian sources. But whether we will finally abandon the old delusion is hard to say: false doctrines die hard. Furthermore, the charm of the American experiment lies with its promising the most focused version of the contest, in promising to combat naturalism. That is no longer a parochial quarrel, but it cannot go forward without gaining a measure of rapprochement with the most congenial European movements.

The foregoing may be put more compendiously. If Cartesian realism were valid—not merely about the "mind-independent" world but about assurances that our cognitive powers could discern that that was so—then the preservation of late American philosophy, that is, the naturalism Davidson and Rorty share and Putnam approaches only because he cleaves, ambiguously, to a more generic Cartesianism, might be honored as a valiant struggle against the bewitchment of the entire post-Kantian dénoument. But the fact remains that it was the post-Kantians, building on Kant's immense advance, who first completely exposed the paradoxes of the Cartesian vision and sketched the minima adequate for its correction.

Furthermore, both the pragmatists and the naturalists of our end-of-century draw back from the classic forms of Cartesianism. It seems hardly to have dawned on them that to give up the classic Cartesian resources was to

give up the prospect of recovering *any* part of Cartesian realism: witness
Davidson and Putnam. But that means that only a constructive realism could
possibly be viable.

In a curious way (a way one might overlook), Putnam is aware that his
rejection of any principled disjunction between the subjective and the objective makes provision for "constructive" choices within the bounds of realism.
But he does not see (apparently) that realism itself must be constructivist all
the way down. As we shall see, that is the element that is missing in Putnam's
turn to (what he now calls) "natural realism," *a fortiori* what is missing in
McDowell's realism, which Putnam now guides himself by. In Putnam, the
constructivist theme leads only to a form of "pluralism" that brooks no chance
for a relativist or incommensurabilist or historicist form of realism itself. (I
shall come back to this before I end this chapter.)

I must take a moment to explain the multiple equivocations on the
term "constructivism" (or "constructive realism"). Both Kant and Hegel are, of
course, constructivists: Kant is a transcendental constructivist, Hegel is not.
Minimally, constructivism signifies that there is no principled disjunction
between metaphysics and epistemology or between cognizing subjects and
cognized objects or between appearances (*Erscheinungen*) and the real world
(call all these variant constructivisms forms of "symbiosis.")

Kant, of course, believes that the "subjective" side of perception and
belief can be exclusively assigned the pure intuitions of space and time and
the categories of the understanding. In that sense, Kant *is* an idealist, for the
objective world that we perceive is, on Kant's theory, actually formed, composed, constituted, "made," by the cognizing mind (the transcendental Ego).
But Hegel is no idealist, for, apart from the formative role of history—which,
in "internalist" terms, is said to affect our concepts—constructivism is confined to the minima mentioned just above. Hegel defeats the strong division
between the ontic and the epistemic in terms of which the "idealist" accusation alone makes sense.

There is no reason to deny that there is an independent world, though
that is not to say that everything that is real *is* uniformly "mind-independent":
certainly, the things of the world of human culture, artworks and machines
for instance—and, I should say, selves—are fully real, exist robustly, but are
hardly "mind-independent."[33] Also, even if we admit the independent world,
that is not to say (agreeing with Davidson) that we *have evidence* for the same;
nor is it to say (contrary to Davidson) that we have *reason* (rather than
evidence) to affirm the same, *if* by that we mean (as Davidson plainly does)
to justify saying that "most of our beliefs are true." Surely, that is the old
Cartesianism under diminished auspices (possibly the obscure equivalent of
epistemic *tertia*). If so, then appropriate answers to metaphysical questions
about what exists in the independent world cannot be independent of our
answers to the matched epistemological questions about our cognitive

competence to know *that*—contrary to what Michael Devitt, for one, has tried to demonstrate.[34]

There is no cognitive way to establish *that* our admitted cognitive powers (perception, for instance) ever discern what there is in the "independent" (noumenal) world. To say that we have "reason" to believe that we know the independent world by perceptual means, but have neither evidence nor reason for believing that this particular belief or that is true, is irretrievably vacuous; and to say, with Davidson, that, nevertheless, we do have reason to believe that "most of our beliefs are true" is to put the cart before the horse—to argue in a completely arbitrary way. Surely, only if we know *to be true* (or have reason to believe we know) a large number of determinate (true) beliefs, could we possibly venture to say that "most of our beliefs are true." That alone would hardly enlarge our knowledge of the world. But it would be to recover the true nerve of Hegel's criticism of Kant: we would be reclaiming two centuries of misplaced history.

Still, it *is* reasonable to hold that we know the independent world and know, as by exercising our perceptual powers, that a great many of our beliefs about the world *are* true! But the "reason" that supports us here is thoroughly "constructive," not a privileged reason, not a Kantian reason, not anything that might vindicate a form of Cartesian realism—*or of naturalism*. That is what Davidson misses. Remember: both Davidson and Rorty insist on eliminating "epistemic intermediaries" (*tertia*); they are prepared to give up the classic Cartesian position, but only because they wrongly suppose they can hold on to *this* part of Cartesianism (which they require) *by other means*. That is the proper lesson of Davidson's, Rorty's, and Putnam's diminished realisms. To speak in the constructivist way is to concede the inseparability of metaphysical and epistemological questions, but it is also to refuse any regulative principle of truth or knowledge. Davidson's and Putnam's theories are but the inseparable halves of the same failed undertaking.

Constructivism holds that the objectivity of our beliefs and claims about the world *is itself a constructive posit* that we impose holistically and without privilege of any kind. It proceeds dialectically as a *faute de mieux* maneuver. Nothing hangs on it "except" these two very modest but all-important gains: (1) that we must (and may) put away every Cartesian longing; and (2) that, admitting (1), we must conclude that the appraisal of every logic, every semantics, every metaphysics and epistemology, proceeds only within the holism of our constructive posit: it never exits from it.

The supposed disjunction between realism and idealism (or between realism and antirealism) is made completely pointless by adopting the least version of post-Kantian symbiosis. Constructivism signifies that the realist standing of all our sciences is an artifact of our symbiotized world, and that alone subverts the naturalist's economy in disallowing "epistemic intermediaries."

I said a moment ago that I was repeating Hegel's criticism of Kant and the pre-Kantians. It's true enough but hard to discern in the prose of Hegel's *Phenomenology*. Let me risk a few lines from the *Phenomenology's* Introduction to confirm Hegel's mastery of the Cartesian *aporia* Descartes and Kant share and the purely verbal difficulty of matching what I have been saying and what Hegel himself says. I won't attempt an exegesis—but I am recovering Hegel's point, if we can find it in Hegel's problematic text:

> It is a natural assumption [Hegel affirms] that in philosophy, before we start to deal with its proper subject-matter, viz. the actual cognition understanding about cognition, what is regarded either as the instrument to get hold of the Absolute, or as the medium through which one discovers it. A certain uneasiness seems justified, partly because there are different types of cognition. . . . This feeling of uneasiness is surely bound to be transformed into the conviction that the whole project of securing for consciousness through cognition what exists in itself is absurd, and that there is a boundary between cognition and the Absolute that completely separates them. For, if cognition is the instrument for getting hold of absolute being, it is obvious that the use of an instrument on a thing certainly does not let it be what it is for itself, but rather sets out to reshape and alter it. If, on the other hand, cognition is not an instrument of our activity but a more or less passive medium through which the light of truth reaches us, then again we do not receive the truth as it is in itself, but only as it exists through and in this medium. Either way we employ a means which immediately brings about the opposite of its own; or rather, what is really absurd is that we should make use of a means at all.[35]

The bearing—on Descartes, Locke, and Kant, and even Davidson—of what Hegel says here may, I hope, be recovered without too much difficulty. Hegel implies that the entire Cartesian project is impossible *sans phrase*, but he does not say that it is therefore impossible to claim to speak of the independent world! The last is what constructivism secures. We cannot know the independent world as it is "absolutely" independent of cognitive conjecture, but we can construct a reasonable sense of what to characterize as the independent-world-as-it-is-known-(and knowable)-to-us. The correction of *any* particular belief will be an artifact internal to that same holism. We have never surpassed Hegel in this regard.

If you allow this small concession to history without yielding to Hegel's grandiose conceptions, you cannot fail to see that Rorty's *Philosophy and the Mirror of Nature* is quite literally a Hegelian critique of a large part of

Western philosophy.[36] Fine: that serves to remind us of an essential part of the pragmatist's original inheritance of the post-Kantian discoveries. But it also confirms the disastrous equivocation on interpretive *tertia* (or "intermediaries," in Davidson's idiom) that both Rorty and Davidson espouse. For the "intermediaries" Hegel opposed included *any epistemic "instrument"* or *"medium"* that operated *relationally* between cognitively separable consciousness and reality; whereas the "intermediaries" Davidson and Rorty oppose (pointedly, in Davidson's "A Coherence Theory of Truth and Knowledge") *are any "epistemic intermediaries" at all*. But that now verges on incoherence.[37]

Davidson and Rorty rule out all constructivist intermediaries, even those "intermediaries" that disallow any initial separation between consciousness and reality (the upshot of a symbiotized world). But that *is* Cartesianism without benefit of argument. Doubtless, Davidson's rationale trades on the fact that constructivism would defeat reductive physicalism and extensionalism at one blow, though it need never put at risk the usual rigor or achievement of any of our sciences. Put in the simplest terms, Rorty cannot support both Davidson and Hegel—or Davidson and the pragmatists.

The entire history now falls easily into place. Devitt, for example, appears as a Cartesian innocent when he confesses at the start of the second edition of *Realism and Truth*: "There is something a little shameful about spending one's time defending something so apparently humdrum as the independent existence of the familiar world"—which he urges in accord with the maxim, "Settle the metaphysical issue before any epistemic or semantic issue."[38] This "cannot" have been written later than the seventeenth or eighteenth century!

Similarly, though he is incomparably more interesting than Devitt, Michael Dummett, for all his "anti-realism" (which Devitt exploits against him), is hardly more than an abler Cartesian when he remarks:

> although we no longer regard the traditional questions of philosophy as pseudo-questions to which no meaningful answer can be given, we have not returned to the belief that a priori reasoning can afford us substantive knowledge of fundamental features of the world. Philosophy can take us no further than enabling us to command a clear view of the concepts by means of which we think about the world, and, by so doing, to attain a firmer grasp of the way we represent the world in our thought. It is for this reason and in this sense that philosophy is about the world. Frege said of the laws of logic that they are not laws of nature but laws of the laws of nature. . . . Reality cannot be said to obey a law of logic; it is our thinking about reality that obeys such a law or flouts it.[39]

This, of course, is a kind of Fregean Kantianism[40]—Cartesianism, in effect. It's for this reason that Dummett believes he can afford to yield on excluded middle (but not on bivalence) and therefore gives cognitive priority to logic over metaphysics; whereas, on the constructivist account, logic (Dummett's sort of logic) is itself a form of metaphysics,[41] a metaphysics "by other means."

V

I offer, finally, some remarks drawn from John McDowell's "John Locke Lectures" (1991), which may be the most promising of these contemporary variations on the Cartesian theme. They are important, beyond their explicit contribution, partly because of Putnam's reliance on McDowell's argument in abandoning his own "internal realism,"[42] partly because they suggest a way of bridging the gap between pragmatism and Cartesianism (by way of Kant), and partly because they do not venture far enough to specify a realism adequate on both metaphysical and epistemological grounds. Putnam believes McDowell's argument enables *him* to recover his pragmatism as a form of "natural realism" (as he now terms it), but the argument is not yet clear.

McDowell's avowed objective is "to consider . . . the way concepts mediate the relation between minds and the world," to which he adds at once: "Representational content cannot be dualistically set over against the conceptual." By these two sentences, McDowell allies himself (with important qualifications) with Kant (*and* Hegel) and against Davidson and that part of Rorty that agrees with Davidson.[43] McDowell then draws the perfectly sensible inference: "*That things are thus and so* is the conceptual content of an experience, but if the subject of the experience is not misled, that very same thing, *that things are thus and so,* is also a perceptible fact, an aspect of the perceptible world."[44] This marks very clearly McDowell's attraction to the pragmatist recovery of the main accomplishment of the post-Kantian movement, but hardly dissallows a Cartesian recovery *of that.* There's the puzzle of McDowell's account.

There is no way to gainsay this duality. What is so astonishing about McDowell's analysis—and Putnam's interest in it—is that *that* is very nearly the entire gist of what McDowell offers: the rest is more Cartesian than pragmatist. McDowell does draw attention to the deep equivocation on "intermediaries" that I've flagged in Davidson and Rorty; and, as I say, that much supports the judgment that McDowell aligns himself with Kant (*sans* Kant's transcendentalism) as well as with Aristotle and Hegel (very lightly), both of whom he reads conformably. But that's all! There's nothing in the way of an epistemologically-centered realism (say, "a realism worth fighting for," in Devitt's phrase) or, if there is, what there is is inexplicit and undefended regarding whatever differences separate pragmatism and Cartesianism.

McDowell may be a closet Cartesian of an extremely attenuated "Kantian" or even "Hegelian" sort. This much, however, is clear: if we adopt McDowell's formulation, then the whole of Davidson's objection to "epistemic intermediaries" instantly fails—is, in fact, rendered irrelevant. That, I concede, is an enormous plus. But, in his defense of realism, McDowell seems to have found it sufficient to retrace *that* argument alone from Kant to Hegel, which is certainly not enough. That is, McDowell himself fails to consider all that is required of "intermediaries."

To have stopped where he does (In *Mind and World*) is to fail to distinguish between a Kantian and a Hegelian view of the symbiotized world: in effect, to fail to distinguish between a "Cartesian" and a pragmatist account of realism. It's not enough (though it is correct as far as it goes) to say that our *concepts* qualify our perception of the real world: the question is whether the constructivist account of the "real world" proves to be a form of idealism or a Kantianized Cartesianism or a pragmatist Hegelianism that eludes the snares of the other options. What (in effect) McDowell very neatly shows is that our "epistemic intermediaries" (our "concepts," in McDowell's idiom) need not be *relationally* defined (in the way Putnam found so disastrous for his own internal realism).

I agree entirely with McDowell here; but I go on to say that the "*tertia*" Rorty dismisses, in agreement with Davidson (obviously a misnomer for the epistemic resources of any constructive realism), mediates *adverbially* in epistemic contexts. But the way in which they are assumed to do so is altogether different in Kant and Hegel: there is, for instance, no recognition in Kant (or in Aristotle, for that matter) of the possibility (the Hegelian and, I would add, the pragmatist possibility) that our interpretive competence is itself a hybrid artifact of our historical culture, not in any way part of an assured and relatively changeless, commensurable, "natural," even essential faculty of reason. As I read him, McDowell does not broach this matter as an inseparable part of the realist question he himself pursues. History or *Bildung* provides (in McDowell's account) for a selection from our conceptual resources, but it does not signify the constructed nature of our concepts themselves.

I have not found in any of McDowell's more recent publications, for instance in the Woodbridge Lectures (1997) or the papers on Wittgenstein,[45] reason to modify my finding. In "The Woodbridge Lectures," McDowell pretty well assimilates Hegel to Kant;[46] and the excellent papers on Wittgenstein, being essentially *explications*, disclose very little that bears directly on a "constructivist" view of language and thought that might actually decide the matter between the Kantian (and Aristotelian) cast of *Mind and World* and a robustly historicized account (Hegelian, on my reading) of our categories and concepts. It is, of course, the historicized treatment of social life that obliges us to consider certain strenuous epistemological and realist puzzles that never surface in *Mind and World*—relativism, incommensurabilism, historicism itself. Putnam and McDowell simply stop short of sketching the main lines of the "natural realism" they seem to share.

It is very difficult to elicit more from McDowell that bears on the fate and prospects of realism. McDowell wishes to avoid Kant's appeal to the "supersensible" (or transcendental), which claims a conceptual source completely "separable" from sensory "receptivity." (I have dubbed that a "Cartesian" feature in Kant, which, on McDowell's reading, correctly accounts for Kant's "idealism."[47]) McDowell is bent on securing a thoroughly "natural" (I would say, an Aristotelian) reading of "empirical thinking" that depends on man's acquiring a "second nature" as a result of *Bildung* or enculturation, which finds alternative treatments in Aristotle and Hegel but not in the original Kant.[48] Here, McDowell opposes epistemological dualisms and any reliance on the "supersensible": the transcendental, the supernatural, the "rampant Platonist."[49] He hardly ventures an account of what *he* finally means by our "natural" endowment, or what he does offer is a Kantianized or Aristotelian Hegel.

So McDowell brings us to the very edge of the quarrel between a fresh pragmatist treatment of the realist issue and a "naturalistic" treatment. The following is nearly all McDowell says on the matter:

> we can regard the culture a human being is initiated into as a going concern; there is no particular reason why we should need to uncover or speculate about its history, let alone the origins of culture as such. Human infants are mere animals, distinctive only in their potential, and nothing occult happens to a human being in ordinary upbringing. If we locate a variety of platonisms in the context of an account of *Bildung* [that is, a "natural platonism" like Aristotle's, a sense of natural, culturally featured predicative regularties] that insists on those facts, we thereby ensure that it is not a rampant platonism [that is, that posits a separable world of Forms, an occult domain].[50]

What McDowell says here is not unwelcome. McDowell positions himself in a no-man's-land between pragmatism and a "natural Platonism," though he clearly favors the latter. In any case, he cannot reconcile the two. By "Platonism," McDowell means (I surmise) an accessible source of objective predicates that runs true and more or less uniformly through the species; by "natural," I take him to mean that the conceptual competence answering to our predicative efforts belongs primarily to our biology but may, in some measure, manifest differences in saliency as a result of our encultured "second nature" (our *Bildung*). It's the open-ended and historically variable (constructed) nature of (what Rorty misleadingly calls) *tertia* that generates the contemporary realist quarrel between the naturalizers and the pragmatists. That is what McDowell fails to address.

I should add, here, that I find three very different treatments of *tertia* (or, better, intermediaries): the first, the one Davidson and Rorty dismiss (quite rightly), the one featured so disastrously in Putnam's "internal realism,"[51] which assigns "epistemic intermediaries" a relational, a Cartesian or Lockean, representationalist role; the second, the one McDowell favors in the passage just cited, which signifies that mind and world are indeed "mediated" (adverbially, as I suggest) by "concepts" that belong to our biological endowment but are selected or featured by our *Bildung* (our "ordinary upbringing"); and a third, the one I recommend (against McDowell's "Cartesian"—or Kantian or Aristotelian—proclivities), which treats our interpretive intermediaries as both "adverbial" (rather than "relational") and as "hybrid" (rather than merely "natural" in the biological sense), that is, as historicized, variable, artifactual, and open to the puzzle of reconciling realism and, say, relativism or incommensurabilism. In my view, to admit conceptual *tertia* is to make our realism constructivist from the start and throughout; there is no fallback objectivism to take for granted.

McDowell, therefore, begins *Mind and World* at the wrong point. "The overall topic I am going to consider in these lectures," he advises, "is the way concepts mediate the relation between minds and the world." He favors a Kantian complication at once and warns: "The more we play up the connection between reason and freedom [which is to account for the accessibility of 'meaning,' the natural way in which our second-natured concepts are already engaged in intelligible experience], the more we risk losing our grip on how exercises of concepts can constitute warranted judgements about the world. What we wanted to conceive as exercises of concepts threaten to degenerate into moves in a self-contained game."[52] Put thus, McDowell's effort is essentially a rearguard, but thoroughly recuperative, move. The telltale signs appear in his speaking of "warranted judgments about the world" and of locating a "variety of [natural] Platonisms in the context of . . . *Bildung.*"

The matter is important enough to press a little more insistently. Two qualifications should serve. For one, when McDowell speaks of "second nature" (which is how he brings Hegel and Aristotle together in reinterpreting Kant), he speaks of the "acquisition of a second nature, which [he says] involves responsiveness to meaning." That is what (that is all) he has in mind in speaking of a "normal upbringing": it is meant to defeat (and does defeat) any purely reductive naturalism in which, say, the autonomy and intelligence of a human agent can be explained entirely in biological terms.[53] *That* much is certainly fair: it's what McDowell gains from Kant. But it does not quite touch on the *metaphysics* of our cognitive powers vis-à-vis realism. Or, rather, it assumes the validity of a "naturalistic" account of our conceptual sources and reconciles their mastery with human freedom. Second, when he speaks of the distinction between "sensory experience" and its being intelligible, McDowell is concerned to avoid the empiricist option of the "non-conceptual" representationality of mere sensation (along the lines developed by Gareth Evans). McDowell's entirely sensible account runs as follows: "To say that an experience is not blind is to say that it is intelligible to its subject as purporting to be awareness of a feature of objective reality: as a seeming glimpse of the world."[54] Yes, of course. But that goes no further than the second sense of "*tertia.*"

It is in this sense that a pragmatism poised at the turn of the new century could easily recover in a single stroke its original promise and "second" energy: by redefining realism in a way that could not have been perceived in its first incarnation and by rereading with care the anti-Cartesian strategies developed by the European progeny of the post-Kantian world (the Marxists, the early Frankfurt-Critical movement, the Hegelianized Kantians, the historicists, the Heideggerian hermeneuts, the European pragmatists, the existential phenomenologists, the Nietzscheans, the poststructuralists, genealogists, sociologists of knowledge), who never suffered the conceptual break with the post-Kantian world that Anglo-American philosophy imposed on itself.

Tertia, construed in my third sense, do play an ineliminable epistemic role (contrary to Davidson and Rorty); do apply adverbially, not relationally (in agreement with McDowell); *and* are culturally and historically formed and transformed (in the historicizing sense Hegel introduces). But if that is so, then the recovery of realism—in particular, pragmatism's recovery of realism—harbors more troubling questions than the ones broached by Putnam, Davidson, Rorty, or McDowell.

NOTES

1. See Richard Rorty, "Private Irony and Liberal Hope," *Contingency, Irony, and Solidarity* (Cambridge: Cambridge University Press, 1989).

2. See Richard Rorty, "Overcoming the Tradition: Heidegger and Dewey," *Consequences of Pragmatism (Essays, 1972–1980)* (Minneapolis: University of Minnesota Press, 1982).

3. Rorty, *Consequences of Pragmatism*, Introduction: "Pragmatism and Philosophy," xiii.

4. Richard Rorty, "Pragmatism, Davidson and Truth," in Ernest Lepore, ed., *Truth and Interpretation: Perspectives on Donald Davidson's Philosophy* (Oxford: Basil Blackwell, 1986).

5. Donald Davidson "The Structure and Content of Truth," *Journal of Philosophy*, LXXXVII (1990) (Davidson's "Dewey Lectures").

6. Richard Rorty, "Is Truth a Goal of Inquiry? Donald Davidson versus Crispin Wright," *Truth and Progress: Philosophical Papers, vol. 3* (Cambridge: Cambridge University Press, 1998), 21–22.

7. See Davidson, "The Structure and Content of Truth," 332.

8. Rorty, "Is Truth a Goal of Inquiry?" 23.

9. Davidson, "The Structure and Content of Truth," 309; cited by Rorty.

10. See Alfred Tarski, "The Concept of Truth in Formalized Languages," *Logic, Semantics, Metamathematics*, trans. J. H. Woodger; 2nd ed., ed. John Corcoran (Indianapolis, Ind.: Hackett, 1983), particularly §7: Postscript.

11. Richard Rorty, *Philosophy and Social Hope* (Harmondsworth, U.K.: Penguin, 1999), 24.

12. See Hilary Putnam, "Sense, Nonsense, and the Senses: An Inquiry into the Powers of the Human Mind" (Putnam's "Dewey Lectures," 1994), *Journal of Philosophy*, XCI (1994).

13. Hilary Putnam, "Values, Facts and Cognition," *Reason, Truth and History* (Cambridge: Cambridge University Press, 1981), 216.

14. For a very brief sense of this, see Hilary Putnam, "William James's Ideas" (1989), written with Ruth Anna Putnam, *Realism with a Human Face*, ed. James Conant (Cambridge, Mass.: Harvard University Press, 1990), 225, 226.

15. See, further, Hilary Putnam, "Bernard Williams and the Absolute Conception of the World," *Renewing Philosophy* (Cambridge, Mass.: Harvard University Press, 1992). I find this paper particularly revealing about Putnam's dialectical strategy.

16. Putnam, "Values, Facts and Cognition," 216.

17. Richard Rorty, "Solidarity or Objectivity?" (1985), in John Rajchman and Cornel West, eds., *Post-Analytic Philosophy* (New York: Columbia University Press, 1985), 10.

18. See Donald Davidson, "A Coherence Theory of Truth and Knowledge," in Ernest Lepore, ed., *Truth and Interpretation* (New York/Oxford: Blackwell, 1986).

19. Hilary Putnam, "Two Conceptions of Rationality," *Reason, Truth, and History*, 126.

20. See, for a sense of Putnam's reasoning, "Objectivity and the Science/Ethics Distinction," *Realism with a Human Face*, which seems to be the original from which "Bernard Williams and the Absolute Conception of the World" is a spin-off. The larger paper appears as well in Martha Nussbaum and Amartya Sen eds., *The Quality of Life* (Oxford: Clarendon, 1993), which helps to confirm (though there is additional evidence) that Nussbaum's recent invocation of Aristotelian essentialism—"pragmatized," in effect—owes a great deal to the convergence of Putnam and Habermas. See Martha C. Nussbaum, "Human Capabilities, Female Human Beings," in Martha Nussbaum

and Jonathan Glover eds., *Women, Culture and Development: A Study of Human Capabilities* (Oxford: Clarendon, 1995). I believe the project fails, for essentially the same reason Putnam's and Habermas's versions fail. See, also, Jürgen Habermas, "Discourse Ethics: Notes on a Program of Philosophical Justification," *Moral Consciousness and Communicative Action*, trans. Christian Lenhardt and Shierry Weber Nicholsen (Cambridge, Mass.: MIT Press, 1990).

21. See John McDowell, *Mind and World* (Cambridge, Mass.: Harvard University Press, 1994, 1996).

22. Davidson, "A Coherence Theory of Truth and Knowledge," 309.

23. Hilary Putnam, *Pragmatism: An Open Question* (Oxford: Blackwell, 1995), 64–65. I have paraphrased (possibly emended) Putnam's first two points, though they seem in accord with what he says here.

24. Davidson, "The Structure and Content of Truth," 279–282. See, also, John Dewey, *Reconstruction in Philosophy* (New York: Holt, 1920), 156 (cited by Davidson). Dewey's book has been reissued in an enlarged edition by Beacon Press, 1957.

25. Davidson, "The Structure and Content of Truth," 304–305.

26. The essential loci for their respective views in this regard appear in Davidson, "A Coherence Theory of Truth and Knowledge" and Rorty, "Pragmatism, Davidson and Truth."

27. Davidson, "A Coherence Theory of Truth and Knowledge," 312.

28. Ibid., 314.

29. Rorty, "Pragmatism, Davidson and Truth," 335.

30. Hilary Putnam, *The Many Faces of Realism* (La Salle, Ill.: Open Court, 1987), 28.

31. See Putnam, "Sense, Nonsense, and the Senses," Lecture I.

32. See Michael de Montaigne, *The Complete Essays*, trans. M. A. Screech (London: Penguin Books, 1993).

33. Here I agree with John Searle's finding, but not with his reasoning. See John R. Searle, *The Construction of Social Reality* (New York: Free Press, 1985).

34. See Michael Devitt, *Realism and Truth*, 2nd ed. (Princeton, N.J.: Princeton University Press, 1997), Introduction.

35. G. W. F. Hegel, *Phenomenology of Spirit*, trans. A. V. Miller (Oxford: Oxford University Press, 1977), Introduction §73 (p. 46).

36. See Richard Rorty, *Philosophy and the Mirror of Nature* (Princeton, N.J.: Princeton University Press, 1979).

37. For a sense of Davidson's difficulties, see Donald Davidson, "Afterwords, 1987," in Alan R. Malachowski, ed., *Reading Rorty: Critical Responses to Philosophy and the Mirror of Nature (and Beyond)* (Oxford: Basil Blackwell, 1990).

38. Devitt, *Realism and Truth*, vii.

39. Michael Dummett, *The Logical Basis of Metaphysics* (Cambridge, Mass.: Harvard University Press, 1991), 1–2.

40. Ibid., 198–199.

41. See ibid., 9–15.

42. See Putnam, "Sense, Nonsense, and the Senses," 445–447; and "Pragmatism and the Contemporary Debate," *Pragmatism*, 64–68.

43. John McDowell, *Mind and World* (Cambridge: Harvard University Press, 1996), 1–7, 85–86.

44. Ibid., 26.

45. See John McDowell, "Having the World in View: Sellars, Kant, and Intentionality" ("The Woodbridge Lectures," 1997), *The Journal of Philosophy*, XCV (1998); and *Mind, Value, and Reality* (Cambridge, Mass: Harvard University Press, 1998), Part III.

46. McDowell, "Having the World in View," 490.

47. McDowell, *Mind and World*, 41–44.

48. Ibid., 83–84.

49. Ibid., 92.

50. Ibid., 163.

51. See Putnam, "Sense, Nonsense, and the Senses," 461–464.

52. McDowell, *Mind and World*, 3, 5.

53. Ibid., 124.

54. Ibid., 54. See the rest of Lecture III and Gareth Evans, *The Varieties of Reference*, ed. John McDowell (Oxford: Clarendon, 1982), Chs. 5–9.

Selected Bibliography

COMPILED BY MICHAEL LIEGL

OVERVIEW - AND DICTIONARY - ARTICLES

Richard J. Bernstein, "The Resurgence of Pragmatism," in *Social Research* 59 (1992): 813–840.

Peter Dews, "Die Historisierung der analytischen Philosophie," in *Philosophische Rundschau* 41 (1994): 1–17.

Susan Haack, "Pragmatism," in *The Blackwell Companion to Philosophy*, ed. Nicholas Bunnin and E. P. Tsui-James (Oxford: Blackwell, 1996): 643–671.

James T. Kloppenberg, "Pragmatism: An Old Name for Some New Ways of Thinking?," in *The Journal of American History* 83 (1996): 100–138.

Ludwig Nagl, "Das neue (post-analytische?) Interesse an der Prä-analytischen Philosophie," in: *Philosophische Rundschau* 37 (1990): 257–270.

Richard Rorty, "Pragmatism," in *Routledge International Encyclopedia of Philosophy* 7 (1998): 632–640.

ARTICLES

Barry Allen, "Putnam und Rorty über Objektivität und Wahrheit," in *Deutsche Zeitschrift für Philosophie* 42 (1994): 989–1005.

Barry Allen, "Ewige Wahrheit: Rorty und Heidegger," in *Die Wiederentdeckung der Zeit. Reflexionen-Analysen-Konzepte* (Darmstadt: Primus, 1997): 27–40.

Richard J. Bernstein, "What is the Difference that Makes a Difference? Gadamer, Habermas, and Rorty," in *Philosophy of Science Association* 2 (1982): 331–359.

Robert Brandom, "From Truth to Semantics: A Path through *Making It Explicit*," in *Philosophical Issues* 8 (1997): 141–154.

Robert Brandom, "Heideggers Kategorien in Sein und Zeit," in *Deutsche Zeitschrift für Philosophie* 45 (1997): 531–549.

Robert Brandom et al, "Book Symposium on Robert Brandom's *Making It Explicit*," in *Philosophy and Phenomenological Research* LVII (1997): 153–204.

Robert Brandom, "Pragmatistische Themen in Hegels Idealismus. Unterhandlung und Verwaltung der Struktur und des Gehalts in Hegels Erklärung begrifflicher Normen," in *Deutsche Zeitschrift für Philosophie* 47 (1999): 355–381.

Robert Brandom, "Interview: Robert Brandom," in *Epistemologia* 22 (1999): 143–150.

Hauke Brunkhorst, "Rorty, Putnam and the Frankfurt School," in *Philosophy & Social Criticism* 22 (1996): 1–16.

John Capps, "Dewey, Quine, and Pragmatic Naturalized Epistemology," in *Transactions of the Charles S. Peirce Society* 32 (1996): 634–667.

Donald Davidson, "On the Very Idea of a Conceptual Scheme," in *Proceedings and Addresses of the American Philosophical Association* 47 (1974): 5–20; reprinted as: *Inquiries into Truth and Interpretation* (Oxford: Clarendon Press, 1984): 183–198.

Paul D. Forster, "The Limits of Pragmatic Realism," in *Philosophy Today* 38 (1994): 243–258.

Paul D. Forster, "Problems with Rorty's Pragmatist Defence of Liberalism," in *Journal of Philosophical Research* 25 (2000): 345–362.

Leszek Koczanowicz, "The Choice of Tradition and the Tradition of Choice: Habermas' and Rorty's Interpretation of Pragmatism," in *Philosophy and Social Criticism* 25 (1999): 55–70.

Anton Leist, "Rorty, oder: Kann man alles bestreiten und dennoch Philosoph bleiben?," in *Deutsche Zeitschrift für Philosophie* 44 (1996): 255–258.

Joseph Margolis, "Skepticism, Foundationalism, and Pragmatism," in *American Philosophical Quarterly* 14 (1977): 119–127.

Joseph Margolis, "Pragmatism without Foundations," in *American Philosophical Quarterly* 21 (1984): 69–80.

Joseph Margolis, "Pragmatism, Phenomenology and the Psychological Sciences," in *Perspectives On Mind*, ed. Herbert R. Otto, (Dordrecht: Kluwer, 1988): 341–354.

Joseph Margolis, "Pragmatism, *Praxis*, and the Technological," in *Philosophy of Technology*, ed. Paul T. Durbin, (Dordrecht: Reidel, 1989): 113–130.

Joseph Margolis, "The Passing of Peirce's Realism," in *Transactions of the Charles S. Peirce Society* Vol. 29 (1993): 293–330.

Joseph Margolis, "Donald Davidson's Philosophical Strategies," in *Artifacts, Representations and Social Practice*, ed. Carol C. Gould and R. S. Cohen, (Netherlands: Kluwer Academic Publishers, 1994): 291–322.

Joseph Margolis, "Peirce's Fallibilism," in *Transactions of the Charles S. Peirce Society* 34 (1998): 536–569.

Joseph Margolis, "Dewey in Dialogue with Continental Philosophy," in *Reading Dewey. Interpretations for a Postmodern Generation*, ed. Larry Hickman, (Bloomington: Indiana University Press, 1998): 231–256.

Thomas McCarthy, "Private Irony and Public Decency: Richard Rorty's New Pragmatism," in *Critical Inquiry* 16 (1990), 355–370.

Thomas McCarthy, "Postscriptum: Ironistische Theorie als Beruf," in *Ideale und Illusion. Dekonstruktion und Rekonstruktion in der kritischen Theorie* (Frankfurt a. M.: Suhrkamp, 1993), 52–64.

John J. McDermott, "Symposium on Rorty's Consequences of Pragmatism," in *Transactions of the C. S. Peirce Society* 21 (1985): 1–48.

John McDowell, "Putnam on Mind and Meaning," in *Philosophical Topics* 20 (1992): 35–48.

Robert G. Meyers, "Putnam and the Permanence of Pragmatism," in *Transactions of the Charles S. Peirce Society*, 34 (1998): 346–364.

Mark Migotti, "Peirce's First Rule of Reason and the Bad Faith of Rortian Post-Philosophy," in *Transactions of the Charles S. Peirce Society* 31 (1995): 89–136.

Georg Mohr, "Die antiquierten Absichten der Bewußtseinsphilosophen. Rorty über Unkorrigierbarkeit und eliminativen Materialismus," in *Analytische Theorien des Selbstbewußtseins*, ed. Manfred Frank, (Frankfurt a. M.: Suhrkamp, 1993), 577–586.

Ludwig Nagl, "Ist die analytische Philosophie 'erneuerungsbedürftig'? Hilary Putnams kritischer Blick auf den angloamerikanischen 'mainstream'," in *Deutsche Zeitschrift für Philosophie* 43 (1995): 1045–1052.

Kai Nielsen, "Taking Rorty Seriously," in *Dialogue* 38 (1999): 503–518.

Nicholas Plants, "Therapeutic Interpretation: Rorty's Pragmatic Hopes and Fears," in *American Catholic Philosophical Quarterly* 8 (1998): 139–147.

Hilary Putnam, "Pragmatismus und Verifikationismus," in *Deutsche Zeitschrift für Philosophie* 43 (1995): 219–231.

Hilary Putnam, and Ruth Anna Putnam, "The Real William James: Response to Robert Meyers," in *Transactions of the Charles S. Peirce Society* 34 (1998): 366–381.

W. V. O. Quine, "Two Dogmas of Empiricism," in *From a Logical Point of View* (Cambridge, Mass.: Harvard University Press, 1953).

Bjørn Ramberg, "Dennett's Pragmatism," in *Revue International de Philosophie* 53 (1999): 61–86.

Tilman Reitz, "Rortys Theoriepause und die Möglichkeit politisch-philosophischer Theorie," in *Das Argument* 220 (1997): 335–338.

Richard Rorty, "Pragmatism, Categories, and Language," in *Philosophical Review* 70 (1961): 197–223.

Richard Rorty, "Transcendental Argument, Self-reference, and Pragmatism," in *Transcendental Arguments and Science,* ed. Peter Bieri and Rolf-Peter Horstmann, Lorenz Kruger, (1979): 77–103.

Richard Rorty, "Heidegger wider die Pragmatisten," in *Neue Hefte der Philosophie* 23 (1984): 1–22.

Richard Rorty, "Truth and Freedom: A Reply to Thomas McCarthy," in *Critical Inquiry* 16 (1990): 633–643.

Richard Rorty, "Sind Aussagen universelle Geltungsansprüche?," in *Deutsche Zeitschrift für Philosophie* 43 (1994): 975–988.

Richard Rorty, "Pragmatism as Anti-Authoritarianism," in *Revue Internationale de Philosophie* 1 (1999): 7–20.

Steffen Schluter, "Deutscher Realismus und Amerikanischer Pragmatismus," in *Deutsche Zeitschrift für Philosophie* 47 (1999): 183–201.

Richard Shusterman, "Dewey on Experience: Foundation or Reconstruction?," in *The Philosophical Forum* 26 (1994): 127–148.

Udo Tietz, "Der gemäßigte Kontextualismus Richard Rortys - Ein postanalytisches Pendant zur poststrukturalistischen Vernunftkritik," in *Poststrukturalismus—Dekonstruktion—Postmoderne*, ed. Klaus W. Hempfes, (Stuttgart: Steiner, 1992), 129–160.

Ernst Tugendhat, "Überreden und Begründen," in *Deutsche Zeitschrift für Philosophie* 44, (1996): 245–247.

Wolfgang Welsch, "Richard Rorty oder Von der Erkenntnistheorie zur bildenden Philosophie und zum Denken der Kontingenz," in *Vernunft. Die Zeitgenössische Vernunftkritik und das Konzept der transversalen Vernunft* (Frankfurt a. M.: Suhrkamp, 1995), 211–244.

Robert B. Westbrook, "A New Pragmatism," in *American Quarterly* 45 (1993): 438–444.

Bruce Wilshire, "Pragmatism, Neopragmatism, and Phenomenology: the Richard Rorty Phenomenon," in *Human Studies* Vol. 20 (Amsterdam: Kluwer Academic Publishers, 1997), 95–108.

Uwe Wirth, "Abductive Reasoning in Peirce's and Davidson's Account of Interpretation," in *Transactions of the Charles S. Peirce Society* 35 (1999): 115–127.

MONOGRAPHS AND ANTHOLOGIES

Karl-Otto Apel, *Die Transformation der Philosophie* (Frankfurt a. M.: Suhrkamp, 1973).

Barry Allen, *Truth in Philosophy* (Cambridge and London: Harvard University Press, 1993).

Robert Brandom, *Making It Explicit: Reasoning, Representing, and Discursive Commitment* (Cambridge, Mass. and London: Harvard University Press, 1994).

Robert Brandom (ed.), *Rorty and His Critics* (Oxford: Blackwell's Publishers, 2000).

Michael Brint and William Weaver, *Pragmatism in Law and Society* (Oxford and Boulder, Colo.: Westview Press, 1991).

Robert W. Burch and Herman J. Saatkamp Jr., *Frontiers in American Philosophy, Volume Two* (College Station: Texas A&M University Press, 1996).

Harvey Cormier, *The Truth is What Works* (Lanham, Md.: Rowman & Littlefield Publishing Group, 2000).

Morris Dickstein (ed.), *The Revival of Pragmatism: New Essays on Social Thought, Law, and Culture* (Durham, N.C.: Duke University Press, 1998).

John Patrick Diggins, *The Promise of Pragmatism. Modernism and the Crisis of Knowledge and Authority* (Chicago and London: The University of Chicago Press, 1994).

Paul Fairfield, *Theorizing Praxis: Studies in Hermeneutical Pragmatism* (Frankfurt a. M., New York: Peter Lang, 2000).

Arthur Fine, *The Shaky Game: Einstein, Realism and the Quantum Theory* (Chicago: University of Chicago Press, 1986).

Volker Gadenne, *Kritischer Rationalismus und Pragmatismus* (Amsterdam: Rodopi, 1994).

Russel B. Goodman, *Pragmatism: A Contemporary Reader* (London and New York: Routledge, 1995).

Jürgen Habermas, *Knowledge and Human Interests* (Boston: Beacon Press, 1972).

Jürgen Habermas, *The Theory of Communicative Action: Reason and the Rationalization of Society (The Theory of Communicative Action, Vol. 1)* (Boston: Beacon Press, 1985).

Jürgen Habermas, *The Theory of Communicative Action: Lifeworld and System: A Critique of Functionalist Reason* (Boston: Beacon Press, 1989).

Jürgen Habermas, *Postmetaphysical Thinking (Studies in Contemporary German Social Thought)* (Cambridge, Mass.: MIT Press, 1994).

Jürgen Habermas, *Between Facts and Norms (Studies in Contemporary German Social Thought)* (Cambridge, Mass.: MIT Press, 1998).

Jürgen Habermas, *The Inclusion of the Other (Studies in Contemporary German Social Thought)* (Cambridge, Mass.: MIT Press, 2000).

Jürgen Habermas, *The Postnational Constellation (Studies in Contemporary German Social Thought)* (Cambridge, Mass.: MIT Press, 2001).

David L. Hall, *Richard Rorty. Prophet and Poet of the New Pragmatism* (Albany: State University of New York Press, 1994).

Larry A. Hickman, *Reading Dewey: Interpretations for a Postmodern Generation* (Bloomington and Indianapolis: Indiana University Press, 1998).

Larry A. Hickman, *Philosophical Tools for Technological Culture: Putting Pragmatism to Work* (Bloomington: Indiana University Press, 2001).

Robert Hollinger and David J. Depew, *Pragmatism: From Progressivism to Postmodernism* (Westport, Conn.: Praeger, 1995).

Konstantin Kolenda, *Rorty's Humanistic Pragmatism. Philosophy Democratized* (Tampa: University of Florida Press, 1990).

Ronald A. Kuipers, *Solidarity and the Stranger, Themes in the Social Philosophy of Richard Rorty* (Lanham, Md.: University Press of America, 1997).

Lenore Langstorf and Andrew R. Smith (eds.), *Recovering Pragmatism's Voice: The Classical Tradition, Rorty, and the Philosophy of Communication* (Albany: State University of New York Press, 1995).

Ben H. Letson, *Davidson's Theory of Truth and Its Implications for Rorty's Pragmatism* (New York: P. Lang, 1997).

Steven Mailloux, *Reception Histories: Rhetoric, Pragmatism, and American Cultural Politics* (Ithaca, N.Y.: Cornell University Press, 1998).

Steven Mailloux (ed.), *Rhetoric, Sophistry, Pragmatism* (Cambridge: Cambridge University Press, 1995).

Alan Malachowsky (ed.), *Reading Rorty: Critical Responses to Philosophy and the Mirror of Nature (and Beyond)* (Oxford: Blackwell Publishers Ltd, 1990).

Joseph Margolis, *Pragmatism without Foundations* (Oxford und New York: Basil Blackwell, 1986).

John McDowell, *Mind and World* (Cambridge, Mass. and London: Harvard University Press, 1996).

Louis Menand (ed.), *Pragmatism: A Reader* (New York: Vintage, 1997).

C. J. Misak, *Truth, Politics, Morality: Pragmatism and Deliberation* (London and New York: Routledge, 2000).

H. O. Mounce, *The Two Pragmatisms: From Peirce to Rorty* (London and New York: Routledge, 1997).

John P. Murphy, *Pragmatism. From Peirce to Davidson* (Boulder, Colo. and Oxford: Westview Press, 1990).

Ludwig Nagl, *Pragmatismus* (Frankfurt a. M.: Campus, 1998).

Ludwig Nagl and Chantal Mouffe (eds.), *The Legacy of Wittgenstein: Pragmatism or Deconstruction* (Frankfurt a. M. and New York: Peter Lang, 2001).

David K. Perry (ed.), *American Pragmatism and Communication. (Lea's Communication Series)* (Mahwah, N.J.: Lawrence Erlbaum Associates, 2001).

Sami Pihlstrom, *Structuring the World: The Issue of Realism and the Nature of Ontological Problems in Classical and Contemporary Pragmatism* (Helsinki: Philosophical Society of Finland, 1996).

Sami Pihlstrom, *Pragmatism and Philosophical Anthropology: Understanding Our Human Life in a Human World* (New York: P. Lang, 1998).

Hilary Putnam, *Reason, Truth, and History* (Cambridge: Cambridge University Press, 1981).

Hilary Putnam, *The Many Faces of Realism. The Paul Carus Lectures* (La Salle, Ill.: Open Court, 1987).

Hilary Putnam, *Realism with a Human Face*, ed. James Conant, (Cambridge, Mass.: Harvard University Press, 1990).

Hilary Putnam, *Words and Life*, ed. James Conant, (Cambridge, Mass. and London: Harvard University Press, 1993).

John Rajchman and Cornel West (eds.), *Post-Analytic Philosophy* (New York: Columbia University Press, 1985).

Marie-Louise Rater and Marcus Willaschek (eds.) *Hilary Putnam und die Tradition des Pragmatismus* (Frankfurt a. M.: Suhrkamp 2002).

Richard Rorty, *The Linguistic Turn: Essays in Philosophical Method. With Two Retrospective Essays* (Chicago: University of Chicago Press, 1967).

Richard Rorty, *Philosophy and the Mirror of Nature* (Princeton, N.J.: Princeton University Press, 1979).

Richard Rorty, *Consequences of Pragmatism. Essays: 1972–1980* (Minneapolis: University of Minnesota Press, 1982).

Richard Rorty, *Solidarität oder Objektivität?* (Stuttgart: Reclam Verlag, 1988).

Richard Rorty, *Contingency, Irony, and Solidarity* (Cambridge: Cambridge University Press, 1989).

Richard Rorty, *Essays on Heidegger and Others: Philosophical Papers, Vol. 2* (Cambridge: Cambridge University Press, 1991).

Richard Rorty, *Objectivity, Relativism, and Truth: Philosophical Papers, Vol. 1* (Cambridge: Cambridge University Press, 1991).

Richard Rorty, *Eine Kultur ohne Zentrum. Vier philosophische Essays* (Stuttgart: Reclam, 1993).

Richard Rorty, *Hoffnung statt Erkenntnis. Einleitung in die pragmatische Philosophie* (Vienna: Passagen Verlag, 1994).

Richard Rorty, *Truth and Progress: Philosophical Papers Vol. 3* (Cambridge: Cambridge University Press, 1998).

Richard Rorty, *Hinter den Spiegeln*, ed. Udo Tietz (Frankfurt a. M.: Suhrkamp, 2001).

Richard Rorty, *Vom Linguistic Turn zum Neopragmatismus. Ausgewählte Aufsätze*, ed. Mike Sandbothe (Weilerswist: Velbrück Wissenschaft, 2001).

Robert J. Roth, *Radical Pragmatism. An Alternative* (New York: Fordham University Press, 1998).

Herman J. Saatkamp, (ed.) *Rorty and Pragmatism: The Philosopher Responds to His Critics* (Nashville, Tenn.: Vanderbilt University Press, 1995).

Mike Sandbothe, (ed.) *Wozu Wahrheit ? Schlüsseltexte der Davidson—Rorty—Debatte* (Weilerswist: Velbrück Wissenschaft, 2001).

Patrick Shade, *Habits of Hope: A Pragmatic Theory (Vanderbilt Library of American Philosophy)* (Nashville, Tenn.: Vanderbilt University Press, 2000).

Richard Shusterman, *Vor der Interpretation. Sprache und Erfahrung in Hermeneutik, Dekonstruktion und Pragmatismus* (Viennai: Passagen, 1996).

Richard Shusterman, *Practicing Philosophy. Pragmatism and the Philosophical Life* (London and New York: Routledge, 1997).

John J. Stuhr, *Geneaological Pragmatism. Philosophy, Experience, and Community* (Albany: State University of New York Press, 1997).

Shannon Sullivan, *Living Across and Through Skins: Transactional Bodies, Pragmatism, and Feminism* (Bloomington: Indiana University Press, 2001).

H. S. Thayer, *Meaning and Action. A Critical History of Pragmatism* (Indiana: Hackett Publishing Company, 1981).

Cornel West, *The American Evasion of Philosophy: A Genealogy of Pragmatism* (Madison: University of Wisconsin Press, 1989).

Kathleen Wheeler, *Romanticism, Pragmatism and Deconstruction* (Oxford: Blackwell, 1993).

Frederick L. Will, *Pragmatism and Realism* (Lanham: Rowman and Littlefield, 1997).

Contributors

Barry Allen is Professor of Philosophy at McMaster University, Hamilton. He is the author of *Truth in Philosophy* (Cambridge, M.A.: Harvard University Press, 1993).

William Egginton is Assistant Professor of Romance Languages and Literatures and Comparative Literature at the University at Buffalo. He is the author of *How the World Became a Stage: Presence, Theatricality, and the Question of Modernity* (Albany: SUNY Press, 2003).

Arthur Fine is Professor of Philosophy at the University of Washington. He is the author of *The Shaky Game: Einstein, Realism and The Quantum Theory* (Chicago: University of Chicago Press, 1986).

Antje Gimmler is Professor of Social Theory at Aalborg University (Denmark). She is the author of *Institution und Individuum. Zur Institutionentheorie von Max Weber und Jürgen Habermas* (Frankfurt a. M. and New York: Campus, 1998) and *Hegel und der Pragmatismus* (forthcoming).

Joseph Margolis is Laura H. Carnell Professor of Philosophy at Temple University Philadelphia. His books include *Pragmatism without Foundations: Reconciling Relativism and Realism* (Oxford: Blackwell, 1986), *Science without Unity: Reconciling the Natural and the Human Sciences* (Oxford: Blackwell, 1987), *Texts without Referents: Reconciling Science and Narrative* (Oxford: Blackwell, 1989), *The Truth about Relativism* (Oxford: Blackwell, 1991), *Life without Principles: Reconciling Theory and Practice* (Oxford: Blackwell, 1996), and *Reinventing Pragmatism: American Philosophy at the end of the Twentieth Century* (Ithaca, N.Y.: Cornell University Press, 2002).

Ludwig Nagl is Professor of Philosophy at Vienna University. His books include *Charles Sanders Peirce* (Frankfurt a. M. and New York: Campus, 1992),

Pragmatismus (Frankfurt a. M. and New York: Campus, 1998), and *The Legacy of Wittgenstein: Pragmatism or Deconstruction* (Frankfurt a. M., London and New York: Peter Lang, 2001).

Hilary Putnam is Emeritus Professor of Philosophy at Harvard University. His books include *Philosophical Papers I–III* (Cambridge: Cambridge University Press, 1975–1983), *Reason, Truth and History* (Cambridge: Cambridge University Press, 1981), *Realism with a Human Face* (Cambridge, Mass.: Harvard University Press, 1990), *Renewing Philosophy* (Cambridge, Mass.: Harvard University Press, 1992), *Pragmatism: An Open Question* (Oxford: Blackwell, 1995), *Words and Life* (Cambridge, Mass.: Harvard University Press, 1994), and *The Threefold Cord: Mind, Body and World* (New York: Columbia University Press, 2000).

Richard Rorty is Professor of Comparative Literature at Stanford University. His books include *Philosophy and the Mirror of Nature* (Princeton: University of Princeton Press, 1979), *Consequences of Pragmatism* (Minneapolis: University of Minnesota Press, 1982), *Contingency, Irony, ,and Solidarity* (Cambridge: Cambridge University Press, 1989), *Philosophical Papers I–III* (Cambridge: Cambridge University Press, 1991–1998), *Achieving Our Country: Leftist Thought in Twentieth-Century America* (Cambridge, Mass.: Harvard University Press, 1998), and *Philosophy and Social Hope* (London: Penguin, 2000).

Mike Sandbothe is Professor of Cultural and Media Studies at Friedrich Schiller University Jena. He is the author of *The Temporalization of Time* (Lanham and New York: Rowman & Littlefield, 2001) and *Pragmatische Medienphilosophie* (Weilerswist: Velbrück Wissenschaft, 2001; Engl. translation forthcoming).

Albrecht Wellmer is Emeritus Professor of Philosophy at Free University Berlin. His books include *Critical Theory of Society* (New York: Herder and Herder, 1971), *The Persistence of Modernity: Essays on Aesthetics, Ethics, and Postmodernity* (Cambridge, Mass.: MIT Press, 1991), *Endgames: The Irreconcilable Nature of Modernity* (Cambridge, Mass.: MIT Press, 2000).

Wolfgang Welsch is Professor of Theoretical Philosophy at Friedrich Schiller University Jena. His books include *Aisthesis. Grundzüge und Perspektiven der Aristotelischen Sinneslehre* (Stuttgart: Klett-Cotta 1987), *Unsere postmoderne Moderne* (Weinheim: VCH Acta humaniora, 1987, 6th edition Berlin: Akademie Verlag, 2002), *Ästhetisches Denken* (Stuttgart: Recalm, 1990, 6th edition); *Vernunft. Die zeitgenössische Vernunftkritik und das Konzept der transversalen Vernunft* (Frankfurt/Main: Suhrkamp, 1995), *Undoing Aesthetics* (London: Sage, 1997), and *Aesthetics and Beyond* (Changohun, PR China: Jilin, 2002).

Index

Dewey, John, 1, 9, 12, 14, 31–2, 43,
48, 50–4, 57–9, 61–2, 63n. 9, 65n.
41, 82–3, 90n. 97, 121, 147, 151–2,
164, 174, 184n. 55, 201, 203–4, 223–
4, 226–8, 230
Dilthey, 233
Dölling, Evelyn, 86n. 22
Doyle, Connan, 137
Dummett, Michael, 79, 88n. 71, 135,
139–40, 239–40
Dunn, John, 155

Eddington, Arthur, 115–7, 122–3, 126
Egginton, William, 8–10
Einstein, 115–6, 124, 127, 139, 154
Ess, Charles, 91n. 108
Evans, Gareth, 244

Fernández Garrido, Miguel, 10
Feyerabend, Paul, 6, 118
Fichte, 233
Fine, Arthur, 6, 7, 129n. 22, 131–6,
138–40, 142
Fish, Stanley, 44n. 5, 215
Forster, E. M., 156
Foucault, Michel, 1, 160n. 14, 203–4,
209–10, 233
Frege, 4, 43, 46n. 41, 141, 184n. 55, 239
Freud, 25, 147, 187–8, 210

Gadamer, Hans-Georg, 56, 65n. 34,
142, 233
Galison, Peter, 128n. 14
Ganeles, Diane, 10
Gauchet, Marcel, 3, 12, 23–5, 28n. 40
Geraets, T. F., 65n. 42
Gibson, Roger, 87n. 51
Gimmler, Antje, 4–5, 65n. 44
Glaspell, Susan, 128n. 6
Gloy, Karen, 66n. 52
Goebbels, 160n. 17
Goldstein, Sheldon, 129n. 22
Goodman, 173
Günther, Klaus, 113n. 21

Habermas, Jürgen, 3–4, 6, 18, 24–5,
28n. 40, 42, 46n. 40, 47, 52, 65n. 36,

83–4, 91n. 106, 97–8, 100, 118, 209,
228–9, 245n. 20
Hahn, Lewis Edwin, 87n. 47
Hance, Allen, 63n. 5
Hanly, Charles, 216n. 5
Harris, H. S., 65n. 42
Hartshorne, Charles, 45n. 30
Hegel, 1, 4–5, 9, 47–62, 63n. 6, 65n.
36, 65n. 41, 65n. 42, 66n. 52, 80,
131, 141–2, 166, 173, 183n. 55, 204,
233, 236–44
Heidegger, 1, 14, 27n. 23, 57, 89n. 74,
105, 140–2, 164, 168–9, 190, 198,
202, 209, 223, 233–4
Heldke, Lisa M., 128n. 12
Heller, Kevin, 10
Henrich, Dieter, 87n. 50
Herf, Jeffrey, 160n. 17
Herschel, 123
Hitler, 39, 152
Hobbes, 142
Horkheimer, 233
Horstmann, Rolf-Peter, 57
Hull, David, 128n. 17
Hume, 50
Husserl, 140, 234

Inkpin, Andrew, 10

Jakobson, 206
James, William, 3–4, 9, 11–26, 26n. 13,
27n. 28, 28n. 40, 31–43, 44n. 7, 44n.
8, 48, 57–8, 82–3, 134, 151, 184n.
55, 223–8, 230, 232, 234

Kant, 1, 5, 9, 13–5, 18, 21, 34, 35, 48,
57–8, 63n. 6, 63n. 7, 65n. 36, 65n.
41, 65n. 42, 69, 72, 77, 80, 93–4,
118, 131, 137, 141, 146, 166, 174,
184n. 56, 204, 233–8, 240–3
Kellert, Stephen, 128n. 12
Kenny, Anthony, 85n. 21
Kepler, 112n. 17
Kierkegaard, 54
Köhnke, Klaus Ch., 85n. 3
Kojeve, Alexandre, 65n. 33
Kripke, 139, 140, 142